Contents

LONGMAN LINGUISTICS LIBRARY

Multilingualism in the British Isles

Multilingualism in the British Isles I The Older Mother Tongues and Europe

edited by
Safder Alladina
Viv Edwards

LONGMAN
LONDON AND NEW YORK

Longman Group UK Limited,
Longman House, Burnt Mill, Harlow,
Essex CM20 2JE, England
and Associated Companies throughout the world.

*Published in the United States of America
by Longman Inc., New York*

First published 1991

British Library Cataloguing in Publication Data
Multilingualism in the British Isles. – (Longman linguistics
Library).
1: The older mother tongues and Europe
1. Great Britain. Languages
I. Alladina, Safder   II. Edwards, Viv
409'.41

ISBN 0-582-01964-8 CSD
ISBN 0-582-01963-X PPR

Library of Congress Cataloging-in-Publication Data
Multilingualism in the British Isles/edited by Safder Alladina, Viv
Edwards.
p.   cm. – (Longman linguistics library)
Includes bibliographical references.
Contents: v. 1. The older mother tongues and Europe – v.
2. Africa, Asia, and the Middle East.
ISBN 0-582-01964-8 (v. 1). – ISBN 0-582-01963-X (pbk.: v. 1). –
ISBN 0-582-06366-3 (v. 2). – ISBN 0-582-06365-5 (pbk.: v. 2)
1. Multilingualism.   I. Alladina, Safder, 1943–   .   II. Edwards,
Viv. III. Series.
P115.M8   1990
306.4'4'0941 – dc20   89–13672
CIP

Produced by Longman Singapore Publishers (Pte) Ltd.
Printed in Singapore

Foreword

It was found in the Language Census of 1987 that there were 172 different languages spoken by children in Inner London Education Authority Schools. The reaction in many quarters was stunned disbelief. One British educationalist told me that England has become a third world country. After believing in the supremacy of English as the universal language, it was difficult to acknowledge that the UK was now one of the great immigrant nations of the modern world. It was also hard to see that the current plurality is based on a continuity of heritage.

The arrogance of colonialism led many to believe that English was the only language needed by the world and that all other languages were somehow inferior to it. This was a view reflected at home as well as abroad. Having denounced the three indigenous languages (Gaelic, Irish and Welsh) as less than equal, it is not at all surprising that the languages of the Black, Browns and Yellows would be considered deficient and unfit for educational attention.

The multicultural debate in the UK, unfortunately, has since then got bogged down in the spurious controversy between multicultural and antiracist education. Instead of discussing cultural variation and the cultural interaction between shared values and culture-specific values, this debate has been lost in the metalanguage of models and the muddles they have created.

The description of different speech communities in this volume for the first time draws attention to the cultural renewals taking place within the value frame of each community. For the first time there is an indication of the formation of a cultural mosaic through structural incorporation of cultural elements from different ethnic groups. The cultural exchange across cultures can only lead to an overarching framework of values, which can give proper justification to a multilingual and pluricultural Britain.

This, however, has to be seen in the context of the prevailing monolingual view of the world in Britain. There is a curious contradiction in the approach to bilingualism. On the one hand, it is considered a quantum leap signifying acquisition of two languages. On the other, it is seen as a threat to English. No wonder that the Swann Report 'Education for All' (1985) rejected the twin ideas of bilingual education and mother-tongue maintenance as a single educational aim. This ambivalence has resulted in favouring selective élite bilingualism, while resisting bilingualism for minority language speakers.

The most forceful monomodel is provided by the US, despite its cultural variation. Fishman characterises the US Bilingual Education Act as primarily an Act for Anglification of non-English speakers, an act against bilingualism.[1] The US provides for wholly inadequate bilingual education for speakers of Spanish and some other migrant language speakers without hiding its bias for Anglicization and the elimination of conditions favouring bilingualism. Britain, which closely follows the footsteps of the US in such matters, is also intolerant of minority languages and works towards deculturalisation of these groups and their eventual Anglicization.

Language use has serious educational consequences. There is evidence that a dominant language speaker studying through either a dominant or minority language medium does well in both. There is evidence too that wherever second or foreign language education is securely based on mother-tongue education the children do well in both. Substitution of the mother tongue for a second/foreign language is debilitating and creates *anomie*, alienation and frustration. In face of such evidence, usurpation of the language of minorities and migrants creates an unequal society. The British have traditionally been known for their policy of divide and rule. They have followed a policy of exclusion at home which does not embrace but rejects, plays one side against the other, group against group, region against region. The outsider, the immigrant and the oppressed have been perpetually marked and condemned, first for not learning English, second for not learning the right kind of English.

[1] Fishman, J. (1989) *Language and Ethnicity in Minority Sociolinguistic Perspective*. Multilingual Matters, 405.

As the identity of the various oppressed groups is threatened, identity assertion movements ensue. These identities are built around languages, religions, ethnicities, regions and similar factors. When two or more such factors are combined, forming ethnolinguistic or ethnoreligious groups or regions, then sometimes these movements are directed towards recognition of specific regions or areas of such concentration, or consolidation of language leading to language maintenance. Hugo Baetens Beardsmore shows how a combination of political process, education and language has arrested massive language shift in Brussels.[2] In the British Isles the Irish ethnic movement thrives on a combination of nationalism, religion and language. Sometimes a home language is given up in order to maintain a distinctive identity. The Vietnamese Chinese in the UK giving up their language in favour of Cantonese is a case in point.

Identities are so apportioned between the majorities and minorities in the UK that the majority has no mother tongue. 'Mother tongue' refers to minority languages. The majority has no one ethnicity: ethnic language refers to minority and migrant languages. The majority is not a community: community language refers to minority and migrant languages. Ethnicity, which in the literature in variously expressed as assertion of cultures, communal upsurges, revival of religions, voices and movements of marginalised peoples, regions and nationalities, hurts the power elites. It represents the affirmation of diversity, of indigenous identity, of organic as against televised or museumised cultures or classicised cultures as found in ancient texts. At a time when only the commercial value of language is emphasised it is no wonder that ethnicity should be condemned, its diverse facets appearing to be in opposition to one another.

In England none of the minority languages have the ethno-linguistic vitality to present a threat to the omnipotence of English. And yet English feels threatened and the managers of education lack the enthusiasm to provide educational support to these minority languages alongside English. As Smolicz rightly observes, 'frequently it is the country's dominant language which represents the majority's core, although its attempted imposition on others may be camouflaged under the guise of concern for the 'life chances' of minority children, the need to preserve the cohesion of the State, conceived in a way which reflects

[2] Beardsmore, H. B. (1989, forthcoming) *The Evolution and current status of Brussels as a Bilingual City.*

the majority's own cores and cultural predilections'.[3]

The minority's linguistic tenacity and the majority's tolerance of linguistic pluralism determine the maintenance of minority language and cultures. Britain is on the crossroads. It can take an isolationist stance in relation to its internal cultural environment. It can create a resilient society by trusting its citizens to be British not only in political but in cultural terms. The first road will mean severing dialogue with the many heritages which have made the country fertile. The second road would be working together with cultural harmony for the betterment of the country. Sharing and participation would ensure not only political but cultural democracy. The choice is between mediocrity and creativity.

DEBI PRASANNA PATTANAYAK

[3] Smolicz, J. J. (1989, forthcoming) *Language Core, values in Australia: Some Polish, Welsh and Indian minority experiences*

Acknowledgements

This book is the end point of a long and often very exciting process. In the attempt to chart the dimensions of linguistic diversity in the British Isles, we have often needed to look beyond the universities, polytechnics and colleges of higher education which are the normal locations for academic writers. One reason for extending the search is the racism which is an everyday reality for large numbers of British people. There is ample evidence, for instance, of the ways in which Black people are systematically denied access to employment in all sections of the job market and there is no evidence that higher education is an exception to this general rule. Another reason is the low priority which has been given in British Universities to languages, in general, and non-European languages, in particular. We have therefore needed to cast our net much further afield to locate potential contributors to this volume. Our thanks are due to all those who have helped us in a fascinating exercise in networking.

We would also like to thank those who have offered information, helped us to develop our own thinking and commented on various aspects of the book. We are particularly grateful to Jagiro Goodwin, D. P. Pattanayak, Ryte Piskowyk, S. Thalib, Aleksas Vilkinskas and students past and present in the Department of Applied Linguistics at Birkbeck College, University of London.

Finally, we would like to acknowledge the following for permission to reproduce material from their books: Colin Baker and Multilingual Matters Ltd for the map depicting the distribution of Welsh speakers in Volume 1, Chapter 6, from *Aspects of Bilingualism in Wales* (Multilingual Matters, 1985: 12); for Volume 2, figures 2.2 and 3.2, The Office of Population Censuses and Surveys for data from Table 51, *National Report (Part 2)*

Great Britain, Census 1981 (HMSO, 1983); for the map in Volume 1, Chapter 4, Mouton de Gruyter for an adaptation of a map from Commins, P. (1988) 'Socioeconomic development and language maintenance in the Gaeltacht' *International Journal of the Sociology of Language*, 70; for a selection of Chinese characters (Volume 2, Figure 13.3), the selection is reprinted from *Speaking of Chinese* by Raymond Chang and Margaret Scrogin Chang, by permission of W.W. Norton & Company, Inc. Copyright © 1978 by W.W. Norton & Company, Inc.

The bringing together of thirty-one different writers to describe the thirty-three different communities covered in the two-volume sequence has been a highly complex task. It has sometimes involved extremely difficult editorial decisions. It has certainly required a great deal of patience, a spirit of compromise and considerable generosity on the part of all concerned. We hope that both the contributors and the wider readership for this volume and its companion will be satisfied with the end product.

Safder Alladina
Viv Edwards

Chapter 1

Many people, many tongues: Babel and beyond

It is a well-established tenet of folk linguistics that multilingualism is a bad thing and that for efficient human communication we need to work towards a monolingual norm. Yet this is contrary to what history tells us. For many centuries, extensive contact and co-operation between the speakers of different languages has been the norm. We know, for instance, of the interaction in various periods of world history between the Chinese, South Asian, Middle Eastern, African, Greek and Roman civilizations. Within South Asia, there is no shortage of evidence to show that the Gujjars from north India built temples in the south and that builders from south India helped to construct the Sun Temple at Konarka in the north (Pattanayak 1987). In a similar vein, the building of the Taj Mahal drew upon the skills of artisans from all over South Asia and beyond. In the European context, the Dark Ages can be·equated with a period of introverted monolingualism and the Renaissance as a period of outward going and necessarily multilingual thirst for knowledge.

Developments in the last quarter of the twentieth century – the phenomenal leaps that have been made in world travel and communication, advances in print technology, translation and language generation – should lead us seriously to challenge monolingual prejudice. The legacy of negative attitudes towards multilingualism, however, lives on. Pattanayak (1985, 1987), for instance, analyses the attitudes of a range of modern scholars: recent work in this area has equated linguistic diversity with linguistic and economic backwardness; presented a causal relationship between multilingualism and low levels of Gross National Product (GNP) or economic underdevelopment; advocated that a common language would make for a more unified and cohesive society; and asserted that monolingualism is a necessary precondition for modernism. It has also been claimed that complete equality of status is possible only in countries that have one or at the most three languages and that, in a modern society, two languages are a nuisance, three languages are uneconomic and many languages are absurd. In reply, Pattanayak (1987) argues that in the multilingual reality, many languages are a fact of existence, any restriction in the choice of language is a nuisance, and one language is not only uneconomic but absurd. For genuine equality of opportunity and participation in democracies, people's right to use and maintain their mother language is a prerequisite.

Thus the folk wisdom regarding multilingualism has established itself in the edifices of academe in spite of the fact that, in this era of technology, many modern and 'economically advanced' societies like the Netherlands, Norway, Sweden and Japan operate very successfully using an international language like English while continuing to use their mother tongue. It would seem that mother tongue maintenance only becomes an issue when language groups that do not hold political and economic power are under discussion.

A history of intolerance

Bilingualism has been an important fact of life for many sections of the population throughout the history of the British Isles. Successive movements of European peoples have contributed to the development of British culture throughout the centuries, each group interacting with the ones who went before and contributing to the process of cultural and linguistic change. The English language today is a living testimony to this process. The Angles, the Saxons, the Vikings and the Normans all helped to shape its development and continue to exert an influence on its present form. It is possible to show, for instance, that the ancient divisions of the Anglo-Saxon kingdoms correspond closely to the regional dialects of twentieth-century English some 900 years after the demise of the monarchies themselves.

The gradual imposition of English has been a story of power struggles and resistance. Political and economic forces began to make inroads on the Celtic languages as early as the eleventh century, although nineteenth- and twentieth-century phenomena such as industrialization and economic restructuring have considerably accelerated the process. The fact that small but significant minorities of Welsh and Scots and Irish Gaelic speakers continue against all odds to assert their right to use their mother tongues is a powerful reminder of the potent symbolism of language in ethnic identity.

Within the education system, however, the policy has been to replace the language of the home with standard English. The 1847 Report of the Church Commissioners on schools in Wales, for instance, viciously attacked the Welsh language on the grounds that it isolated 'the masses' from the 'upper portions of society', denied its speakers access to the top of the social scale and kept them 'under the hatches'. In the classroom there were cruel attempts to humiliate Welsh speakers by making anyone heard using the language wear a wooden halter known as the 'Welsh not'. The humiliation of having to wear the halter was compounded by the pressure to 'grass' on classmates, since the last person wearing the not at the end of the day was subjected to corporal punishment.

However, the targets for the Establishment throughout this period were not simply bilingual speakers on the Celtic fringes but other linguistic varieties at odds with what was seen as the norm. Speakers of regional dialects were also subjected to a range of unpleasant tactics, the effect of which was to leave no doubt as to the desirability of standard English. As recently as 1920 there were reports of Lancashire teachers who were deliberately sent out into the school yard at playtime 'to detect lapses of speech among children when amusing themselves outside school buildings' (Hollingworth 1977). The 1921 Newbolt Report on the teaching of English in England reflects this preoccupation with the unworthiness of dialect, heaping opprobrium on children whose speech is 'disfigured by vulgarisms'. Seventeen years later, the 1938 Spens Report talks in similar terms of the 'slovenly, ungrammatical and often incomprehensible' nature of the English 'of common usage'.

The work of the sociologist Basil Bernstein in the 1960s (see, for instance, Bernstein 1973) did much to perpetuate these long-standing prejudices. He postulated two polar codes – the elaborated code and the restricted code and argued that the different distribution of these codes might account for the evidence that working-class children tend to underperform at all stages of education. Although Bernstein has strenuously denied that this was ever his intention, his work was widely interpreted as suggesting that the standard language could be equated with the elaborated code and non-standard dialects with the restricted code.

Bernstein's work has been severely criticized on many different fronts. It has been suggested, for instance, that his theory of language codes is both untestable and unrelated to linguistic evidence. He has also been severely taken to task for failing to take situational factors into account. More recently evidence has emerged from the work of writers like Tizard and Hughes (1984) and Wells (1987) that the main differences in language use occur not between working- and middle-class children but between school and home. None the less, the legacy of Bernstein lives on. The highly influential Bullock Report, published in 1975, advocates that health visitors should urge parents to 'bathe their children in language'. In 1980, a project launched in the Ladywood area of Birmingham tried to put this policy into practice. Speech therapists, health visitors and social workers made contact with mothers in neighbourhood supermarkets and distributed their children with 'Mum talk to me' stickers (Edwards 1983).

Since Bullock, notions of criticism and rejection have – on a policy level, at least – been replaced with the notion of appropriateness. The 1981 Rampton Report, for instance, argues that the imaginative and creative use of a child's home language helps in developing awareness of different forms of language including standard English – and their appropriateness for different situations. This theme is further developed in the Cox Report (DES and Welsh Office 1988). The extent to which official policy is actually implemented in many schools, however, remains an open question. Children's views on dialect collected as part of the Survey of British Dialect Grammar (Edwards and Cheshire 1989) included the following comment from a fourth-year secondary-school child in Rotherham:

> Teachers always correct the way I speak and also the way I write. They correct the way I write more than anything. When I write a story and include talking, I write it how I would speak. But sometimes teachers cross it out and put in how they would talk. I don't think they should do that. They should leave it as it is.

This comment underlines the naïvety of attempts to modify children's speech through formal education. It has been estimated that less than 10 per cent of the population speak standard English, and, of these, perhaps as few as 3 per cent speak standard English with the Received Pronunciation traditionally associated with the public schools or broadcasting (Hughes and Trudgill 1978). The considerable pressures for linguistic conformity exerted by schools and the job market beyond would therefore seem to be singularly unsuccessful in achieving their aim. The evidence points to little change between the numbers of speakers of non-standard dialects of English leaving school at the end of compulsory schooling and the numbers who embarked on the process some eleven years earlier. Those who wish to change children's speech, either by eradicating the non-standard dialect or by extending their repertoire to include standard English, have usually been guilty of underestimating the potency of language as a symbol of identity.

New horizons

Any attempt to understand reactions to bilingualism in recent years thus needs to take into account this history of linguistic intolerance towards both speakers of Celtic languages and, in a broader context, regional dialects of English. It is also important to take into account the ways in which intolerance of this kind has tended to make linguistic diversity of all kinds more or less invisible. To take an extreme example, most British people are completely ignorant of the nature of British Sign Language (BSL), the normal language of interaction of an important section of the deaf community in Britain. Linguists have now shown that BSL is as complex and flexible as any spoken language and that it fulfils all the communication needs of its speakers. Yet, it is often not recognized as a language in these respects at all and, for most of the last century, it has been outlawed from schools for the deaf in much the same way as Welsh or Gaelic or non-standard English. In the same way, most people are unaware that Gypsies speak an ethnolect completely unintelligible to *gaujos* or outsiders.

Even when children are recognized as speaking a *bona fide* language, the attitudes of both schools and wider society are often extremely ambivalent. Many people show a marked hierarchy of preferences in their attitudes towards other languages. Thus children who speak French, either because they have a French parent or because they have lived in France, are considered to be very fortunate and are encouraged to make efforts to maintain their fluency in the language. The same is true of other Western European languages such as German, Spanish and Italian. In contrast, the bilingualism of the Gujarati or Panjabi or Hakka-speaking child is often undervalued or ignored.

Bilingualism has traditionally been considered in negative terms in Britain and elsewhere. We have already discussed the ways in which educators tried to argue that the use of Welsh would hold its speakers back. Such views were by no means restricted to the

Celtic fringe: it has been commonplace throughout the last thirty years for bilingual parents to be told that it is in their children's best interests only to hear English in the home. A large number of studies undertaken between 1920 and 1960, reporting that bilingual children tended to perform more poorly than their monolingual peers, added weight to arguments for the undesirability of bilingualism. There has been a gradual recognition, however, of the serious shortcomings of these studies (cf Peal and Lambert 1960). In some cases, working-class children from under-resourced schools in poor areas were compared with middle-class monolingual peers. Other studies failed to take account of the fact that one language is usually dominant in bilingual speakers and have compared verbal scores on tests of the children's weaker language with those of monolingual pupils.

The 1970s marked the first official recognition of the positive value of linguistic diversity. The Bullock Report (1975: 293–4) described bilingualism as 'an asset, as something to be nurtured, and one of the agencies which should nurture it is the school'. Developments in the decade which followed were often very exciting. Schools began to value the language skills which children brought to school and bilingualism, for the first time, was seen in a positive light. The work of various researchers on the cognitive and intellectual benefits of bilingualism (see, for instance, Cummins 1984; Swain and Cummins 1986) was widely disseminated and teachers began to think in terms of language transference skills rather than language interference. Local education authorities such as the Inner London Education Authority (ILEA), Brent and Leicester and individual schools and colleges started to collect information on the language repertoire of their pupils.

National and international developments have often acted as a catalyst or reinforced the interest of educators in this area. As early as 1976, a draft of an EC directive on the language education of the children of migrant workers was issued to interested parties throughout Europe (EC Commission 1976). It was proposed that member states should offer free tuition in the national languages of migrant workers as part of the curriculum for full-time education. By the time the directive was published in the following year, however, important modifications had been made: member states were required only to 'promote mother tongue teaching' . . . . 'in accordance with their national circumstances and legal systems' (Council of Europe 1977). Considerable scepticism has been expressed about government willingness or ability to achieve even the modest aims set out in the revised version of the directive (Bellin 1980). It has been pointed out by some that the *raison d'être* of the EC directive may be to facilitate the future repatriation of non-EC nationals to their countries of origin. None the less, the issue of linguistic minorities has been put very firmly on the political agenda. Developments in Europe need to be seen in a world-wide context. In the USA, the Bilingual Education Act, which entitled educational establishments to financial assistance for their language teaching programmes, was passed in 1968. Although the Act was essentially assimilationist in that its primary concern was with the acquisition of English, the *Lau* v. *Nichols* case of 1974 established the right of a non-English-speaking child (in this case, of Chinese origin) to a meaningful education which acknowledges the child's home language. The Black English trial in Ann Arbor represented another major achievement, when Black parents won their argument that, if their children were to have access to equality of educational opportunity, all teachers in the school system needed to learn about and respect the language background of the home (Labov 1982). These advances, however, were short-lived. The Bilingual Education Amendments Act of 1981 and the Bilingual Education Improvements Act of 1982 began to erode the achievements of the 1960s and 1970s. In 1988, the Heritage Foundation which advises the President on cultural issues recommended that English be declared the official language of the United States. This is a glaring example of a politically dominant group imposing its language on all members of society, disregarding the multilingual reality and denying equality of opportunity and outcome in the educational and political processes. Such a move is in marked contrast to the Declaration of Language Rights supported, among others, by the International Association of Applied Linguists (AILA) and the International Association for Crosscultural Communication (AIMAV), which reads as follows:

The XXII Seminar of AIMAV on Human Rights and Cultural Rights held at the School of Law at the Universidad Federal de Pernambuco (Recife, Brazil), October 7–9, 1987, chaired by Francisco Gomes de Matos,

Considering that the ideals and principles of equality, solidarity, freedom, justice, peace and understanding, which have inspired international legislation and instruments on human rights, share a crucial linguistic dimension,

Recognizing that the learning and use, maintenance and promotion of languages contribute significantly to the intellectual,

educational, sociocultural, economic and political development of
individuals, groups and states,

Noting that the Universal Declaration of Human Rights, the
International Covenants related to human rights and other
international universal instruments make provision for cultural
rights,

Mindful of the need to arouse and foster awareness, within and
across cultures, of the recognition and promotion of the linguistic
rights of individuals and groups,

Asserting that linguistic rights should be acknowledged, promoted
and observed nationally, so as to bring about and assure the
dignity and equity of all languages,

Aware of the need for legislation to eliminate linguistic prejudice
and discrimination, and all forms of linguistic domination,
injustice, and oppression, in such contexts as services to the
public, the place of work, the educational system, the courtroom,
and the mass media,

Stressing the need to sensitize individuals, groups and States to
linguistic rights, to promote positive societal attitudes towards
plurilingualism and to change societal structures toward equality
between users of different languages and varieties of languages,

Hence, conscious of the need for explicit legal guarantees of the
linguistic rights of individuals and groups to be provided by the
appropriate bodies of the member states of the United Nations,

Recommends that steps be taken by the United Nations to adopt
and implement a Universal Declaration of Linguistic Rights which
would require a reformulation of national, regional and
international language policies.

The pattern of developments in the United States has been mirrored, to some extent at least, in the UK. After a considerable
period of neglect and decline, leading in the case of Cornish and
Manx to actual language death, linguistic minorities have gradually begun to assert themselves. Irish has been enshrined as an
official language in the constitution of Eire; Welsh has achieved
official status in Wales; and bilingual education programmes have
been developed in Ireland, Wales and, to a lesser extent, Scotland. With the drive to recruit labour from the New
Commonwealth and the arrival of political refugees from
countries such as Uganda, Vietnam and Iran, the mother tongue
issue has become part of a much wider political platform. Many
well-established communities, such as the Italians, Lithuanians
and Poles who had first settled in Britain at the start of the cen-

tury, had been subject to considerable pressure to assimilate to the English-speaking majority. However, the arrival of new groups of migrants in the post-war period, and the new atmosphere of ethnic self-assertion, has seen the rekindling of interest in, and commitment to, the mother tongue.

In an atmosphere such as this, teachers began to feel the need for information on the linguistic backgrounds of their children. The languages of ethnic minority children had in fact received remarkably little attention until the 1980s, and, even at this stage, it is possible to argue that linguistic diversity remained an under-researched field. Trudgill's (1984) *Language in the British Isles*, for instance, a work which might reasonably have been expected to give extensive coverage of this area, devotes only five out of thirty-three chapters to non-indigenous languages. Some progress has none the less been made. Black British English has perhaps fared best with three books and one edited collection of papers (Edwards 1979, 1986; Sutcliffe 1982; Sutcliffe and Wong 1986), supported by a wide range of material published on Caribbean language (*eg* Bailey 1966, Cassidy and Le Page 1966; Dalphinis 1985). The language of the Italian community forms the subject of Tosi (1983); Mobbs (1985) provides a brief overview of South Asian languages in Britain; and Taylor (1987) pays some attention to language issues in her review of research on the Chinese community in Britain. Various publications (*eg* Edwards 1983; Houlton and Willey 1983; Tansley, Navaz and Roussou 1985; Rosen and Burgess 1980) look specifically at the educational implications of linguistic diversity.

By far the most pertinent work for present purposes, however, is the Linguistic Minorities Project (LMP) (1985) *The Other Languages of England*. Although some attempts (*eg* Rosen and Burgess 1980; ILEA 1978, 1981, 1983) had previously been made to document the extent and nature of diversity, the publication of this work represented the first and most extensive account of this area in a British context. Its scope is impressive: it provides information on the background and history, patterns of language use and mother tongue teaching provision for some eleven different communities; it also discusses bilingualism and education, surveys of school language and sharing languages in the classroom.

A work so ambitious in its aims inevitably attracts both praise and criticism. The difficulties of locating and sampling adult members of linguistic minority communities, for instance, make it extremely difficult to make reliable generalizations (Smith 1984). Although the population census of Britain gives information on the place of birth of respondents, this information is not always useful in determining language background. In certain instances, such as Poland, speculation on the possible home language can be very near the mark. However, respondents born in Cyprus might speak Greek, Turkish, Armenian and/or English as their home language. Similarly those born in Kenya might speak a Bantu language such as Swahili, a Nilotic language such as Luo, one of the South Asian languages or English. Moreover, population censuses do not give information on children who were born in Britain but none the less use a language other than or in addition to English.

Another problem faced by the LMP was the difficulty of formulating questions which were acceptable to both the teachers administering the survey instrument and the children who were completing it (LMP 1984). Other factors, too, threaten the validity of their findings. As Nicholas (1988) points out:

> In at least three respects, the classroom stands between the survey and the elicitation of responses from plurilingual respondents. There is pressure from peers – the fear of exhibiting 'alienness'. . . . There is the fact that the survey is conducted in 'the language of the classroom': in a constrained situation and discourse, and in English only. There is the problem of untrained and unsuitable elicitors, teachers co-opted as interviewers.

In spite of criticisms of this kind, *The Other Languages of England* remains the most extensive, sensitively designed survey of linguistic diversity in Britain to date, and it is the intention of this volume to build on these foundations. One of the ways in which we hope to achieve this end is by extending the number of communities under discussion from eleven to thirty-one. When one considers that the 1987 ILEA *Language Census* recorded a total of 172 different languages, our own attempt can be seen as the tip of the iceberg. Nevertheless it represents an important step forward in the documentation of diversity.

Another significant feature of the present volume is the attempt to break down the 'them and us' mentality. All of the writers are themselves bilingual and, in the vast majority of cases, they are describing their own speech communities. This is a radical departure. The overwhelming majority of books on linguistic diversity in Britain have, in fact, been produced by writers who are describing speech communities other than their own. The disadvantages of being an outsider in this situation, while not insurmountable, are very real. There is a danger, for instance, of defining research questions from the perspective of the dominant society, thereby overlooking issues which are felt to be important by minority communities themselves. It is also possible to interpret the findings of such research through one's own cultural matrix, thus distorting the information which has been gathered. There are political considerations, too. For as long as writers choose to work on and be recognized as experts on a community other than their own, they are effectively setting themselves up in competition with members of minority communities for extremely limited research funding; they may also inadvertently engage in academic paternalism in which the hidden message is 'We understand your situation much better than you do yourselves.'

In attempting to document the sociolinguistic situation of a wide range of speech communities, many of the contributors to these volumes have had to confront the problem of unevenness of information. At one end of the continuum, there is a considerable body of research on the various Celtic speech communities; at the other end of the continuum there is virtually no published work on British communities who speak European languages like Hungarian and Lithuanian; or South Asian languages like Tamil and Sinhala; or African languages like Hausa and Yoruba; or East Asian varieties like Singaporean and Malaysian English. The task facing writers attempting to describe these various speech communities is thus necessarily more introspective than would be the case for those dealing with well-documented languages. It is very much to their credit that some modest start has been made in this direction.

The structure of the book

There are various ways in which the book might be organized. It would be possible, for instance, to divide the various language groups, purely on the basis of the size, into major and minor speech communities. Such a classification, however, might have the effect of blurring points of similarity between the various different groups and of creating the impression that the situation of the larger communities is in some way more valid or more important than is the case for the smaller ones. It would also detract from one of the aims of the present volume which is to provide information on many of the smaller communities which, up until very recently, have failed to attract the attention of researchers.

Alternatively it might be possible to arrive at some kind of chronological classification: those languages which have been a feature of the linguistic landscape of Britain for a century or more; those which arrived before the Second World War; those which arrived in the period of economic expansion of the 1950s and 1960s; and those which have arrived with political refugees in the 1970s and 1980s. This approach, however, assumes a unitary pattern of settlement for the different groups. The reality is very different. Most South Asians arrived in Britain in the post-war period. They were, however, joining a migration 'chain' which had been established at the beginning of the twentieth century by sailors who were abandoned by the shipping companies and who decided to remain in England (see Visram 1986). Similarly most Eastern European migrants arrived in Britain in several quite distinct waves of population movement.

We finally decided to organize the book along geolinguistic lines (see Fig. 1.1, Geolinguistic areas). There are seven main sections: the older mother tongues – Welsh, Gaelic, Irish and British Sign Language and Romanichal which have been established in the British Isles for many centuries; the languages of Eastern Europe – Hungarian, Lithuanian, Polish, Ukrainian, Yiddish; the languages of the Mediterranean – Greek, Italian, Moroccan Arabic, Spanish, Portuguese and Turkish; the languages of South Asia – Panjabi, Urdu, Hindi, Bengali, Gujarati, Tamil, Sinhala; the languages of West Africa and the Caribbean; the language of East Asia as spoken in Hong Kong, Japan, Singapore and Malaysia, the Philippines and Vietnam; and the languages of the Middle East – Hebrew and Farsi. The languages included in the volumes are, of course, only a small sample of those spoken by the various speech communities in the British Isles and their inclusion is as much a function of the availability of writers as any other factor.

The decision to divide the book along geolinguistic lines is not without problems of its own. It is not always clear to which area a particular language should belong, nor where the boundaries should be drawn. Where, for instance, do we place Romanichal, a language with historical roots in South Asia but which has come to the British Isles via Eastern Europe? This situation is complicated further by the fact that Romanichal has been established here for a sufficiently long period for it to be considered as one of the 'older mother tongues', alongside Welsh, Gaelic and British Sign Language.

None the less a geolinguistic approach has several advantages. It is politically neutral and does not in any way imply that some language minority communities are more important than others. It also allows us to identify the many broad trends which draw together different speech communities since patterns of migra-

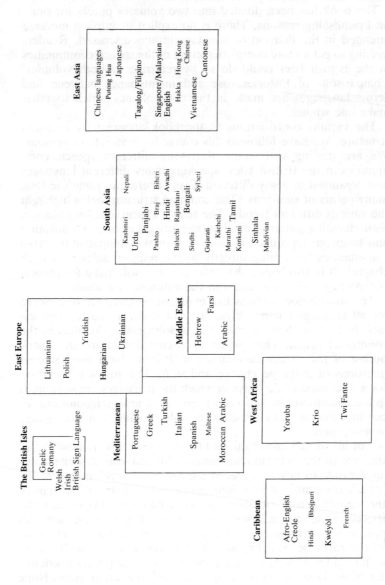

FIGURE 1.1 Geolinguistic areas

tion, as well as the sociolinguistic situation, tend to be broadly similar within a given geolinguistic area.

The book has been divided into two volumes purely for practical publishing reasons. There is no explicit or implicit message intended in the division of language groups discussed. Readers wishing to get a more complete picture of the speech communities of the British Isles could do so by referring to both volumes. Comparisons of histories, use and maintenance between and across languages are made in the two volumes which together make one whole.

The various contributions to the book adhere to a common structure. We have followed this course for a variety of reasons. We are dealing with some thirty-one different speech communities in the British Isles, speaking many different languages and organized in many different ways. There are, none the less, many points of similarity. The common structure helps highlight the various different trends. The reader concerned, for instance, with changing patterns of changing language use, or education and language reproduction, is able to make comparisons across communities by turning directly to the relevant section of each chapter. It is also hoped that this approach will make for greater consistency and cohesiveness in the volumes as a whole.

The contributors address five main issues which are of concern for all language communities, large or small, recent or well established. First they describe the sociolinguistic situation in the country of origin. They go on to discuss the nature and distribution of the speech community in Britain. Next they address questions of language change and shift. This forms a backdrop for a discussion of the ways in which the languages are supported in the community by various aspects of cultural, religious and social life. Finally, they consider the role of education in language reproduction.

Not all speech communities fit neatly into this framework. In the case of the older mother tongues for instance, it seems more appropriate to talk in terms of the historical development of the speech communities and their geographical distribution than of the sociolinguistic situation in the country of origin and the speech community in Britain. Similar problems are posed for Yiddish which currently has no country of origin, and for Hebrew, whose roots lie well beyond the modern state of Israel. Some communities such as the Japanese are only temporary residents, for whom language maintenance and shift are not an issue. None the less, most contributions fit with relative ease into the schema outlined above.

The sociolinguistic situation in the country of origin

Each contribution starts with a description of the sociolinguistic situation in the country of origin. For instance, which languages are spoken and what is their status? The fact that multilingualism is the norm in most societies becomes apparent from the various chapters. This multilingualism has been widely recognized in relation to Africa and South Asia, but it is possible to demonstrate a high degree of diversity even in countries which are usually perceived to be linguistically homogeneous. Thus Japan has significant populations of Korean speakers. And Spain has speakers of Catalan, Vasco and Gallego in addition to the various dialects of Spanish.

The standard language question is also of considerable importance. In Italy, for instance, the dialect of Florence forms the basis of a national literary language used in education and government. However, it is estimated that only 2.5 per cent of the population were able to use this variety on the unification of Italy in 1861 and highly divergent local dialects are still used very widely throughout the country. By the same token, most settlers from Bangladesh are speakers of Sylheti rather than standard Bengali, the national language; and most Urdu speakers in Britain speak Panjabi as the language of the home. In all these cases, however, the expectation is that children should be educated through the medium of the standard language. Information on the linguistic situation in the country of origin is of great relevance in a British context, because this same expectation applies to mother tongue teaching. Italian parents would expect mother tongue classes to focus on standard Italian rather than the southern dialect which many of them speak; Bangladeshi parents usually expect their children to learn Bengali, not the Sylheti spoken in the home; Panjabi Muslims associate Urdu, not Panjabi, with literacy and religious learning. Standard and non-standard varieties thus exist in a situation of diglossia in which the standard is reserved for formal domains such as education and literacy, while non-standard varieties are used in more intimate domains such as conversations with family and friends.

Traditions of literacy in the various countries of origin are also interesting and relevant for the description of language use and maintenance of minority communities. Patterns and expectations are highly variable. At one end of the scale, countries like the Ukraine, Poland and Japan have almost universal literacy. At the other end of the scale are the pre-literate communities in parts of Africa whose small-scale, decentralized organization results in a greater dependence on the spoken than on the written word. There are also different kinds of literacy: the rote learning and calligraphic skills associated with Qur'ānic learning are very different, for instance, from the recent development of creative writing skills in many British schools.

Minority speech communities in the British Isles

Each contribution goes on to describe the history of the arrival and settlement of the different speech communities. For instance, the Poles and Ukrainians of the immediate post-war period, the Hungarians in the 1950s, the Vietnamese refugees in the 1970s and the Tamils in the 1980s, have sought asylum in Britain as political refugees. In contrast, settlers from India, Pakistan, Bangladesh and the Caribbean, have, in the main, come from areas of high unemployment for economic reasons. It is not possible, of course, to make a simple split between political and economic migrants since, even within the same group, motivation differs through time. The Eastern Europeans who have arrived in Britain since the Second World War have come for political reasons; in many cases, however, they were joining earlier settlers trying either to escape poverty in the home country or to better their lot. Most Hong Kong Chinese came to Britain originally for economic reasons but, with the transfer of Hong Kong to China in 1997, the motivation is becoming increasingly political.

It is also possible to make a distinction between the long-established communities such as the Italian, South Asian and African which have maintained a presence – albeit numerically small – for several hundred years and communities like the Vietnamese who have arrived more recently in Britain. A further distinction can be made between these groups and the 'annual migrant' Saudi Arabic speakers living in the more expensive areas of London or the Japanese who are sent to work in Britain by their companies for varying lengths of time.

Even within the longer-established groups there is significant variation. Bangladeshis, for instance, differ in many important ways from the other larger South Asian groups. They tended to cling more tenaciously to the 'myth of return' and, although most Bangladeshis arrived in Britain in the 1950s and 1960s, they sent for their wives and children much later than other South Asians. Because of increasingly stringent immigration legislation, there have often been long delays in reuniting families. One of the consequences is that Bengali-speaking children form the most recent and largest linguistic minority within the ILEA; and, because the majority of children have been born in Bangladesh, they are inevitably in greatest need of language support within the schools.

Remaining with South Asian communities, there are also important differences between those who have come direct from South Asia and those who have arrived via East Africa. Settlers from north India and Pakistan come from predominantly rural areas and have, in the main, received little formal education. In contrast, most of those who have lived in East Africa were traders, industrialists and middle-level professionals and artisans. In this respect East African Asians are closer to Sri Lankans – a highly educated élite who chose to stay in Britain after completing their higher education – than to their north Indian kinfolk.

A further important factor in the discussion of the various minority communities in Britain is the pattern of settlement. Some groups are concentrated into a relatively small geographical area which makes it possible to develop and maintain strong social networks; others are highly dispersed and consequently find it far more difficult to maintain a sense of community. Thus most Spaniards, Turks, Greeks and Vietnamese are to be found in London. Panjabis, Ukrainians, Poles, Tamils and Sinhala, however, are scattered throughout the country. In the case of Poles and Panjabis, the communities outside London are sufficiently large to be able to sustain an active community life; in the case of Ukrainians, Tamils and Sinhala the small numbers and the dispersed nature of the community makes the task of forging a separate linguistic and cultural identity a great deal more difficult.

Groups who have little or no contact with the home country also face very real difficulties. Lithuanians, Latvians, Ukrainians and Estonians, for instance, cannot travel freely to the country of origin; they cannot receive visits from the families they left behind; nor is there the possibility of new immigration which would have the effect of revitalizing the community in Britain. None the less, those groups which find themselves isolated in this way have shown considerable resolve to maintain their ethnic identity, not only through community involvement in the UK, but by building links with similar groups in Europe and in the USA and Canada.

Changing patterns of language use

The inevitable consequence of settlement in Britain is a shift from the mother tongue to English. The extent of this shift will vary, of course, according to individual factors such as degree of identification with the mother tongue and culture; it will also depend on group factors such as the size of the community, its degree of organization and the length of time it has been established in Britain. For more recently arrived communities such as the Bangladeshis and the Vietnamese, the acquisition of English is clearly more urgent a priority than the maintenance of the mother tongue. In the case of Eastern Europeans, however, where the present generation are the grandchildren of the original post-war settlers, the shift to English is such that mother tongue teaching is often an urgent community priority.

In the case of the first generation, language shift is evident in the adoption of a wide range of loan words for objects and concepts peculiar to the new country, though very often these words are used within the morpho-syntactic framework of the mother tongue (cf for instance, Muir on Polish (ch. 9) and Cervi on Italian (ch. 13)). In the case of the second and subsequent generations, there is a much wider range of adaptation: incidence of both code-mixing and code-switching is likely to increase and sometimes words from the mother tongue are inserted into an English syntactic structure rather than the reverse (cf Mahandru on Panjabi (Vol. 2, ch. 8) and Estebanez on Spanish (ch. 15)); English variants are sometimes substituted for phonemes in the original language (cf Jenkala on Ukrainian (ch. 10)); children may aquire only a passive knowledge of the mother tongue, choosing to reply to their parents in English (cf de Zoysa on Sinhala (vol. 2, ch. 10) and Mehmet Ali on Turkish (ch. 12)).

Several factors, however, can bring about language stability. The 'new ethnicity' which has been well documented in the USA and Canada, is beginning to make itself felt in a British setting, too. The realization that a language may be lost completely from the community can often greatly focus the mind: the astonishing cultural renaissance in Wales, Ireland and Scotland is no doubt largely a response to the very real threat of extinction for these indigenous minority languages. The rapid burgeoning of mother tongue classes in the 1970s suggests a similar reaction on the part of the indigenizing language communities. Many young adults are consciously seeking to learn or improve their skills in the mother tongue: Italian classes have recently been set up for the first time in Llanelli in Wales, for instance, where the Italian community has been settled since the early years of this century. In a similar vein, there are reports of British-born Ukrainians and Yiddish-speaking Jews who were brought up in predominatly English-speaking homes who are now striving to produce a Ukrainophone or Yiddophone environment for their own children.

Language, culture and community

Most settler families in Britain have very strong links with the country of origin in the form of letters, visits and investment in land and property. The advent of the international telephone network, satellite television and the free availability of videos have also served to strengthen this ongoing contact. As we have already indicated, even in those cases where there is no access to the home country, strong links are cultivated with communities in exile in other parts of the world.

No individual, indeed no family, exists in a social vacuum and the role which the wider minority community plays in the maintenance of language and culture is clearly critical. The extent of community provision varies enormously. Later arrivals, such as the Portuguese, the Spanish, the Filipinos and the Moroccan Arabs, who work in jobs with long, antisocial hours in the hotel and catering industry very often have little time or energy to devote to community organization. Longer-established groups, however, often offer an impressive range of social, political, religious and cultural activities.

In many communities the church, mosque, *gurdwara* or temple plays a central part in the social life of the group, fulfilling an important welfare and cultural role as well as providing for spiritual needs. In some cases, life revolves around the family and the place of worship. Religious festivals such as 'Id, Christmas, Diwali and Vesak, and life-cycle celebrations, such as naming ceremonies, weddings and funerals, form an important focus for community life.

In most cases, however, there is also an extensive secular organizational network. Sometimes the focus is political, reflecting either political divisions within the country of origin (*cf* Mahandru on Panjabi (Vol. 2, Ch. 8) and Mehmet Ali on Turkish (Ch. 12)) or on issues such as anti-racism or housing which are of more immediate relevance for life in Britain (*cf* Husain on Bengali (Vol. 2, Ch. 5) and Nwenmely on Kwéyol (Vol. 2, Ch. 4)). There is also a wide range of organizations, some religious, some secular, which focus on cultural activities such as music (eg Khan on Urdu (Vol. 2, Ch. 9); Papadaki d'Onofrio and Roussou on Greek (ch. 12), dance (eg Dave on Gujarati (Vol. 2, Ch. 6) and Perinpanayagam on Tamil (Vol. 2, Ch. 10)), drama (*eg* Nwenmely on Kwéyol (Vol. 2, Ch. 4)) and art (eg Husain on Bengali (Vol. 2, Ch. 5)). A wide range of local, regional, national and international ethnic publications mirrors this cultural and political activity. Many communities also have extensive political activity. Many communities also have extensive sporting networks, such as the eastern Caribbean cricket teams or the Turkish Cypriot football leagues.

Most communities have developed an extensive ethnic economy which services the needs of the community. In areas of important settlement, it is possible to find a wide range of cafés, restaurants, travel agents, food shops, clothing shops and video outlets run by and for a given minority community. In many of the larger minority communities, this ethnic economy provides employment for large numbers of workers and creates an environment in which it is often more natural to use the mother tongue than English. The workplace is thus an important factor in language maintenance.

Education and language reproduction

Formal language teaching is not always a community priority. Dalphinis (Vol. 2, Ch. 2), for instance, talks of the ways in which many speakers of British Black English maintain distinctively Black speech patterns as a symbol of resistance to a racist White society, in spite of the fact that both parents and teachers have encouraged them to use British English. In a similar vein, Hancock (Ch. 5) describes the strong ethnic identity which insulates Gypsies from the hostility of mainstream society and which ensures that Romanichal is transmitted with 100 per cent success to the youngest generation without recourse to any formal teaching. On the contrary, school represents a considerable threat by teaching values which are often directly contrary to those taught in a Gypsy home.

For most minority communities, however, it is possible to identify three main strands in language reproduction: family, community and school, and successful transmission from one generation to the next will usually depend on all three strands working in harmony. Responsibility for teaching minority languages in a British context began in the home. In the earlier days, before there were any well-developed community activities, parents took it upon themselves to maintain the language and culture within the family. Quite often this was because they felt that their stay in Britain would be temporary and many harboured the illusion that they would return to the homeland.

Parents were often anxious that their children were drifting away from traditional cultural and religious values. Sometimes there was a genuine breakdown of communication between grandparents and young children. Gradually, there was a realization that responsibility for language maintenance lay not only with the family but with the wider community and the first efforts to organize more formal mother tongue teaching were initiated.

In some cases, the impetus and many of the resources came from the government of the group concerned. Thus mother tongue teaching in the Italian, Spanish, Portuguese, Greek and Turkish communities is supported in varying degrees by the Embassy or High Commission in London. In other cases, religious bodies have played an important role. Thus, historically, the Nonconformist Church has played a key role in the transmission of Welsh and the Catholic Church in the teaching of Polish, Ukrainian and Lithuanian; mosques have fulfilled a similar role in the transmission of Qur'ānic Arabic and Urdu, gurdwaras in the teaching of Panjabi and viharas in the teaching of Sinhala. Increasingly, however, the organization of mother tongue teaching is being taken on board by non-religious groups, especially parent associations.

In the early years, mother tongue classes were supported entirely by the community. As time went by, increasing numbers of LEAs began to recognize this provision, sometimes paying teachers' salaries, sometimes allowing rent-free accommodation, and occasionally providing both salaries and accommodation. The number of classes and of pupils involved in community language teaching is enormous. The LMP (1985) survey of mother tongue teaching provision in 1981–82, for instance, recorded 106 classes and 1,894 students in Coventry, 183 classes and 3,586 students in Bradford and 143 classes and 3,042 students in Haringey. These figures indicate that there is greater vitality in the area of language maintenance than is officially recognized.

The problems faced by those teaching the classes were not, of course, restricted to finance. All have had to come to terms with the shortage of suitable materials for use with children in Britain. Very often the content of books and courses produced in the home country fail to speak to the interests and experience of British-born children and the linguistic level for a given age range is too advanced. Although some improvements are being made in this area (see, for instance, Dave (Vol. 2, Ch. 6) in relation to the examinations of the Gujarati Literary Academy and Cervi (Ch. 13) in relation to new materials for overseas Italians), the only solution in most cases is for teachers to produce their own materials, an extremely time-consuming task.

Teaching methodology also offers many challenges. Staff who have been trained overseas often structure their teaching in a way which is markedly different from the relatively informal and child-centred approach of most primary classrooms, or indeed the communicative language-teaching strategies which have recently gained ground in modern language teaching. In the case of teachers seconded by an overseas government, the lack of familiarity with the children's everyday experience in school can further exacerbate this problem. However, there are signs of progress. Many communities provide their own training programmes (see *eg* Jenkala on Ukrainian (Ch. 10) and Dave on Gujarati (Vol. 2, Ch. 6)); many teachers make their own arrangements for professional training, seeking, for instance, places on Royal Society of Arts diploma courses on community languages (see for instance, Taheri White on Farsi (Vol. 2, Ch. 16)); and increasing numbers already work within the state system as recognized teachers or as instructors.

The gulf between community and state provision has been the subject of a great deal of concern in recent years and there have been many attempts to bridge the gap between the two kinds of provision. This has been done in various different ways. In some cases, the community language has been introduced as a school subject. This initiative has much to recommend it. The exclusion of community languages from mainstream education can only have the effect of lowering their status in the eyes of Anglophone and minority-language-speaking children alike and recognition for the linguistic diversity within our midst is long overdue. However, the introduction of community languages has often been problematic. Sometimes they are taught at the same time as higher status subjects and the take-up rate is low. Sometimes they are offered as an option against the so-called 'low status' subjects on the school curriculum like art, craft or sport, or in the lunch time or after school rather than being integrated into the timetable. This kind of organization reinforces the low status of the languages on offer in schools. Sometimes community languages *are* integrated into the timetable but are taught in the same way as modern languages. This approach fails to recognize that, while the children concerned may have native speaker proficiency, their passive competence and productive abilities are well in advance of modern language students.

A broader concern about the introduction of community language teaching into state schools concerns the amount of control which is exercised over the content of teaching. For most communities, language teaching cannot take place in isolation but must address the history, culture and religion of the people (*cf* Muir on Polish (Ch. 9) and Wong on Chinese (Vol. 2, Ch. 13 and 15)). There is thus, understandably, a fear that the teaching which takes place outside the community may not satisfy these needs.

There are political considerations, too. The growth in community language teaching has produced a demand for teachers which cannot be satisfied from the pool of currently qualified teachers. Yet there is no shortage of experienced teachers within the various minority communities. The problem lies on the one hand in the Department of Education and Science's reluctance to recognize overseas qualifications and, on the other hand, it their failure to provide sufficient places and funding for the further training which would make this recognition possible. As a result, very many people are currently working is schools as instructors. The low pay, low status and insecurity associated with the post of instructor is a source of widespread dissatisfaction for minority communities.

Community languages find their way into state schools in a variety of other ways. There have been moves, for instance, to acknowledge linguistic diversity in the hidden curriculum, by ensuring the availability of a wide range of books, posters and music; by writing children's names and captions on drawings in a variety of scripts; by inviting parents to tell stories in the mother tongue. Sometimes community languages feature as part of language awareness programmes which explore children's own language use and the language of the wider community. A growing number of schools now offer community languages as part of a 'carousel' or 'taster' programme of language teaching in the early years of secondary school, where children are exposed to a variety of languages for short periods of time. In many schools, bilingual language support teachers work alongside the classroom teacher in a team-teaching situation.

Some experimentation has taken place on the effectiveness of bilingual education. In an international context, of course, there is no shortage of evidence to support the use of the mother tongue as a medium as well as a subject of education for children from minority communities (cf Skutnabb-Kangas and Cummins 1988; Garcia and Otheguy 1987). The findings of British initiatives, in the form of the Bedfordshire Mother Tongue Project (Simons 1979) and Mother Tongue and English Teaching Project (Fitzpatrick 1987), also argue forcefully for the value of bilingual education. It would seem, however, that no progress will be made on this front in the foreseeable future. The Swann Report (1985), for instance, makes it clear that 'we cannot support the arguments put forward for the introduction of programmes of bilingual education in maintained schools in this country. . . we would regard mother tongue maintenance. . . as best achieved within the ethnic minority communities themselves'.

The unveiling of plans for the National Curriculum also indicates a waning of enthusiasm for minority languages. The only minority language which is likely to benefit from the National Curriculum is Welsh. However, even in this case, the benefits are likely to be extremely limited. No reference was made to Welsh in the earliest formulations of policy and even its current recognition is somewhat grudging, DES (1987: 9):

> In some counties of Wales it would be appropriate – and in line with existing practice in schools – for Welsh to be made a foundation subject. But the linguistic pattern in Wales is varied, and in some areas the Secretary of State would expect that it would not at present be appropriate to require the study of Welsh throughout the period of compulsory education for pupils who study through the medium of English. At the least, the legislation will provide for attainment targets, programmes of study and assessment arrangements for Welsh wherever it is taught.

More cynical observers might thus be tempted to interpret the writing in of Welsh into the National Curriculum as an afterthought in recognition of the present situation rather than a serious attempt to promote the language.

Equally pertinent for the present discussion, the National Curriculum has precisely nothing to say about community languages or bilingualism outside of the Welsh context. It allows for 10 per cent of curriculum time to be spent on modern foreign languages at secondary level, but there is no mention of the potential role of community languages in the cursory references to language teaching. It would seem that this is yet another case of an opportunity missed. It might also be argued that the government has failed to recognize the inherent dangers of an Anglocentric approach for large number of bilingual pupils.

The key feature of the National Curriculum is in fact the way in which testing and assessment procedures are such an integral part of the package. The government very clearly lays out its intention to set objectives to be reached by the ages of 7, 11, 14 and 16 and can only leave us to conclude that its aim is to centralize control not only of the curriculum but also of teaching. The likely consequences of developments in this direction are a limiting of the teachers' ability to exercise their judgement in responding to children's needs and a narrow, Eurocentric curriculum. More worrying still is the possibility that any group which does not conform to the norms against which the test is referenced will suffer discrimination. We may well be on target for a return to the pathological model' of language where any speaker – working class, Black, or bilingual – who departs from the norm is labelled as deficient.

Bilingual children, however, may well be doubly disadvantaged. First, English may not be their dominant language but there is only provision for testing in English. Second, in order to meet the requirements of the test, teachers may decide that it is in children's best short-term interests to be taught using structural rather than communicative teaching techniques. This would inevitably have the effect of making access to the curriculum more difficult still for bilingual children.

The preoccupation with testing and objectives is likely to involve us in a downward spiral: bilingual children who are not fully fluent in English are likely to underachieve; their underachievement is likely to have an adverse effect on teacher expectations; this in turn, will lead to further depressed performance and so on. The repetition of the situation in the 1960s and 1970s where ethnic minority children were seriously over-represented in ESN schools and low-ability groups is almost inevitable: any system which relies heavily on assessment procedures of the kind proposed is likely to result in bilingual children being wrongly assessed and wrongly placed.

The pressing issues for minority language communities are thus not limited to timetabling, resources and pedagogy. They extend to the legitimate needs of large numbers of bilingual children to be recognized in the formulation policy. Any commitment to equality of opportunity in education must go beyond mere lip service to involve genuine community consultation, and a willingness to resource the implications of linguistic diversity.

Postscript

The failure of central government to take on board the needs of bilingual children is certainly a subject of concern. It is unlikely, however, that insensitivity of this kind will blunt the enthusiasm for the positive aspects of bilingualism on the part of either educators or minority language communities themselves. There are other developments, too, which may well foster more positive attitudes toward linguistic diversity; 1992, the Year of Europe, may well mark the dawning of a new era in this respect. The process of European integration has extremely important implications for minority languages and the central role which these languages play in the cultural identity of communities and individuals. As we move towards a wider multinational, multi-linguistic and single Europe, many people are becoming aware of the new contexts and wider contacts which are opening up for speakers of lesser-used languages. The European Centre for Traditional and Regional Cultures (ECTARC) (1988), for instance, points out that: 'A notable feature of recent European development has been the revitalization of the regional concept and this will surely have a stimulating effect upon the promotion of lesser used languages. Will these languages, then, be the vital elements of, and the means towards intercultural and interpersonal understanding in the future?' While the ECTARC comments are focused more specifically on indigenous minority languages such as Welsh, Frisian and Catalan, the impact of a single Europe without boundaries will clearly be no less significant for the more recent indigenizing minority languages throughout the European Community.

If we are to judge by the experience of other multilingual areas of the world, the solution will lie not in the imposition of any one natural or synthetic language but in the recognition of multilingual reality. Modern history is replete with tales of linguistic repression and resistance: the repression of Welsh in Wales and the legal – and illegal – action taken to counter it; language martyrdom in Bangladesh by Bengali speakers desperate to maintain the place of their mother tongue rather than the Urdu language imposed upon them by West Pakistan after partition from India; language riots in Belgium provoked by the perceived injustices of Flamand speakers in relation to the Walloon majority; cries of 'Vive le Québec libre!' and, by implication, 'Vive la langue française!' uttered by Charles de Gaulle on a state visit to Canada. In these, and many similar cases, social order and a sense of justice have depended on the recognition of the rights of linguistic minorities rather than the imposition of the language of the dominant group. If we wish to bring about equality of opportunity, access and outcomes, we need to create conditions which will support and encourage multiliterate and multilingual development.

This book is an attempt to bring to the attention of readers the wealth and history of languages in the British Isles today. It is just a beginning. The users and speakers of the languages themselves are identifying areas for further research and issues which deserve the urgent attention of teachers, administrators and educational policy-makers. It is hoped that those with the power to make decisions will listen. It is also hoped that the various speech communities will learn from the experience and efforts of others in the area of language maintenance. And most of all, it is hoped that the British people of the twenty-first century will recognize and value the heritage of a multilingual Britain.

References

BAILEY, B. (1966) *A Transformational Grammar of Jamaican Creole.* Cambridge: Cambridge University Press.
BELLIN, W. (1980) ' The EEC Directive on the Education of the Children of Migrant Workers: a comparison of the Commission's proposed directive and the Council directive together with a parallel text', *Polygot* **2**, fiche 3.
BERNSTEIN, B. (1973) *Class, Codes and Control,* vol. 1. London: Routledge & Kegan Paul.
Bullock, Sir A. (1975) *A Language for life.* London: HMSO.
CASSIDY, F and LE PAGE (1966) *Dictionary of Jamaican English.* Cambridge: Cambridge University Press.
Council of Europe (1977) *Council Directive on the Education of the Children of Migrant Workers* (77/48b/EEC). 25 July.
DALPHINIS, M. (1985) *Caribbean and African Languages.* London: Karia Press.
Department of Education and Science (DES) and Welsh Office (1988) *English for Ages* 5–11: *Proposals of the Secretary of State for Education and Science and the Secretary for Wales.* London: HMSO.
CUMMINS, J. (1984) *Bilingualism and Special Education: Issues in Assessment and Pedagogy.* Clevedon, Avon: Multilingual Matters.
Department of Education and Science (DES) [and the] Welsh Office (1987) National Curriculum 5–16: a consultative document. London: HMSO.
EDWARDS, V. (1979) *The West Indian Language Issue in British Schools.* London: Routledge & Kegan Paul.
EDWARDS, V. (1983) *Language in Multicultural Classrooms.* London: Batsford.
EDWARDS, V. (1986) *Language in a Black Community.* Clevedon, Avon: Mutilingual Matters.
EDWARDS, V. and CHESHIRE J. (1989) 'A Survey of British Dialect Grammar'. In J. Cheshire, V. Edwards, H. Münstermann and B. Weltens (eds) *Dialect and Education: Some European Perspectives,* Clevedon, Avon: Multilingual Matters, *pp* 200–18.
The Euporean Centre for Traditional and Regional Cultures (EC-TARC)(1988) Literature for Conference on '*Lesser-Used Languages in a Europe wihout Boundaries*', 25–27 November. Llangollen: EC-TARC.
European Communities Commission (1976) *An Education Policy for the Community. Resolution of the Council and of the Ministers of Education.* Meeting within the Council of 9 February 1976. Background note published 26 March 1976.

FITZPATRICK, B. (1987) *The Open Door*. Clevedon, Avon: Multilingual Matters.

GARCIA, O. and OTHEGUY, R. (1987) 'The bilingual education of Cuban – American children in Dade County's ethnic schools', *Language and Education* 1 (2): 83–96.

HOLLINGWORTH, B. (1977) 'Dialect in school: an historical note', Durham *and Newcastle Research Review* 8: 15–20.

HOULTON, D. and WILLEY, R. (1983) *Supporting Children's Bilingualism*. York: Longman for the Schools Council.

HUGHES, A. and TRUDGILL, P. (1978) *English Accents and Dialects. An Introduction to Social and Regional Varieties of British English*. London: Edward Arnold.

Inner London Education Authority (ILEA) (1978, 1981, 1983, 1985, 1987) *Language Census,* London: ILEA Research and Statistics.

LABOV, W. (1982) 'Objectivity and commitment in linguistic science: the case of the Black English trial in Ann Arbor', *Language and Society* 11: 165–201.

Linguistic Minorities Project (LMP) (1984) *Schools Language Survey Manual of Use*. University of London Institute of Education.

Linguistic Minorities Project (LMP) (1985) *The Other Languages of England*. London: Routledge & Kegan Paul.

MOBBS, M. (1985) *Britain's South Asian Languages*. London: Centre for Information on Language Teaching and Research.

NEWBOLT, H. (1921) *The Teaching of English in England*. London: HMSO.

NICHOLAS, J. (1988) 'British Language Diversity Surveys (1977–1987): a critical examination', *Language and Education* 2(1): 15–33.

PATTANAYAK, D. P. (1985) *Language and Power*. Conference Report, London: North London Community Group.

PATTANAYAK, D. P. (1987) *Multilingualism and Multiculturalism: Britain and India*. Occasional Paper No. 1, International Association for Intercultural Education, University of London Institute of Education.

PEAL, E. and LAMBERT, W. (1960) 'The relation of bilingualism to intelligence', *Psychological monographs* **76**: 546

RAMPTON, A. (1981) *West Indian Children in our Schools* (Interim report of the Committee of Inquiry into the Education of Children from Ethnic Minority Groups.) London: HMSO.

ROSEN, H. and BURGESS, A. (1980) *The Languages and Dialects of London Schoolchildren*. London: Ward Lock Education.

SIMONS, H. (1979) *Mother Tongue and Culture in Bedfordshire*. EC Pilot Project, First External Evaluation Report, Cambridge: University of Cambridge Institute of Education.

SKUTNABB-KANGAS, T. and CUMMINS, J. (eds) (1988) *Minority Education: From Shame to Struggle*. Clevedon, Avon: Multilingual Matters.

SMITH, G. (1984) *Sampling Linguistic Minorities: A Technical Report on the Adult Language Use Survey*. LMP/CLE/LINC Working Paper No. 4, London: University of London Institute of Education.

SPENS, W. (1938) *Report of the Consultative Committee on Secondary Education with Special Reference to Grammar Schools and Technical High Schools*. London: HMSO.

SUTCLIFFE, D. (1982) *British Black English*. Oxford: Basil Blackwell.

SUTCLIFFE, D. and WONG, A. (1986) *The Language of the Black Experience*. Oxford: Basil Blackwell.

SWAIN, M. and CUMMINS, M. (1986) *Bilingualism and Education*. London: Longman.

SWANN, LORD (1985) *Education for All*. London: HMSO.

TANSLEY, P., NAVAZ, H. and ROUSSOU, M. (1985) *Working with Many Languages: A Handbook for Community Language Teachers*. London: School Curriculum Development Committee.

TAYLOR, M. (1987) *Chinese Pupils in Britain: A Review of Research into the Education of Pupils of Chinese Origin*. Windsor: National Foundation for Educational Research/Nelson.

TIZARD, B. and HUGHES, M. (1984) *Young Children Learning*. London: Fontana.

TOSI, A. (1983) *Immigration and Bilingual Education*. Oxford: Pergamon.

TRUDGILL, P. (ed.) (1984) *Language in the British Isles*. Cambridge University Press.

VISRAM, R. (1986) *Ayahs, Princes and Lascars*. London: Pluto.

WELLS, G. (1987) *The Meaning Makers: Children Learning Language and Using Language to Learn*. London: Hodder & Stoughton.

Part one

The older mother tongues of the British Isles

The 'older mother tongues' is an expression which, to the best of our knowledge, was first introduced by James (1978) in an edited volume with contributions on Welsh, Gaelic and Irish. Following the new waves of immigration of the twentieth century, particularly those of the post-war period, it had become necessary to develop terminology which would distinguish between, on the one hand, the newer 'indigenizing' and, on the other hand, the longer-established 'indigenous' linguistic minorities of the British Isles.

It is speculated that the Celtic languages first made their appearance in the British Isles in the Iron Age and that, by the beginning of the Christian era, all areas were predominantly Celtic-speaking with the exception of the Pictish areas in the north and north-east of Scotland. Two forms of Celtic began progressively to grow apart. One branch, Goedelic or Gaelic, later developed into separate Scots, Irish and Manx varieties. However, during the so-called 'Dark Ages', there was no substantial divergence, for instance, between Old Irish and Early Scottish Gaelic, and throughout the medieval period, the two languages shared a common literary standard, sustained by hereditary literary orders and travelling bardic schools (Jackson 1951; Thomson 1984). The Celtic language spoken in Ireland is generally referred to as 'Irish', in order to distinguish it from Scots Gaelic, although in Irish the name of the language is *Gaeilge*. Welsh, Cornish and Breton developed from another branch of the Celtic language family, the Brythonic or British, and later diverged in ways similar to Irish and Scots Gaelic and Manx.

Celtic languages draw on modes of grammatical organization which are markedly different from the majority of Indo-European languages, especially English. Thus, sentences are structured with

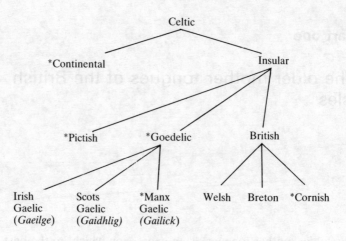

FIGURE PI.I The Celtic Sub-family of Indo-European languages

the verb first, followed by the subject, object and the rest of the predicate; there is a system of prepositional pronouns where prepositions are marked for person; consonant mutations in the form, for instance, of lenition and nasalization, carry syntactic and semantic information.

The story of the Celtic languages has been one of long decline. The expansion of the Angles and Saxons in the fifth century marked the beginning of a process which has been under way ever since. Cornish began to die out about the end of the eighteenth century and Manx came to a formal conclusion with the death of the last native speaker in December 1974. Scots Gaelic has retreated to the Highlands and islands and Irish to the far west. Welsh has similarly undergone an assault from the south-east and the border counties. Industrialization, famine, emigration, economic restructuring and the in-migration of English speakers have all helped to accelerate this process.

The inevitability of imminent language death is not, however, by any means assured. The growth of the ethnic revival during the late twentieth century is a force to be reckoned with. And while there are quite clearly many differences between the situation of the older Celtic tongues and the 'indigenizing' languages, the presence of many new language minorities within the British Isles, and the increasing confidence with which they are beginning to assert their legitimate needs and rights, has served to heighten the longer-standing plight of their Celtic predecessors.

By the same token, speakers of the newer mother tongues have much to learn from the situation of the Celtic languages which have, in many areas, made substantial progress in terms of official recognition and the provision of bilingual education. Much more work remains to be done but there are none the less many lessons to be learned: the importance of a co-ordinated language policy which involves central government, local authorities and individual schools; the pooling of resources and the sharing of information; the vital role which the media and, in particular, broadcasting, have to play.

Discussion up until this point has focused on the Celtic languages and the similarities and differences between these older mother tongues and the newer indigenizing language minorities of the twentieth century. However, if we choose to make the entry to the twentieth century the majoi division between the various minority languages, we would be committing a serious sin of omission by limiting the older mother tongues to the Celtic languages. At least two other groups should be included. The first are the Roma, otherwise known as Gypsies or Travellers. Thought to have come from India, possibly in the fifth century, they gradually made their way across Europe, reaching the UK by the fifteenth century. The extreme hostility of the various host societies, combined with the Roma concept of ritual purity or *mukadi kovels*, has ensured the maintenance of autonomous Romani varieties through the centuries.

Significantly, the legacy of suspicion and distrust on the part of the mainstream society has been sufficiently strong for most members of mainstream society to remain totally ignorant of the linguistic and cultural traditions maintained by Gypsies over the centuries. Today, the British variety, sometimes known as Anglo-Romani, has lost the inflected grammar of its continental neighbours and is limited to certain elements of grammar, such as prepositions and pronouns, and a common lexical pool of Romani origin. Anglo-Romani none the less fulfils the same function as its inflected predecessors: it marks a strong sense of Romani identity and insulates the Traveller community from the *gaujos* or outsiders.

Another seriously misunderstood group which must surely be included among the older mother tongues are users of British Sign Language (BSL). Although BSL was widely used to some considerable effect in deaf education in the nineteenth century, the twentieth century has seen a dramatic reversal of this trend. Signing has been dismissed as a 'telegraphic', 'ugly', 'ungrammatical', 'broken' and totally inadequate form of communication; in many quarters it is not even accorded the status of a true language. Yet close linguistic analysis shows that BSL shares many of the features of spoken languages, especially creoles, and is able to fulfil the same range of communicative functions as any other variety.

Many deaf people argue that the consequences of this stance for deaf children have been catastrophic. Hearing parents have been urged to use speech not sign with their deaf children, a situation which has given rise to considerable frustration for children and parents alike. In some cases, sign has been banned from schools for the deaf; in others, only the use of contrived sign systems which follow the word order of English – and which are therefore akin to foreign languages for the deaf learner – is sanctioned. Only in the last decade have significant moves been made in deaf education towards a 'total communication' approach, which includes the use of BSL.

The clear picture which emerges from the older mother tongues – the Celtic languages, Romani and BSL alike – is that the dominant group is often extremely intolerant of difference and can react both cruelly and punitively to those who dare to fall out of step either linguistically or culturally. Against this background, the slow but sure movement during the post-war period to a greater appreciation of diversity is simultaneously a source of great hope for members of minority communities and of great enrichment for the dominant majority. The recognition of the many strong links between indigenous and indigenizing mother tongues is a vital part in this ongoing process.

References

JAMES, C. (ed.) (1978) *The Older Mother Tongues of the British Isles*. London: Centre for Information on Language Teaching and Research.

JACKSON, K. H. (1951) *Language and History in Early Britain*. Edinburgh: Edinburgh University Press.

STENSON, N. (1981) *Studies in Irish Syntax*. Tubingen: Narr.

THOMSON, R. L. (1984) 'The history of the Celtic languages in the British Isles'. In P. Trudgill (ed.) *Language in the British Isles,* Cambridge: Cambridge University Press, *pp* 241–58

Chapter 2

The British Sign Language community

Paddy Ladd

The sign-language deals mainly with material objects. It dreads and avoids the abstract.... There is, of course, a wide gulf between such a language as this and the cultivated and refined languages of the world.

REVEREND J. KEEP (1871)

BSL is a language with a grammar specifically suited for vision; it is a language which is capable of very fine nuances of expression; it is a language capable of wit, drama and poetry; and – finally – because it evolved for the eye rather than for the ear – it is a language which gives us many clues to the nature of human language itself.

URSULA BELLUGI (1976)

British Sign Language (BSL) has not only been a language struggling for its existence – it has also had a struggle to be accepted as a bona fide language at all. It was not until the beginning of the 1980s that linguists were able to confirm that the gestures and facial expressions associated with deaf people were actually bound by grammatical structures to the same extent as spoken languages. The findings of linguists are, however, still in the early stages of dissemination and many people still look upon deaf people as handicapped rather than as a linguistic minority.

British Sign Language has been traced back to the 1500s, but is probably as old as Jewish Sign Language which has been documented as early as the sixth century AD (Miles 1988). Originally it would have been used only in isolated families and villages, but communities of users developed as the population concentrated in towns during the Industrial Revolution. Deaf schools and clubs began to appear in the early 1800s and by the end of the nineteenth century covered the United Kingdom; BSL, deaf culture, deaf art and deaf pride all made rapid progress in this period, still described by deaf people as 'The Golden Age'.

The growth of the deaf schools in the nineteenth century, and thus of deaf marriages and public awareness of BSL, began to alarm many people who feared that, at this rate, the numbers of deaf people would start to swamp the population. They proposed that BSL should be banned in deaf schools and that deaf teachers should be removed from their posts and they tried to outlaw deaf marriages and deaf clubs (Lane 1987). In the first two of these aims they were successful: sign languages and deaf teachers were outlawed following the 1800 Congress of Milan, called to discuss the future of deaf education. By the turn of the century BSL had been driven underground with dire consequences for the educational performance of deaf children (see section on education and language reproduction, below). It continued to thrive, however, in the deaf clubs and in the families of the 10 percent of deaf children born to deaf parents.

The BSL community currently numbers between 50,000 and 100,000. No government has yet expressed an interest in establishing accurate figures. It is spread throughout the UK, with over 250 clubs or local communities, although not all deaf people attend the clubs. Since many members attended deaf schools and continue to meet each other at regional and national gatherings, there is a high level of national awareness and cultural consciousness. Hearing people are also members of the community – many hearing children of deaf parents, for instance, have BSL as their first language. Likewise, friends of deaf people join the community or marry into it.

The linguistic status of BSL

There is ample evidence of the disregard of deaf people as full and feeling human beings. It was suggested as recently as 1974 by the headteacher of the most influential deaf school in Europe that deaf people should be discouraged from marrying each other (*British Deaf News* 1974: 342). There have been frequent reports that deaf parents of deaf children have been completely ignored and excluded from organizations of parents with deaf children, from school PTAs and from deaf children's mother and toddler groups. Operations to sterilize deaf women without their consent have also been uncovered (Montgomery, Hay and Holmes 1979).

It should come as no surprise that the low status attached to deaf people extends to their language. There has always been a condescending attitude on the part of speakers of the dominant language towards signing which has been described variously as 'broken', 'ugly' and 'telegraphic'. It is interesting to note, however, that the same structures which are cited as examples of the limitations of sign languages (see, for example, Namir and Schlesinger 1978) occur commonly in certain spoken languages. Thus, non-inflection of nouns and verbs, as well as zero copulas, are regular features not only of sign languages but also of creoles world-wide. Compare the following examples of BSL written glosses (upper case) and Jamaican Creole (lower case) together with their English translations:-

BOY TWO CAR HAVE – The boy has got two cars
De bwoy got two car

YESTERDAY BOY WALK SCHOOL – The boy walked to school yesterday
De bwoy walk to school yesterday

JOHN HAPPY – John is happy
John happy

A strong case has in fact been made by various writers for considering sign languages as creoles on both structural and socio-historical grounds (Fischer 1979; Ladd and Edwards 1982; Deuchar 1984).

There have also been suggestions that sign languages are necessarily restricted. Crystal and Craig (1978: 147), for instance, argue that: 'Physical and perceptual limitations must necessarily limit the range of iconic vocabulary and hinder the use of various processes found to be important in the analysis of speech – for example, the process of extension and restriction in metaphorical expressions and the like'. The premise that sign language is iconic (*viz* the meaning is transparent from the sign), however, is false. Although we would expect a greater degree of iconicity for visual signs than for auditory words, signs tend to become more arbitrary as time goes by (Frishberg 1979). The fact that hearing people do not understand signing and frequently make wildly inaccurate guesses at the meaning of individual signs (Bellugi 1976) also throws suspicion on the notion of iconicity. Moreover, close examination of BSL shows that it is in fact rich in metaphor. The great potential of sign language in this area can be shown, for example in the sign for a certain campaigner for deaf rights well known for the opposition which his views often provoke. The sign for his name (which begins with 'G') consists of two clenched fists, but instead of simply holding one on top of the other as you would in finger spelling, the fists are rotated in a clockwise direction one over the other, signifying 'G, the stirrer'.

It has been suggested, too, that sign language is necessarily context dependent (Trevoort 1975). This assumption derives partly from the fact that the object of study is often the language of young children who have not yet been exposed to adult signing and partly because of an inadequate understanding of the organizing principles of sign language. Observation of BSL in normal social settings, however, can leave no doubt that its users can express both context-bound and context-free meaning in the same way as 'normal' language.

The linguistic status of sign languages was finally established only in the late 1970s and 1980s thanks to the efforts of linguists who have finally established their rule-governed nature and communicative efficiency (cf Woll, Kyle and Deuchar 1981; Kyle et al 1985; Deuchar 1984; Edwards and Ladd 1985). Sign language is not, as is commonly thought, universal, and the many different national sign languages are by no means mutually intelligible. This can be illustrated for instance, by reference to the way in which BSL has followed English around the globe. Whereas Australian and New Zealand sign languages have a significant proportion of BSL signs, American Sign Language (ASL) is quite different and poses communication difficulties for signers from other parts of the English-speaking world. Within BSL, regional dialects are very strong, partly because, as we will see, sign language was forced underground at the end of the nineteenth century and partly because of the absence of a written form. BSL is particularly strong in the north of England and Scotland where the ban on its use came later than in the south. This is still a rich, untapped field for dialectologists.

Changing patterns of language use

The twentieth century has seen a dramatic decline in the use and status of BSL following on the 1880 Congress of Milan. The outlawing of sign from schools for the deaf had serious social consequences well beyond the domain of education. Whereas deaf people had previously taken an active role, for instance, in founding schools and clubs, there was a marked decline in self-confidence which led to the domination of the deaf community by hearing 'missioners' and welfare workers. The population at large now saw not BSL users but 'hearing-impaired individuals' in permanent need of social work help.

The ability of the deaf community to communicate in a full range of situations in BSL diminished. The core of the community has always been the 10 per cent of deaf children who learn the language from their deaf parents and play a crucial role in transmitting the language. The other 90 per cent of deaf children, born to hearing parents, were now forced to learn BSL outside the classroom from the other children, especially those with deaf parents.

Even where sign language was allowed in schools, teachers chose to use not BSL but various forms of contrived sign systems which followed English word order (see section on Education and language reproduction, below). Partly as a result of this, a continuum of usage developed, ranging from BSL at one pole to what has been called Pidgin Signed English (Woodward 1973) at the other (see Dalphinis and Nwenmely (Vol. 2, chs 2 and 3) for discussion of a parallel situation for Afro-Caribbean creoles). Pidgin Signed English emerged as the language of upward mobility and its use was reinforced by those who worked with deaf people. It became the favoured variety for formal situations such as church services and contact with the wider society. In contrast, BSL was seen as the language of informal conversation, and those who used it most were (and still are) referred to as 'the less intelligent deaf', 'the stupid deaf' and so on. Negative attitudes such as these threaten to cut off the intelligentsia from the grass roots in a community which has already been seriously damaged by the reluctance of hearing people to acknowledge sign.

The pressures which have been operating against BSL have also produced a high degree of linguistic differentiation between generations. It has been widely noted by the adult deaf community who were educated before oralism was rigidly imposed in schools that children's communication is unsystematic inasmuch as it combines gestures, lip patterns and conventional and *ad hoc* signs. In several schools, colour signs, for instance, are all built around one manual sign with the lips providing the key to the colour intended to be communicated, whereas BSL has separate signs for each colour. In the early teens, however, there is often a rapid development towards BSL: syntax and vocabulary become much more highly developed, and the role of lip patterns as markers decreases. Nevertheless the signing styles of young and old still differ markedly and add to the divisions within the community.

The 1980s have seen increasing pressure from deaf organizations for the recognition of BSL as the natural language of the deaf community. Linguists have at last acknowledged the legitimacy of BSL as a language in its own right. It is wholly appropriate, for instance, that BSL should finally be appreciated as an indigenous language of the British Isles by its inclusion in the present volume. In contrast, however, political legitimation has not yet been achieved. The British pressure group, the National Union of the Deaf (NUD), has attempted to get the United Nations to accept that the world's sign language users constitute linguistic minorities. More recently the main deaf body of the UK, the British Deaf Association (BDA), has begun a serious push for European Community recognition of the sign languages of the member states. The outcome of these initiatives is not yet known but it seems highly likely that recognition will be achieved at some point in the future. The spin-off effects of official status across a wide range of fields will be considerable, as the Swedish example has already shown (see section on Education and language reproduction, below).

Language, culture and community

Deaf organizations around the world were formed after the events of 1880, and the Congress of Milan, but it is only in the last few years that they have begun to show any discernible results for their efforts. Only now, with the use of BSL once more in public places and on television, and with the British population expressing an interest in learning it, is it once again possible to examine the language, its community and its culture.

There are three major organizations which focus on deaf issues. The Royal National Institute for the Deaf (RNID) has been viewed by many deaf people with considerable suspicion because it is not a direct consumer organization and because of its traditional perception of deaf people as handicapped rather than as a linguistic minority. The British Deaf Association (BDA), in contrast, is the major organization *of* (rather than *for*) deaf people with branches in every town in the UK and 18000 members. The BDA was responsible for keeping the BSL community together as a national entity in the decades when oralism threatened to decimate it. Its central focus on its formation in 1890 was on education, but it has only been from the 1970s onwards that any success has been achieved in that field.

The National Union of the Deaf (NUD), a small pressure group, was formed in 1976 and is the only completely deaf-run group. Their work has involved vigorous campaigning in education and establishing the principle of deaf people running their own affairs. Their campaign to get sign language television programmes has also borne fruit in the 1980s and the BSL community has consequently had a higher profile nationally.

A great deal more work, however, remains to be done in educating the public at large to the legitimate requirements of the deaf community. The role of the sign language interpreter, for instance, is crucial to the true integration of the BSL community into mainstream British society. Here again, reactions to the provision of interpreters reflect the same pattern of negative attitudes towards BSL. In the last century, skill in BSL interpreting was widespread. School staff and missioners to the deaf worked together and deaf clubs had a strong tradition of outside speakers coming to give lectures on a wide range of subjects. Individuals wishing to contact statutory authorities used the missioners or members of their family to interpret.

With the decline in the status of BSL in the twentieth century, the number of people capable of interpreting also declined and by the 1970s there was almost no one capable of interpreting from BSL to English. Interpreting in the other direction was mainly in Pidgin Signed English despite the fact that the majority of BSL users could only imperfectly understand the 'interpreter'.

At the time of writing, the onus is still very much on deaf people to use specialist services set up on their behalf rather than on statutory authorities to provide interpreters of their own accord. Hospitals, solicitors, employers, Citizens' Advice Bureaux, museums, unions, colleges, local authorities have yet to accept their responsibility for providing their own interpreters. One exception to this overall trend is the Greater London Council. They provided, among other things, interpreters for staff meetings and training courses for their deaf staff, and hopefully this model will spread.

It is clear that the more confident deaf people become and the more they wish to assert themselves in society, the more work there will be for interpreters. There is already a chronic shortage, exacerbated by neglecting a sizeable section of the population who could become interpreters – hearing children of deaf parents. It is, however, encouraging that the 1980s have seen an upsurge in the numbers of hearing people who wish to learn the language and the BSL Teaching Agency has been set up to train deaf people to teach BSL. This is an important departure. Previously, outsiders who wished to learn to sign were taught by hearing welfare officers who taught a form of Pidgin Signed English which allowed for only very limited communication. The deaf community was then almost completely isolated, with no access to mainstream Britain.

If deaf people are to be able to play a full and equal part in the wider society, attention needs to be paid not only to the provision of interpreters but also to the need for translation. The very low levels of literacy achieved by many deaf children taught by oral methods (see section on Education and language reproduction, below) is a matter for serious concern well beyond the school walls. The sheer mass of information that deaf people find impossible to access is awesome and the main requests to welfare services for help have consistently concerned translating and explaining official documents such as tax forms. Until deaf people achieve the same levels of literacy which were widespread when signing was a legitimate vehicle of education, the need for help in translation of this kind will continue unabated.

The main progress in this area has taken the form of the London Deaf Video Project sponsored in 1985 by the Greater London Council. It aims to translate official information into BSL on video cassettes which are circulated to London deaf clubs. Despite this crucial lead, no other local or central government department has yet accepted their responsibility to translate such information.

Because of the lack of meaningful contact between deaf and hearing communities in the twentieth century, few hearing people are aware of the existence of a rich deaf culture. Like many other aspects of deaf life, deaf culture came under serious threat with the outlawing of sign. In the 1880s there were deaf drama groups performing in BSL and deaf periodicals of the time point to the language being used both playfully and creatively. 'Good signing' was widely appreciated, audiences travelling miles to see a particular 'speaker'. However, with the banning of BSL in schools, the community's drama and poetry started being performed in Pidgin Signed English, even though many people could not understand the proceedings. Plays and poems about deaf cultural experience began to disappear. Word play using sign declined, although puns based on Pidgin Signed English were common among English users, both deaf and hearing.

The only creative mode that survived was story-telling. Although it no longer serves to pass on much of deaf history (no doubt, a consequence of the low self-esteem already discussed), it remains a major part of discourse and an important element in deaf identity. The importance of story-telling as an integral part of conversation has been documented for Black American and other cultures where the written word takes second place (Edwards and Sienkewicz, forthcoming). It is certainly true for BSL. It is very much a case of 'Ask a BSL user a question and you'll get a story in reply'.

With the rise of deaf and BSL pride in the 1980s, creative play with BSL began to grow. Drama incorporating deaf cultural themes is becoming increasingly common, as, too, is the use of BSL. The work of composers like the deaf sign poet, Dorothy Miles, has become more accepted and songs in sign have begun to move out from the church where they have stayed for most of the twentieth century. Deaf cabaret groups have begun to form and the seeds have been sown for a strong resurgence of BSL art in the 1990s.

Even so, users of Pidgin Signed English have continued to dominate arts funding and liaison with the English-speaking theatre. And an indication of the continuing low status of BSL came when *Children of a Lesser God,* an American play about a deaf woman in which signing plays a central role, came to Europe. In many countries, the use of American Sign Language (ASL) in the play provoked strong protest and, in some cases, the play was immediately adapted into the native sign language. However, the play was performed in ASL in Britain with little protest from the deaf community who, ironically, were the only members of the audience not able to follow the play.

None the less, considerable progress has been made and will no doubt continue to be made in the coming years. One likely avenue of development is 'deaf studies', along the lines of the Black studies courses in the USA and Britain in the 1960s and 1970s. Insistence on the medical model which holds that BSL users are simply individual, isolated 'impaired-hearing people' has led to the rejection of the idea that deaf people and BSL have a history and culture. The publication in 1987 of Harlan Lane's seminal work on this area, *'When the Mind Hears'* has, however, started to spark off interest in discovering deaf history and we can expect that 'deaf studies' will become an important issue in the community in coming years.

Education and language reproduction

Following the 1880 Congress of Milan, signing was outlawed in the schools of Europe. Accounts of methods used to enforce this policy are common in the deaf community: deaf children's hands

were tied behind their backs, physical punishment and even tor-
ture were used and older children were set to spy on the others
in tactics that parallel the use of the Welsh not (see ch. 6).

From this point onwards, all communication was conducted by
the mouth or the pen, with disastrous results. In the nineteenth
century deaf schools had been producing professional people:
teachers, missioners, journalists, architects, artists, astronomers
and inventors. A hundred years later, a survey conducted by Conrad (1979) showed that the average reading age of the deaf school
leaver was 8.75 years; the speech of 90 per cent of deaf children
was described as unintelligible; and their lip-reading skill was
found to be no better than that of hearing children (who had
never been taught to use this form of communication).

When some schools finally started to accept that signing had a
place in education they tended to bypass BSL in favour of contrived sign systems such as Signed English and the Paget Gormon
Signed System which followed English word order, inventing
some lexical items and drawing others from BSL. Another
development currently in wide use is Sign Supporting English
which not only follows English word order but uses signed affixes,
prepositions, conjuctions and copulas which are not found in
BSL. However, the introduction of contrived sign systems has
had limited success, partly because no training was available for
teachers; partly because no standards were set from school to
school for language competence; and partly because of the inherent drawbacks to teaching children through sign systems which
attempt to mimic English.

At first sight, it seems reasonable to assume that if one visually
mirrors English to a deaf child, the child will then reabsorb and
reproduce the language. In practice, however, the situation would
seem to be more complex. Some people feel that these systems
have the effect of overloading the visual information and often
obscuring the meaning of utterances between teacher and child.
It has also been pointed out that few people are able to use such
complicated systems fluently. In contrast, the structure of BSL
seems perfectly adapted to the visual medium. Although lexical
items in all the sign languages of the world differ very greatly,
they all seem to have very similar syntactic structure, which might
suggest that the visual medium is subject to even more powerful
linguistic constraints than spoken languages.

Given the profound structural differences between natural and
contrived sign languages, the deaf child being taught through the
medium of a contrived sign system is in a situation very similar
to that of the second language learner in the hearing classroom.

This situation is sometimes complicated still further by the fact that children often reply in BSL which many of the teachers do not understand; there is therefore a tendency for classroom teaching to revert to a teacher-centred model.

In the 1980s pressure for a bilingual education incorporating concepts from mother tongue teaching is gaining ground. A group called 'LASER' has been established, and progress can be expected in the next decade. A similar organization in France, 2LPE (Deux Langues Pour Education), has already had considerable success. Bilingualism, of course, is a qualitatively different concept, since teachers have to change from a philosophy of 'handicapped children needing communication' to one that recognizes the validity of the child's internal language and culture, and teaching from that outwards to English. This is a big step for teachers working in an atmosphere which pathologizes the language of deaf people. The example of Sweden, however, has shown very clearly what can be achieved with a change in attitude towards sign. There, the government has recognized Swedish Sign Language as the first language of the deaf child and Swedish as the second language and set about instituting appropriate training for teachers. Unfortunately, at the time of writing, the Department of Education and Science has shown no signs of recognizing the relevance of this model for the British situation.

A number of other issues must be placed firmly on the political and teaching agenda as priority issues in the coming years. One such issue is the question of the multiracial nature of the present-day British deaf community. Deaf children of Caribbean and Asian origin began to enter the BSL community in the 1970s. Because oralist educational policies were at their height during this period, the literacy, deaf consciousness and ability to join the deaf community of these groups, like their White peers, has been damaged. This has reinforced institutionalized racism, leading to under-representation and involvement in deaf life. Young people of all races do, however, spend a lot of time together and frequently assert that, unlike in the hearing world, racial tension is not a feature of the deaf community. This position is no doubt an accurate reflection of the way in which deaf people divide the world into two groups – deaf and hearing – so that the shared deaf identity takes precedence over everything else.

A related area of concern surrounds the choice of marriage partners for deaf people of Asian origin. The tendency is for the young deaf women to stay at home and, in many cases, to be married to hearing men. Tension is growing as young men, White and Black, begin to outnumber the women in social events. Many deaf people of Asian origin feel their primary culture is BSL culture and that they should have freedom of movement in the deaf community. This is an area which requires great sensitivity on the part of all concerned.

A rather different subject for debate is the effective ban of deaf people from teaching in deaf schools. At present, the numbers of deaf teachers are negligible and these are all people who have become deaf later in life. Schools are beginning to employ classroom aides, but further development is blocked by the Department of Education and Science, who insist that all teachers of the deaf must also have experience of teaching in the mainstream (notice the parallel here with the high proportion of mother tongue teachers who are only accorded instructor status, *passim* both volumes). They argue that any certification for teaching simply in deaf schools would not be a full and equal qualification. However, this proviso deliberately and effectively prevents suitably qualified deaf people from becoming teachers of the deaf because, quite clearly, they cannot function well in mainstream schools.

Many deaf people believe that deaf education will never be effective until the teaching profession is fully opened up to deaf teachers. Not only would deaf teachers have the advantage of competence in BSL, they would also provide a valuable role model for deaf children. Their knowledge of the special ways in which the deaf child thinks would clearly have innumerable applications right across the education system. The situation is currently deadlocked and only continuing political pressure from the deaf community is likely to bring about any change.

Integration is another matter for ongoing concern. The 1981 Education Act has further eroded the position of sign. British Sign Languange and deaf culture have always been nurtured in the community created by deaf schools, even when the teaching practice in these schools has been predominantly or exclusively oralist. The move to integrate handicapped children into the mainstream has meant that only 13 per cent of deaf children now attend deaf schools. The isolation of deaf children from other children who can develop meaningful peer relations through sign has caused great anger in the deaf community. People suspect, for instance, that the literacy levels of deaf children 'lost' in the mainstream are much lower than they should be, and that they may be suffering serious psychological damage. Little headway, however, has been made in modifying the present policy of integration.

The situation has not been helped by the disabled pro-integration bodies who have ironically 'gained' more for deaf than for disabled children. It will be crucial in the future that disabled groups support deaf people in their demands for separate deaf education, just as deaf people have supported disabled people's wishes to integrate. Similarly, it is essential that the public at large must be educated as to the reasons for the deaf community's wishes for separate education and the damage which they are doing by placing deaf children in mainstream schools.

If these problems are resolved, the future may see a workable compromise where deaf children have access to mainstream education on *their* terms and from their own cultural perspective. The integration of deaf children at present is very much a one-sided affair; in genuine integration hearing children would also have access to BSL and deaf culture. The American situation is considerably in advance of the British in this respect; ASL, for instance, can be learned in mainstream schools and is even accepted for some university degrees as a foreign language. In contrast, BSL has not yet made headway in the mainstream curriculum though we can realistically expect some developments in this area in the 1990s. Until this is achieved, however, the touchstone of the argument is, as Steve Biko has put it in a South African context: 'Not integration but de-segregation'.

Political acceptance is crucial if change is to take place. The neglect of deaf people's demands is linked to the pathological view of deaf people as inferior and handicapped. Recognition of BSL, together with the cultural resurgence which will inevitably accompany it, would play a critical role in turning this view of deafness on its head and the consequences of this change in attitude would be felt in very many ways. The form and content of deaf education would be called into question. The provision of interpreters would allow deaf people to follow college and vocational courses to which they are currently denied entry and to be able to access news and entertainment which are available to hearing people. In short, the recognition of BSL would allow deaf people to participate on equal terms in all aspects of public life.

References

BELLUGI, U. (1976) *Attitudes towards Sign Language. Is There a Need for Change?* Carlisle: British Deaf News (1974) British Deaf Association.

CONRAD, R. (1979) *The Deaf School Child.* London and New York: Harper & Row.

CRYSTAL, D. and CRAIG, E. (1978) 'Contrived sign language'. In I. Schlesinger and L. Namir (eds) *Sign Language of the Deaf*, London: Academic Press.

DEUCHAR, M. (1984) *British Sign Language.* London: Routledge & Kegan Paul.

EDWARDS, V. and LADD, P. (1985) 'The linguistic status of BSL', *York Papers in Linguistics* 11: 31–41.

EDWARDS, V. and SIENKEWICZ, T. (forthcoming). *Oral Cultures Past and Present: Rappin' and Homer* Oxford: Basil Blackwell.

FISCHER, S. (1979) 'Sign languages and creoles'. In Siple, P. (ed.) *Understanding language through Sign Language Research,* New York: Academic Press, *pp* 304–31.

FRISHBERG, N. (1979) 'Arbitrariness and iconicity: historical change in ASL', *Language* 51: 696–715.

KEEP, J. (1871) 'The sign-language', *American Annals of the Deaf* 16: 30.

KYLE, J. and WOLL, B. with PULLEN, G. and MADDIX, F. (1985) *Sign Language. The Study of Deaf People and Their Language.* Cambridge: Cambridge University Press.

LADD, P. and EDWARDS, Y. (1982) 'British Sign Language and West Indian Creole', *Sign Language Studies* 35: 101–26.

LANE, H. (1987) *When the Mind Hears.* London: Souvenir Press.

MILES, D. (1988) *British Sign Language.* London: BBC Publications.

MONTGOMERY, G., HAY, J. and HOLMES, M. (1979) *The Integration and Disintegration of the Deaf in Society.* Edinburgh: Scottish Workshop Publications.

NAMIR, L. and SCHLESINGER, I. (1978) 'The grammar of sign language'. In I. Schlesinger and L. Namir (eds) *Sign Language of the Deaf,* London: Academic Press.

TREVOORT, B. (1975) *Developmental Features of Visual Communication.* Amsterdam: North-Holland.

WOLL, B., KYLE, J. and DEUCHAR, M. (eds) (1981) *Perspectives on British Sign Language and Deafness.* London: Croom Helm.

WOODWARD, J. (1973) 'Some characteristics of Pidgin Sign English', *Sign Language Studies* 3: 39–46.

Chapter 3

The Gaelic speech community

Kenneth MacKinnon

Mhair i fòs,	She has nevertheless withstood,
Is cha téid a ghlòir air chall	And neither shall her glory be lost
Dh'aindeoin gò	Despite the deceit
Is mioruin mhòir nan Gall	And the great illwill of the Lowlanders.

ALASDAIR MAC MHÀIGHISTIR ALASDAIR:	ALEXANDER MACDONALD
Moladh na Sean Chànain Gàidhlig (c. 1750)	*The Praise of the Ancient Gaelic Language (c.* 1750)

Théid dualchas an aghaidh nan creag	(Heritage will persist against the rocks.)

(GAELIC PROVERB)

Scotland's linguistic history is complex. Its original inhabitants spoke a form of early Welsh – but there is conjecture concerning what was spoken by the northern Picts (Jackson 1955: 129–60). The Gaelic language originally came to Scotland c. AD 500 with the expansion of the northern Irish kingdom of Dál Riata into the western Highlands and islands of Scotland (Bannerman 1974). The expansion of this settlement and the subsequent absorption of the Pictish kingdom in northern Scotland, the British kingdom of Strathclyde in south-western Scotland and part of Anglian Northumbria in the south-east, established a largely Gaelic-speaking Scottish kingdom roughly coterminous with present-day Scotland by the eleventh century. Celtic Christianity gained influence throughout this area with the coming of Columba from Derry to Iona in 563, and this missionizing Celtic Church first brought literacy and learning not only to the Gaelic Scots and their near neighbours but to most of England also (Green 1911: 43–8).

From the reign of Malcolm III 'Ceannmór' (1054–96), Gaelic lost its pre-eminence first at court, then among the aristocracy to Norman French influences, and subsequently in the Lowlands through the establishment of English-speaking burghs in eastern and central Scotland, to Scots. This distinctive Scottish language originally known as Inglis — and more latterly as Lallans – derives from the Anglian speech of south-eastern Scotland, and the speech of English and Flemish settlers in the burghs of eastern Scotland in the early Middle Ages. As the speech of a mercantile burghal class, it spread westward and northwards displacing the early Welsh of the Strathclyde Britons, and the Gaelic spoken elsewhere (MacKinnon 1974: 19–29). In the northern Highlands and islands, Norse settlement brought about the development of the Norn language in Caithness and the northern isles. By the eighteenth century Norn became extinct as a distinctive vernacular, but has strongly influenced both literary Scots and especially its northern dialects (Geipel 1971: 74–5).

As a West Germanic language, developing separately from English from more specifically Anglian and Celtic roots, with both French and Norn influences, Scots became the language of state administration in medieval Scotland, and developed one of the most vigorous literary traditions of late medieval and Renaissance Europe (Kay 1986: 41–58). Today, with the absorption of the Scottish state into the UK, Scots has become a non-standard congeries of dialects, albeit with some lively continuing vernacular literature. Gaelic also continues as one of Scotland's living indigenous languages but, as a Celtic language, has been better able to resist English influences in its speech forms.

By the seventeenth century Gaelic had retreated to the Highlands and Hebrides, which still retained much of their political independence, Celtic culture and social structure. These differences came to be seen as inimical to the interests of the Scottish and the subsequent British state, and from the late fifteenth century into the eighteenth a number of Acts of the Scottish and British parliaments aimed at promoting English language education first among the aristocracy and subsequently among the general population, at outlawing the native learned orders, and finally on disarming and breaking the clans and outlawing Highland dress and music.

In the nineteenth century, contemporaneously with the

notorious 'Highland Clearances' (the enforced migration of the crofting population), a popular and successful voluntary Gaelic schools system came into being. This was superseded after legislation in 1872 by a national English-medium school system in which Gaelic had little if any place. Some measure of security was given to the crofting community by legislation in 1886. Despite the extension of the franchise, with universal male suffrage from 1867, and the development of local government in the 1880s and 1890s, recognition of Gaelic was very slow in coming.

The neglect of Gaelic in the education system after 1872 resulted in the language surviving as an oral rather than a literary medium for many of its speakers. The purpose of school was to promote *English* literacy. Thus traditional Gaelic literacy was associated with a religious culture which emphasized Bible reading, home worship and the singing of the Metrical Psalms. Calvinism has promoted Gaelic literacy, and in the strongholds of the Free Church and Free Presbyterian Church, adult Gaelic reading ability compares well with English reading ability. Where Protestantism, supportive education policies and high incidence of Gaelic speakers combine, Gaelic literacy can be compared with English literacy levels, as in northern Skye, rural Lewis, Harris and North Uist. Gaelic literacy is lower in Catholic South Uist and Barra, as the religious culture has not emphasized the Gaelic scriptures as has Calvinism. This effect can also be shown as between Gaelic speakers in mainland Catholic and Protestant areas (MacKinnon 1978: 65–7).

In 1981 56.2 per cent of all Gaelic speakers claimed to be able to read Gaelic, and 41.6 per cent to write it. The practice of writing Gaelic – even for personal letters – is very rarely undertaken, and among older Gaelic speakers, and in areas where the language is not taught in the schools, writing ability is weak. Baker (1985: 22–40) has observed that in Wales higher levels of Welsh literacy associate significantly with language retention. There is some census evidence that this is also true for Gaelic. In 1981 Gaelic reading and writing levels correlated significantly with intergencrational language maintenance in Skye and Western Isles enumeration districts (MacKinnon 1987a).

Gaelic usage is typically diglossic, and its character has been studied in a number of Gaelic communities. In east Sutherland, where Gaelic is well on the way to extinction, Dorian (1981b: 112) reported Gaelic being used in high domains (such as the church), and English in low domains (doubtlessly the family). In a study of a rapidly weakening Gaelic community in Mull, although not focusing on diglossia itself, Dorian reported on the unfavourable reactions of non-Gaelic speakers when Gaelic was used in mixed company to exclude non-speakers from a conversational exchange – and of its continuing value to Gaelic speakers (1981a: 176–7).

Diglossic usage of Gaelic and English was examined in studies in Harris in the early 1970s (MacKinnon 1977: 143–57), in Barra and Harris in the late 1970s (MacKinnon and MacDonald 1980: 91–100; MacKinnon 1985a: 73), and in Skye and the Western Isles in the late 1980s (MacKinnon 1988). The general pattern emerging from these various studies seems to indicate that community usage of Gaelic may often stand up better than family usage – especially where children's schoolwork, peer group and sibling exchanges are concerned. The religious domain is weakening and may not function much longer as the bulwark for the language that it once was. In strongly Gaelic communities Gaelic predominates in most work domains – especially crofting – and exchanges with older relations. Local post offices and shops can be pivotal domains for community usage, and where these have been taken over by non-Gaelic-speaking incomers (as in southern Skye) Gaelic may rapidly retreat to within the family.

The geographical distribution of the Gaelic speech community

The Scottish Gaelic speech community today numbers about 80,000. About 23,500 of these are usually resident within the Western Isles Islands Area, about 16,500 in Highland Region, about 6,000 in Argyll and Bute District, and about 500 in the Highland area of Perthshire. These areas, which approximate to the traditional Gàidhealtachd, or Gaelic-speaking area, thus contain about 46,500 – or about 58 per cent – of present-day Gaelic speakers. The remainder live within the rest of Scotland, mainly in the Lowlands, 15,000 of them in the central Clydeside conurbation centred upon Glasgow. In the 1981 Census, the usually resident population of Scotland totalled 5,035,315, of whom 4,843,553 were aged 3+. Of these, 82,620 were able to read, write or speak Gaelic among whom were 79,307 speakers of the language, comprising 1.64 per cent of the national population aged 3+ (Registrar General (Scotland) 1983). Of these 79,307 speakers of Gaelic, only 20,345 resided in local neighbourhoods (census enumeration districts) in which 75 per cent or more of whole inhabitants spoke Gaelic. Those areas, in which Gaelic predominates as community speech at the present time, are chiefly in the Western Isles, the Isle of Skye, the Isle of Tiree, and western parts of Islay. (At the 1981 Census they also included the tiny Isle of Canna and the Kilninian enumeration district in Mull.) In 1981, 28,675 or just over one in three of Scotland's 79,307 Gaelic speakers lived in these and adjacent areas in which 50 per cent or more of the population spoke Gaelic (see Figure 3.1).

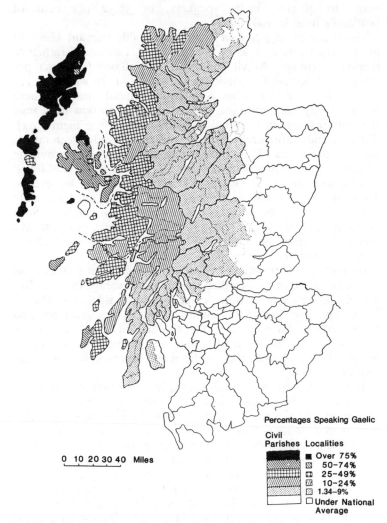

Percentages Speaking Gaelic

Civil Parishes	Localities	
■	■	Over 75%
		50–74%
		25–49%
		10–24%
		1.34–9%
	□	Under National Average

0 10 20 30 40 Miles

FIGURE 3.1 Proportions of Local Populations Speaking Gaelic in 1981

Local native Gaelic speakers, chiefly of the older generation, are still to be found in the western coastal areas of Highland Region and the western coasts and islands of Argyll and Bute District. There are also still some vestiges of native Gaelic in most parts of the mainland Highlands, even in Highland Perthshire. Together with migrant Gaels who have moved to these areas from the more strongly Gaelic west, the Highlands and Hebrides were home to 46,410 Gaelic speakers, or 58.52 per cent of Scotland's total in 1981.

The other 41.48 per cent comprised chiefly migrant Gaels in the principal urban areas of the Lowlands. Lowland Strathclyde Region, excluding Argyll and Bute, had 18,650 (or 23.52 per cent) of all Scotland's Gaelic speakers in 1981, of whom 15,114 lived in the central Clydeside conurbation around Glasgow. There is thus today an important and growing proportion of Gaelic speakers resident in Lowland and urban areas (see Figure 3.2). These trends are undoubtedly continuing and accelerating, through the 1980s. This implies that the concept of providing educational and cultural support for Gaelic only in the traditional 'Gaelic-speaking areas' is rapidly being overtaken by events. There are, for example, growing demands among young articulate city Gaels for Gaelic-medium education for their children. Such demands are difficult to resist under the present government's 'Parents' Charter', which attempts to give parents some choice over their children's schooling.

All parts of the traditional Gàidhealtachd still had a proportion of Gaelic speakers greater than the national average in 1981. But it could no longer be said, as it still sometimes is, that Scotland's Gaelic speakers are to be found mainly in the Hebrides and north-west coastal fringes. Today, the majority are in fact to be found elsewhere in Scotland, resident in areas which could not be described in any sense as Gaelic in either present-day or recent historic character.

The problems which result from this distribution pattern of Scotland's Gaelic speakers mean that contacts within the Gaelic speech community are particularly difficult. The Highland mainland is mountainous and deeply indented by the sea. Thus the small Gaelic populations of the western glens and peninsulas are very much isolated from one another. The islands are today typically connected by modern lines of communication, not so much with one another as through ferry ports on the west coast with road and rail links to the Lowland cities. In the past (prior to the 1975 local government reforms) Highland administrative areas had typically encompassed both thoroughly Gaelic island and

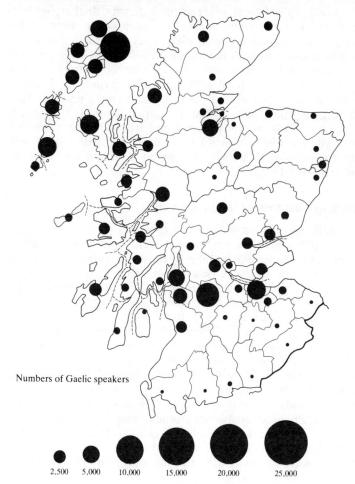

Numbers of Gaelic speakers

2,500 5,000 10,000 15,000 20,000 25,000

FIGURE 3.2 Size and Location of Gaelic Populations: 1981 Census

west-coast areas with the more populous and anglicized east-coast areas – as in the former Highland counties. In these and other ways, the Gaelic areas have in the past been divided from one another, and mutual contacts between them have been reduced. The roles of the present-day broadcasting and education services and policies of local administration are thus of particular importance in overcoming these difficulties.

The Western Isles Islands Area council, Comhairle nan Eilean, is a 'most-purpose' local government authority discharging both district and regional powers. Since its inception in 1975, it has developed a bilingual administrative policy, conducting its affairs and deliberations in both languages, introducing Gaelic on to its public signs and notices, and greatly enhancing its position in education. Four other local authorities have formulated bilingual policies and have constituted Gaelic committees. These are Highland Region, Skye and Lochalsh District, Ross and Cromarty District, and most recently Argyll and Bute District. Although Strathclyde Regional Council has not to date constituted a Gaelic committee as such, it has designated a councillor with responsibility for Gaelic.

Changing patterns of language use

The Gaelic speech community is on the whole an ageing sector of the population – but there have been some recent small increases in Gaelic-speaking abilities. Between 1961 and 1971 a 10 per cent increase in the census figures was a feature of lowland Scotland exclusively (see Figure 3.3). However, between 1971 and 1981 for the first time there were proportional and numerical increases of Gaelic speakers in the Western Isles and parts of Skye (together with some other areas attracting oil-related industry, and suburban fringes of the larger cities). In the Gaelic-speaking areas these general increases were the result of specific age-related increases among older children and young adults, producing a 'bulge' in the population profile. This is a feature not only of the most strongly Gaelic-speaking areas, but more generally of all areas with primary Gaelic teaching schemes. The population profile of Gaelic speakers in the Lowland area, and of Highland areas where Gaelic has not featured in education, is greatly attenuated in the age-ranges of childhood and youth.

There are within the present-day Gàidhealtachd a number of areas in which the proportion of young people (aged 5–24) speaking Gaelic matches or exceeds the proportion in the older age-ranges. These areas may be said to demonstrate some viability in their maintenance of the language. At the 1981 Census, these areas comprised some 30 of the 140 enumeration districts of the Western Isles, chiefly in western Lewis, southern Harris, the Uists and Barra, and some 9 of the 50 enumeration districts in Skye, chiefly in its northern and southern extremities. In some other areas Gaelic maintenance in the 5–24 age-range was within 1–2 percentage points of the older generations, as in

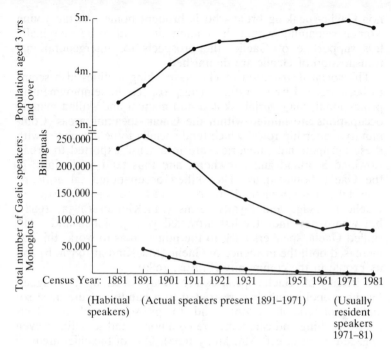

FIGURE 3.3 Numbers of Gaelic Speakers 1881–1981

the Western Isles communities of Barra and Vatersay, or within 3–4 points, as in the remainder of Harris, Scalpay and remoter parts of Lewis (MacKinnon 1987a). In the Isle Ornsay postcode sector of Skye, the incidence of Gaelic was stronger in the 3–24 age-range than among the older population – the likely result of the policies of the local estate, Fearann Eilean Iarmain, in using Gaelic as its language of management (MacKinnon 1985b).

There is some evidence that in the most strongly Gaelic communities, supportive attitudes and usage of the language are less well represented among the younger women, as compared with other age and gender groups. There is also a definite differential migration of younger women as compared with younger men from the most strongly Gaelic areas (MacKinnon 1977, 1984b, 1985a, 1986). Other research suggests that within the occupational continuum of Gaelic communities, Gaelic is best conserved within the semi-skilled agricultural group, which comprises the crofting 'core' of these communities. Supportive attitudes and Gaelic-speaking partners may be sought, but often it will be a non-Gaelic-speaking bride who is brought home. As the young women remaining within the community tend to be marginally less supportive of Gaelic, the prospects for intergenerational transmission of Gaelic are diminished.

The social distribution of Gaelic-speaking abilities also seems to be patterned by migration. The prospects for employment in professional, managerial, skilled non-manual and skilled manual occupations are limited within the Gaelic-speaking areas. Community leadership roles, which tend socially to be associated with these occupational categories, are in a sense exported to urban Lowland Scotland and elsewhere, and thus tend to diminish in the Gaelic home areas. The skilled occupational categories – especially the non-manual group – tend to be less supportive of Gaelic in usage and loyalty terms (MacKinnon 1985a, 1988), but where new industry has attracted young, skilled and semi-skilled Gaelic speakers back to the home areas to work, this has increased both the incidence of Gaelic (MacKinnon 1987a, b) and its profile in the community (Prattis, 1980).

Virtually all Gaelic speakers are today functionally bilingual. Gaelic monolingualism is restricted to a handful of the most socially isolated old people and to pre-school infants. Thus code-switching and calqueing are common – and sometimes even engaged in for effect (MacAulay 1982). One of the chief areas of influence of English upon Gaelic is in the introduction of new terminology. In 1987 a database project was established at Sabhal Mór Ostaig, the Gaelic college in Skye. Such a development was long overdue as academic Celtic departments had tended to concentrate upon historical rather than contemporary lexicography. The Gaelic Department of the BBC has, however, always played a key and conscious role in this respect – and today many Gaelic neologisms in common use were first introduced in broadcasting.

Broadcasting is also a butt for controversies regarding Gaelic dialects and speech varieties. Mainland dialects are today moribund – especially the eastern dialects (which did not diphthongize the long 'e' in words like *meud* (measure), *beul* (mouth), or intrude an 's' between final 'r' and 't', in words like *tart* (thirst), *neart* (strength)). Probably the largest dialect in numbers of speakers is that of Lewis, which has a somewhat 'sing-song' character often and easily parodied by speakers of other dialects (MacAulay 1978; Gleasure 1983). Listeners often state they resent dialects other than their own. Paradoxically, survey informants frequently claim that 'the proper Gaelic' is not spoken in their home area. Such reactions result from lack of exposure to alternative speech varieties and perhaps to some image of 'pulpit Gaelic' or newsreaders' Gaelic as in some way providing a standard variety. Both reactions probably result from deficiencies of the education system in insufficiently developing people's linguistic repertoire and awareness in Gaelic as compared with English.

Language, culture and community

For many years, An Comunn Gàidhealach (The Highland Association) was the most important Gaelic language organization. It has been responsible since 1892, for instance, for organizing the principal Gaelic cultural festival, the annual National *Mòd*. It has also been active in educational, publishing and cultural fields. With the appointment of a professional director in 1966, it involved itself in socio-economic issues and much more active political pressure on both central and local government. In the mid-1980s these roles in public life and education, together with youth work and the media, were taken up by a new organization, CNAG (Comunn na Gàidhlig) funded by the Highlands and Islands Development Board, a governmental development agency. This has left An Comunn with a purely cultural remit. Concurrently, the Board assisted both the newly established Gaelic playgroups organization, Comhairle nan Sgoiltean Araich, and helped to establish a Gaelic learners' organization, Comunn Luchd-Ionnsachaidh (which has since run into financial difficulties after about two years of very effective activity).

In recent years most of the political parties have given some attention to Gaelic, with arguably the Scottish Labour Party and the Scottish National Party coming out with the most articulated policy statements. Somewhat bland official statements of governmental policy on the language were made by the Secretary of State in 1985 (at a CNAG conference at Sabhal Mór Ostaig) and by a Scottish Office spokesman in 1987 (at the Celtic Film Festival in Inverness). The latest statement went little beyond unspecific general support. There are almost no examples of central governmental official usage of Gaelic. After some direct action campaigning the government has acceded to bilingual roadsigns in Skye – and Gaelic-only signs in the Western Isles.

Since 1963 a government-assisted Gaelic Books Council has considerably stimulated Gaelic publishing. The first all-Gaelic magazine *Gairm* has appeared regularly since 1952, and has developed a publishing business. This was followed by a number of other ventures in Gaelic publishing, for example a bilingual fortnightly paper in the late 1960s, a book club in the early 1970s (both now defunct), and most recently the Acair publishing house at Stornoway formed by a consortium chiefly for educational material, and chiefly in Gaelic. There are Gaelic features in local newspapers such as the *Oban Times*, *West Highland Free Press* and *Stornoway Gazette*, and the weekend supplement of *The Scotsman*.

Until it became an early victim of local government and Arts Council economies, a Gaelic theatre company, Fir Chlis (the Northern Lights) based in the Western Isles toured annually between 1978 and 1982. The 7.84 Company has subsequently toured with bilingual productions – but the Arts Council has now axed its grant. Amateur Gaelic drama has become a vigorous and popular scene over the past decade, and deserves a complementary professional theatre. A Gaelic community film unit Sùil (Eye) in the 1970s developed into the Celtic Film Festival with headquarters in Inverness. In 1987 a professional Gaelic film and video unit was established in Lewis, Fradharc Ùr (New Vision) and is training young Gaels in film and video production.

The present pattern of BBC Gaelic radio broadcasting on VHF under the banner Radio nan Gàidheal nationally, also provides services of a more local kind: as Radio nan Eilean in the islands, and as Radio air a' Ghàidhealtachd on the Highland mainland. In total, these stations currently broadcast about 25 hours in Gaelic per week, inclusive of schools' broadcasting. Gaelic is poorly served by television: both BBC and ITV provide merely weekly half-hour news review and cultural features, and short weekday children's programmes.

Gaelic in the media thus takes very much the back seat. It is still true to say that, even in terms of its tiny national proportion of speakers, it is nowhere near having a comparable allocation of airtime on either radio or television. There are four television channels currently available – with the promise of more to come shortly. Something like Sianel Pedwar Cymru in Wales, which Scottish companies help to fund, could in long-overdue justice be done for Gaelic in Scotland. I can only dub its Scottish equivalent 'Chaneil Ceithir Gàidhlig' (Four isn't Gaelic!). There is now the prospect of an £8 million budget for Gaelic television. Had the licence fee been realistically determined, there were plans for an all-day BBC Gaelic radio channel a few years ago. This proposal now deserves to be taken off the back burner.

The more vigorous local branches of An Comunn, and self-help learners' groups, provide Gaelic-medium social events in various places (Edinburgh, Inverness and Dingwall are good examples). There is quite a lively exiles scene in Glasgow, organized by home-area organizations. Outwith Scotland there are Gaelic organizations in places such as London, Manchester and Newcastle which bring down Gaelic entertainers and stage events. It is difficult to estimate how many Gaelic speakers there are to be found living in England – but a conservative estimate, in the absence of a UK language census, should indicate several thousand in the London Gaelic playgroup. With the abolition of ILEA the pros-day class for children in the 1960s which petered out because of travelling difficulties. It was more recently revived by the Highlands and Islands Society of London – and there is talk of a London Gaelic playgroup. With the abolition of ILEA the prospects for any place for Gaelic in London schools is dim – unless through voluntary effort on the lines of the London Welsh school (see Ch. 6). Since 1950 ILEA has run weekly evening classes in Gaelic, and since 1978 Wansfell College, Essex and Holly Royde College, Manchester have run regular residential weekend Gaelic courses.

Education and the reproduction of language

Since 1882 it has been possible to take Gaelic as part of a university degree in Celtic, and the 1918 Education Act provided for Gaelic to be taught 'in Gaelic-speaking areas' – although these were undefined. The Act was similarly unspecific as to whether instruction was to be through the medium of Gaelic – or merely of Gaelic as a specific subject.

Even today, apart from the bilingual administrative and educational policies in the Western Isles, and some place for Gaelic in schooling in Highland, Tayside and Strathclyde Regions, there is no formal recognition of Gaelic as one of Scotland's national languages, nor any general provision for the language nationally in Scotland's school system. However, by the mid-twentieth century some instrumental acknowledgement of Gaelic had been made by the Highland county education authorities, and Gaelic was used as an initial teaching medium in the early primary stages in Gaelic-speaking areas, and the language could be studied as an examination subject in parity with other languages at the secondary stage. Some significant developments in Gaelic education have occurred since 1975, such as bilingual education in the Western Isles and Skye, the introduction of Gaelic as a second language at primary level, the inception of Gaelic-medium primary units from 1985, and public Gaelic nursery schools in 1988

Gaelic enters into the school system in three distinct ways. In the Western Isles and Skye (and in some measure, Tiree) primary education is bilingual. Since 1958 Inverness-shire and Ross-shire had developed the use of Gaelic as an initial teaching medium in the early primary stage in the Gaelic areas. From 1975 the new Western Isles authority developed a pilot bilingual teaching project in thirty-four of its then fifty-nine primary schools, which after 1981 was extended to almost every school as its general policy. A similar scheme has been adopted by Highland Region first for northern Skye, and recently for the whole island, covering all twenty primary schools.

Gaelic is also taught as a second language in 70 primary schools elsewhere in Highland Region, 30 in Argylle under Strathclyde Region, and 18 in Highland Perthshire under Tayside. In all these cases, the effects of primary Gaelic teaching schemes, whether bilingual or second-language, can be shown to have some stabilizing effect upon the speech community and to enhance the local profile of the language (MacKinnon 1984c, 1987c). Gaelic is also taught as a second language in about forty secondary schools in these areas, and three others in Central, Grampian and Lothian Regions (1987 figures).

The third type of schooling is Gaelic-medium education. This was first introduced after parental pressure in Glasgow and Inverness: both essentially urban centres outwith the Gáidhealtachd. Gaelic-medium units were established in two schools in 1985 (MacIllechiar 1985). Subsequently, similar units were established in six further schools in the Western Isles and Skye. The impetus for such schools came from about 1982, and in the following five years established a national organization and about thirty playgroups and parent-and-toddler groups in both Gaelic-area and urban locations, with more currently projected (Scammel 1985).

The peculiarity of Gaelic education at the present time is that it has developed vigorously at the primary and pre-primary stages, but hardly exists except as a second language at the secondary stage. Apart from pilot schemes in the Western Isles, a bilingual secondary education stream commenced in Glasgow in 1988. There might have been a bilingual secondary project in the Western Isles leading on directly from bilingual primary schooling, but the council's nerve failed in 1979, and the scheme was remitted. When the council resolved to continue, the government had changed and the Scottish Education Department insisted on the delaying tactic of an independent evaluation of the primary scheme. This eventually reported (Mitchell *et al* 1987), but as yet there is no forthcoming response from government for assistance for the funding and development of a secondary bilingual project.

Meanwhile the Western Isles has internally funded a more limited project at Lionel. In 1985 the government promised a specific grant fund for Gaelic education – initially of £250,000 – and by 1989/90 this had grown to over £850,000, which greatly assisted such projects.

There are yet further anomalies in Gaelic education. Although pupils can proceed through Gaelic-medium primary education, they cannot yet undertake the secondary stage through the medium of Gaelic. However, since 1983 they could receive a tertiary education through the language, at Sabhal Mór Ostaig Gaelic College in Skye which has been recognized by the Scottish Education Department Council to undertake full-time HND courses through the medium of Gaelic in business and Gàidhealtachd studies. There are no university degree courses taught through Gaelic – and indeed no degree in Gaelic as such, apart from degrees in Celtic at Glasgow, Edinburgh and Aberdeen. Current discussion of a postgraduate diploma taught in Gaelic would complete the picture of Gaelic neatly leapfrogging alternate stages of the Scottish education system!

The merger of Aberdeen and Dundee Colleges of Education, and the proposal to alternate Gaelic teachers between Jordanhill and Northern Colleges in successive years did not instil confidence in the future supply of registered teachers of Gaelic – or of other subjects through Gaelic. This last condition is as yet largely unmet and unexplored by either the Central Committee on the Curriculum or the General Teachers' Council. Thus with developing demand for Gaelic education, a crisis of supply of teachers of Gaelic and teachers trained to use Gaelic as a medium is already upon us.

Education is thus proving to be a most fruitful field for language conservation and enhancement. If present trends are to continue, however, there is an urgent need for the creation of a system and some degree of central co-ordination, preferably involving both professional educators and the affected public. Career structure, movement around the system, initial and in-service training, curriculum development and a national resource centre deserve to be on the agenda. Yet there is not really any national forum where such an agenda could be discussed.

Some form of national Gaelic language unit would be clearly desirable. Something is needed to co-ordinate the various initiatives which have come about in the field of language planning at the corpus level – and some institution in Scotland with the interest and funding to carry out both sociolinguistic and sociology of language research for Gaelic. Teaching schemes and curricular

materials from playgroup to adult learner stages are currently
being developed and merit much more extensive professional ser-
vicing and more generous funding than they are getting.

Changes in the central government policy are also a matter
for concern. If a 'National Curriculum' is imposed on Scotland
there is every likelihood Gaelic will be marginalized with much
else into the 30 per cent available for 'other studies' rather than
be included in the curricular 'core' – as has been conceded for
Welsh in Wales. The chance to formulate a national language
policy involving English, 'modern', indigenous and 'indigenizing'
minority languages in the core curriculum has been missed.

Although the political climate is one of economy, there is at
the present time a vitality about Gaelic issues and Gaelic culture
in Scotland. Gaeldom has seized and pressed opportunities with
success. Policies made to conserve the status quo of the majority
in the south of England can be used under the rule of law to
secure linguistic rights for minority communities in the outer
peripheries. The last two censuses indicated for Gaelic that at its
'eleventh hour' there still exists the possibility of a future for the
Gaelic speech community. The opportunity is there – but it requires some vision and courage to exploit it. As the Gaelic scriptures have it: 'That na raointean geal chum an fhogharaidh . . .
ach tha an luchd-oibre tearc.' ('The fields are white unto harvest
. . . but the labourers are few' John 4: 35; Matthew 9: 37).

Acknowledgements

Thanks are due to Hatfield Polytechnic for support on projects
referred to in this section: for secondment, funding, graphical
and computing assistance; and likewise to various bodies within
the Gàidhealtachd and their staff: Highland Regional Council,
Comhairle nan Eilean, HIDB, An Comunn Gàidhealach, and the
Crofters' Commission.

The results of projects which have been funded by the SSRC
(Research grant HR 4039/L, 1976) and the ESRC (Research grant
GOO 23 23 28, 1985) are acknowleged with thanks. I also wish
to thank personally research colleagues working on these
projects, especially Morag MacDonald and Cathlin Macaulay,
and the many part-time workers and respondents.

Permission to use small area statistics (SAS 1981 and RSAS
1971) supplied by General Register Office (Scotland) is acknowledged with thanks. Material from Crown Copyright records
made available through the Office of Population Census and Sur-

veys, The General Register Office (Scotland) and the Economic and Social Research Council Data Archive has been used by permission of the Controller of Her Majesty's Stationery Office.

Bibliography and references

BAKER, C. (1985) *Aspects of Bilingualism in Wales.* Clevedon: Multilingual Matters.

BANNERMAN, J. (1974) *Studies in the History of Dalriada.* Edinburgh: Scottish Academic Press.

DORIAN, N. C. (1981a) 'The valuation of Gaelic by different mother tongue groups resident in the Highlands'. In *Scottish Gaelic Studies,* Vol. 13, Pt II, pp 169–82. Aberdeen: University of Aberdeen.

DORIAN, N. C. (1981b) *Language Death. The Life Cycle of a Scottish Gaelic Dialect.* Philadelphia: University of Philadelphia Press.

GEIPEL, J. (1971) *The Viking Legacy – the Scandinavian influence on the English and Gaelic languages.* Newton Abbott: David & Charles.

GLEASURE, J. W. (1983) 'Gaelic: dialects, pricipal divisions.' In Thomson, D. S. (ed.) *The Companion to Gaelic Scotland,* Oxford: Blackwell, pp 91–5.

GREEN, A. S. (1911) *Irish Nationality.* London: Home University Library.

HULBERT, J. (ed.) (1985) *Gaelic: Looking to the Future.* Longforgan, Dundee: Andrew Fletcher Society.

JACKSON, K. H. (1951) 'Common Gaelic', *Proceedings of the British Academy* 37

JACKSON, K. H. (1955) 'The Pictish language'. In Wainwright, F. T. (ed.) *The Problem of the Picts,* Edinburgh: Thomas Nelson, pp 129–60 (reprinted 1980, Perth: Melven Press).

KAY, B. (1986) *Scots – the Mither Tongue.* Edinburgh: Mainstream Publishing.

MACAULAY, D. (1978) 'Intra-dialectal variation as an area of Gaelic linguistic research'. In *Scottish Gaelic Studies,* Vol. 13, Pt I, pp 81–97. Aberdeen: University of Aberdeen.

MACAULAY, D. (1982) 'Borrow, calque and switch: the law of the English frontier'. In Anderson, J. (ed.) *Language Form and Linguistic Variation,* Amsterdam: Benjamins.

MACDONALD, M. (1982) *Cor na Gàidhlig – Language, Community and Development: the Gaelic Situation, a Report . . . . with Recommendations for Action,* Inverness: Highlands and Islands Development Board.

MACILLECHIAR, I. (1985) 'Gaelic-medium schools – why? and when?'. In Hulbert, op. cit., pp 28–33.

MACKINNON, K. (1974) *The Lion's Tongue.* Inverness: Club Leabhar.

MACKINNON, K. (1977) *Language, Education and Social Processes in a Gaelic Community.* London: Routledge & Kegan Paul.

MACKINNON, K. (1978) *Gaelic in Scotland 1971*: Some Sociological and Demographic Considerations of the Census Report for Gaelic. Hatfield: Hertis Publications.

MACKINNON, K. (1984b) *Gaelic in Highland Region – the 1981 Census.* Inverness: An Comunn Gàidhealach.

MACKINNON, K. (1984c) *Gaelic Language Regeneration Amongst Young People in Scotland 1971–1981* from Census Data. Hatfield: Hertis Publications.

MACKINNON, K. (1985a) 'The Scottish Gaelic speech-community – some social perspectives', plenary paper give at the First International Conference on the Languages of Scotland, Aberdeen University. Hatfield: Hertis Publications; and in *Scottish Language* No. 5 (Winter 1986), pp. 65–84.

MACKINNON, K. (1985b) 'Gaelic in the census – a tenacious survival'. In Hulbert, J. (op. cit. pp. 11–20.

MACKINNON, K. (1986) 'Gender, occupational and educational factors in Gaelic language-shift and regeneration', paper to Third International Minority Languages Conference, University College of Galway, 20–26 June 1986. Hatfield: Hertis Publications; and in MacEoin, G., Ahlqvist, A. and O⁻hAodha, D. (eds) *Third International Conference on Minority Languages: Celtic Papers*, pp. 47–71, Clevedon: Multilingual Matters

MACKINNON, K. (1987a) 'Language retreat and regeneration in the present-day Scottish Gàidhealtachd', paper to the First International Seminar on Geolinguistics, North Staffordshire Polytechnic, Stoke-on-Trent, 13–15 May 1987. Forthcoming in Williams, C. *Essays in Geolinguistics*, Clevedon: Multilingual Matters.

MACKINNON, K. (1987b) 'Occupation, migration and language-maintenance in Gaelic communities', paper to Ninth International Seminar on Marginal Regions, Skye, 5–11 June 1987. Hatfield: Hertis Publications.

MACKINNON, K. (1987c) *The Present Position of Gaelic in Scottish Primary Education.* Leeuwarden: Fryske Akademy/EMU-Project, and Hatfield: Hertis Publications.

MACKINNON, K. (1988) *Language-Maintenance and Viability in the Scottish Gaelic Speech-Community.* Report to Economic and Social Research Council.

MACKINNON, K. and MACDONALD, M. (1980) *Ethnic Communities: The Transmission of Language and Culture in Harris and Barra.* Report to the Social Science Research Council, Hatfield: Hertis Publications.

MITCHELL, R., MCINTYRE, D., MACDONALD, M. and MCLENNAN, S. (1987) *Report of an Independent Evaluation of the Western Isles Bilingual Education Project.* University of Stirling.

PRATTIS, J. I. (1980) 'Industrialisation and minority-language loyalty: the example of Lewis'. In Haugen, E., McClure, J. D. and Thomson, D. S. *Minority Languages Today*, a selection from the papers read at the First International Conference on Minority Languages held at Glasgow University from 8 to 13 September 1980. Edinburgh: University Press, Ch. 3.

Registrar General (Scotland) (1983) *Census 1981* Scotland, Gaelic Report. Edinburgh: Her Majesty's Stationery Office.

SCAMMEL, K. (1985) 'Pre-school playgroups'. In Hulbert, op. cit., pp. 21–7.

THOMSON, D. S. (1968) 'Gaelic learned orders and literati in medieval Scotland'. In *Scottish Studies,* Vol. 12 (University of Edinburgh School of Scottish Studies).

Chapter 4

The Irish speech community

Tina Hickey

> *Is buaine port ná glór na n-éan*
> *Is buaine focal ná toice an tsaoil*
> (SEANFHOCAL)
> A tune is more enduring than the song of the birds
> A word is more enduring than the wealth of the world
> (PROVERB)

Milis an teanga an Ghaeilge,	Sweet is the Irish language
Guth gan chabhair coigriche,	A tongue sufficient unto itself
Glór, géar-chaoin, glé, glinn, gasta	Witty, refined, vivid, and clear
Suairc, séimhidhe, sult-bhlasta.	Cheering, gentle, pleasing.
Gidh Eabhra teanga is seanda,	Although Hebrew is the most ancient
Gidh Laidin is léannta,	And Latin the most learned tongue
Uathu uirthi níor frith linn	From them we did not borrow
Fuaim no focal de chomaoin.	Sound or word as enhancement.

SEATHRÚN CÉITINN (SEVENTEENTH-CENTURY POET)

Irish has had a long and chequered history. In the 'Golden Age' of the sixth to ninth centuries, a considerable body of literature was produced in the language, so that, as Greene (1966:10) states, Irish has the oldest vernacular literature in Europe after Greek and Latin. It even replaced Latin to a great extent as a religious medium by the eighth century. Newcomers tended to be Gaelicized, even after the Norman invasions of the twelfth century. The disappearance of Irish from most parts of the country is a relatively recent phenomenon. Wall (1969) noted that it was not until the seventeenth century that the language began to be pushed back towards the western seaboard. The use of Irish was penalized from the reign of Elizabeth I, but this initially affected only the area around Dublin, known as the Pale. Plantations of English settlers began in the mid-sixteenth century and continued after the 'Flight of the Earls', which followed the defeat of O' Neill and his Spanish allies at Kinsale in 1601. The defeat and exile of so many Irish chiefs and the influx of English settlers constituted a passing of the Irish order and meant that while Irish was still the majority language at the end of the Tudor period, it was soon to become primarily the language of the peasant class.

The role of the Catholic Church was influential in this phase of the history of the language. While official English policy was directed towards the replacement of Irish by English, in the sixteenth century the Catholic Church appeared to be tied to the language. Following the Reformation, the Irish clergy in rural Ireland looked on Irish as the best protection for their flocks from Protestantism. Wall (1969) notes that there was at that time an awareness of the need for bilingual clergy to minister to Irish-speaking districts. Nevertheless, there was little printing in Ireland of devotional or religious literature for the Catholic population, probably as a result of the low levels of Irish literacy at the time, and the disappearance of the learned classes.

By the middle of the eighteenth century Irish had begun to decline seriously. By the time the Penal Laws were relaxed towards the end of the eighteenth century, the Catholic Church appeared to have accepted anglicization. The founding of Maynooth College by the English in 1795 for the education of the Catholic priesthood was of great significance, as English was the dominant language there. By the beginning of the nineteenth century, the Church was one of the principal proponents of the use of English, unlike the Nonconformist churches of Wales which played a large part in the maintenance of Welsh. Wall (1969) also points to the greater political involvement of the people in the largely English-speaking nationalist movement from the end of the eighteenth century as one of the strongest forces in the displacement of Irish.

Fitzgerald (1984:126) estimates that roughly half of the children in Ireland at the start of the nineteenth century spoke Irish. However, by the 1851 Census only 5 per cent of the total population were Irish monolinguals, while 23 per cent were bilinguals, and by the 1881 Census the proportion of Irish monolinguals had declined to only 1.25 per cent, with bilinguals at 18 per cent of the total population. Nevertheless, there were still areas at that time where Irish was the language of 70–100 per cent of these communities. The Catholic schools which began to be established early in the nineteenth century ignored Irish, and the National schools established by the English in 1831 actively discouraged it. The catastrophe of the Famine occurred in the 1840s, when it is estimated that 1 million people died, while another million emigrated between 1846 and 1851. Since the rural poor who were most severely affected by this disaster also formed the greatest concentration of Irish speakers at that time, Wall (1969:87) argues that a great proportion of those who died or emigrated were Irish speakers.

The history of the language from the mid-nineteenth century is one of attempts to maintain and revive Irish. The Gaelic League was founded in 1893 and became the most important organization in the revivalist effort. It played a significant role in the nationalist movement in the early twentieth century, and many of the political leaders of the Free State were members of the League. Irish was closely tied to the nationalist cause, and was made the first official language at the founding of the Free State in 1922, this provision being enshrined later in the 1937 Constitution. The later history of the language is examined in the sections on language maintenance and education.

While the focus of this discussion is on the Irish language in Ireland, it must be borne in mind that the majority of people in the country are native English speakers. The type of English spoken is most frequently called Hiberno-English (Kallen 1988; Bliss 1972, 1984; Harris 1985; Harris, Little and Singleton 1986), but the terms 'Irish English' (Ó Baoill 1985), 'the English language in Ireland' (Kallen 1985; Ó Muirithe 1977; Bliss 1976) and 'Anglo-Irish' (usually found in literary criticism) are also used. The English language as it is spoken in Ireland has distinctive features in its phonology, syntax, vocabulary and idioms. Many of these features arise from the influence of Irish, while some result from the inheritance of seventeenth-century English variants.

Geographical distribution of the language

The main source of data on the number and distribution of Irish speakers is the Census of Population. Since 1851 the Census has generally included a question on the ability to speak Irish. The question in use in recent censuses is: 'Ability to speak Irish: write "Irish only", "Irish and English", "Read but cannot speak Irish", or leave blank as appropriate.' While speakers of the language, particularly second-language speakers, are distributed throughout the country, those areas in which Irish is the vernacular are designated by the term 'Gaeltacht'. Since the number of monolingual Irish speakers is small, in census returns most native speakers are included with non-native speakers of Irish, as 'speakers of Irish and English'. Thus, estimation of the number of native speakers of the language is made difficult. The varying proportions of native speakers within Gaeltacht areas, and the substantial migration from these areas to the towns and cities, make it difficult to rely on population changes in Gaeltacht areas as an indicator of changes in the number of native speakers.

Gaeltacht, or Irish-speaking areas, are mainly located on the western seaboard, including some islands, with some other small inland areas (see Fig. 4.1). Commins (1988:12) notes that Gaeltacht areas, as currently defined, cover about 7 per cent of the land area of the Irish Republic. According to the 1986 Census, they had a population of 83,000, or 2.3 per cent of the national total. The boundaries of Gaeltacht areas have been altered on political grounds several times in the last thirty years and there is a distinction made between areas known as *ffor-Ghaeltacht* (containing at least 80 per cent Irish speakers) and *breac-Ghaeltacht* (containing 25–79 per cent Irish speakers). Gaeltacht areas are predominantly rural, although those close to Galway have tended to absorb the expansion of the city.

At the turn of the century there were still small pockets of Irish speakers in the mountainous areas of what was to become Northern Ireland. The Census of 1911 was the last to record data on Irish in this area, and it showed that by that time there were no monolingual Irish speakers there, and in all, only 1.7 per cent (or 21,000 people) of the population of the province spoke Irish. The present situation of Irish in Northern Ireland will be reviewed in the course of the discussion on language maintenance and loss.

Changing patterns of language use

Strategics aimed at the maintenance of Irish in the Gaeltacht which were launched with the foundation of the Free State in 1922 would appear to have been unsuccessful. The Committee on Irish Language Attitudes Research (CLAR 1975), for instance, pointed to population loss from these areas through emigration and a 'natural population decrease', resulting from the higher than average representation of old people in the community, with a lower birth rate than the national average. However, it also

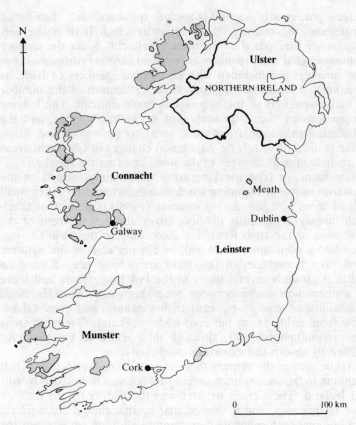

FIGURE 4.1   Ireland: Gaeltacht or Irish-speaking areas (shaded)
Based on Commins (1988: 13)

noted that equally important factors in the decline of the language
were the anglicization of the Gaeltacht which occurred in public
authority and other institutional and commercial domains, where
even state organizations were found to use English frequently in
interaction with the Irish-speaking community. The census
evidence confirms the decline in the number of Irish speakers in
the Gaeltacht, from 87 per cent of the Gaeltacht population aged
three years or over who were returned as Irish speakers in 1961,
to 77 per cent in 1981.

Commins (1988:16) noted that the fundamental problem with
state policies concerning the Gaeltacht until recent decades was
the focus on population stabilization in these areas, without
specific language-directed policies. State intervention initially con-

centrated on providing aids to agriculture and traditional industries, and the improvement of housing and education. In 1958, Gaeltarra Éireann was established to promote local industry and to encourage foreign investment. Údarás na Gaeltachta (the Gaeltacht Authority) was established in 1979, in place of the earlier body, with an extended brief which included the encouragement of Irish as the principal medium of communication in the Gaeltacht, in addition to the promotion of industrial development. However, Commins (1988:17) argues that Údarás is hampered in its attempts to achieve language maintenance objectives by its lack of statutory control in areas such as education, social services and agricultural development.

The increase in industrial/commercial jobs in the 1970s contributed to the reversal of the population decline in the Gaeltacht, but this concealed a more complex picture: there was in-migration of adults in their thirties and forties who were more likely to be English-speaking monolinguals than native Irish speakers (CLAR 1975:138), while the out-migration of young native speakers continued. Among in-migrants to Gaeltacht areas, a higher proportion of men than women were 'returning natives'. Hilliard's (1982) study of the migration history of the parents of school beginners in the Gaeltacht found that the proportion of mothers born outside the Gaeltacht rose from 19 per cent in 1970 to 36 per cent in 1980, whereas the corresponding figures for fathers were 12 and 14 per cent. This influx of non-native women led to an increase in the number of non-joint native speaker marriages and had an inevitable effect on the intergenerational transmission of Irish.

If the census data on 3–4-year-olds is taken to indicate home-generated ability, then the latest figures available for this cohort, from the 1981 Census, showed that 53 per cent (or 6,700 children) of 3–4-year-old children in the Gaeltacht 'knew Irish' (representing about 4.9 per cent of the national cohort of children of this age). However, the proportion of school-going children in the Gaeltacht who were Irish speakers was higher, at 80 per cent, and this is thought to indicate a reliance on the schools for the transmission of the language. Of course this strategy is only effective in producing Irish speakers so long as a critical balance of native to non-native speakers is maintained. In some Gaeltacht schools there has been a language shift to English when that critical balance is upset.

The introduction of new English-using contexts in industry and commerce have also affected the linguistic balance of the Gaeltacht. Commins (1988:20) notes that it is clear that there is now a widespread shift to English there. The Committee on Irish Language Attitudes Research (CLAR 1975) concluded that bilingualism was the dominant pattern in almost half of Gaeltacht communities, and suggested that the maintenance either of stable diglossia or close-to-monolingual Irish usage depends not only on the production of native speakers in the home, but on the transmission of propensity of use as well. That survey indicated that high levels of usage can only be found in communities where at least 80 per cent of speakers have high competence.

While language maintenance in the Gaeltacht has clearly not been very successful, policies directed at language revival in English-speaking areas have had somewhat more success. The increase in the number of Irish speakers outside of the Gaeltacht has not, however, led to the establishment of Irish-speaking communities. Levels of usage are still very low, and the Ó Riagáin and Ó Gliasáin (1984) survey found that fewer than 10 per cent of their respondents reported using Irish in the week preceding the survey. Irish speakers who live outside of the Gaeltacht tend to be too widely dispersed to form Irish-speaking networks, and this also decreases their effectiveness as a source of bilingual reproduction.

The 1981 Census showed that overall more than a million people, or just over 31 per cent of the total population, claimed to be able to speak Irish. It is not possible to ascertain exactly how many of these were native speakers, or what was the general level of proficiency among non-native speakers of the language. However, some data can be gleaned on both these questions from survey evidence. The Committee on Irish Language Attitudes Research (CLAR 1975) conducted a survey of almost 3,000 people in 1973. While this, like the census, used a self-reported measure of competence in Irish, it was a more precise one. Some of the results of this survey, and of the more recent Ó Riagáin and Ó Gliasáin (1984) survey of almost 800 adults, are given in Table 4.1, including each respondent's report on the Irish ability of their mother and their eldest child (where applicable), in order to indicate intergenerational change.

Table 4.1 shows that among respondents' children, there was some improvement at the middle levels of ability during this period. The change in the ability levels of respondents' mothers needs to be assessed in the light of the higher 'Not applicable/no information' figure in 1983. The data on respondents themselves show little change, with 48 per cent reporting that they had little or no Irish, 19 per cent reporting basic ability, 20 per cent

TABLE 4.1 Speaking ability of respondent and selected family members (%)

	Respondent's mother		Respondent		Respondent's eldest child	
	1973	1983	1973	1983	1973	1983
No Irish	50	37	21	16	12	11
The odd word	22	23	27	32	17	12
Few simple sentences	12	13	22	19	22	22
Parts of conversations	5	8	17	20	23	31
Most conversations	3	4	10	10	19	21
Native speaker ability	4	2	3	3	5	2
Not applicable/no information	4	13	—	—	2	1
	100	100	100	100	100	100

Sources: Committee on Language Attitudes Research (1975); Ó Riagáin and Ó Gliasáin (1984).

moderate ability and 13 per cent reporting high levels of competence in the language.

Turning to a survey of the situation of Irish in Northern Ireland, Sweeney (1988) found that 11 per cent of his sample of about 5,000 adults reported some knowledge of Irish. However, this was restricted almost exclusively to Catholics, with 26 per cent of Catholics and only 2 per cent of Protestants in the sample claiming some ability in the language. Irish ability was also most widespread in the under-25 age group. It should be borne in mind that the criteria by which respondents in this survey were asked to judge their Irish ability differed from those used in the surveys in the Republic, and the results are therefore not directly comparable. More than half of those who said that they had a knowledge of Irish said that they could not use it in conversation, 41 per cent of this group said that they could carry on a simple conversation and only 6 per cent of those reporting that they knew Irish thought that they could conduct a complex conversation in the language. Levels of Irish use were not high, with only 16 per cent of those with a knowledge of the language reporting that they use it occasionally, or more frequently, at home. Almost 25 per cent of Catholics expressed an interest in improving their Irish, and 3 per cent of Protestants. Ó Glaisne (1981) noted that there has always been some interest in Irish among Northern Ireland's Protestants, but Sweeney (1988) claims that the historical link between the language and Irish nationalism has curtailed that interest.

In evaluating the success of Irish language policies in the Republic of Ireland there is a paradox to be observed: it appears to be a success story in that more people report themselves as having a knowledge of the language now than did a century ago, yet the numbers using the language are very low. Similarly, attitudes to the language are favourable, but there is widespread pessimism about its future. The reason for the conflicting interpretations of success and failure of the language movement may be attributed to the use of differing yardsticks: Irish has not been restored as the vernacular of the country as was the objective of the Gaelic League at its founding in 1893, yet more people now report that they can speak the language than could at that time. Relative success is measured in the increase in persons in English-speaking areas with a bilingual competence, failure in the declining number of native speakers, and low levels of use of Irish. Ó Riagáin (1988:48), commenting on the 'balance' between the decline of native speakers and the increase in second-language speakers of Irish, noted that this apparent maintenance is very fragile, since it represents the loss of Irish-speaking communities, without their replacement by stable Irish-speaking networks. Overall, it appears that Irish is still in danger of disappearing as a community language, as it was 100 years ago, but given the right conditions, there are enough people with some knowledge of the language to allow it the potential to survive and there is still substantial support for it among the public.

Language, culture and community

An important element of the official strategy for the maintenance of Irish in the Gaeltacht and the revival of the language elsewhere involved the creation of the appropriate context for Irish in the state. This involved the implementation of its constitutional and legal status as first official language, the standardization of the language, and the fostering of Irish publishing and broadcasting.

Ó Baoill (1988:109) notes that the standardization of the grammar and spelling of Irish was one of the most important steps towards the revival of the language. There are three main dialects of Irish (Ulster, Munster and Connácht) but none of the three was or is socially dominant, so there was no obvious norm. Nor was there a cohesive urban Irish-speaking community, among whom such a norm might have developed. The Translation Section of the Dàil (Parliament) was established in 1922 and this body was given the task of standardizing the language, which culminated in the 1958 official guide: *Gramadach na Gaeilge agus*

Litriú na Gaeilge (The Grammar and Spelling of Irish). The Translation Section also abandoned the old Gaelic script which had been used for writing Irish since 1600, and adopted Roman script. There was an encouraging public response to the 1958 publication and it has been reissued at least five times.

In tandem with standardization went the provision of new terms, which are a must for any living language. The Buanchoiste Téarmaíochta (Permanent Terminology Committee) was established in 1927 and has continued, with some interruptions, to the present. The need for this body became clear when new technical subjects were introduced into the curriculum with a consequent need for authoritative terms in teaching. The terms produced are provided in specialized lists and vocabularies, although there is some resistance to using these terms instead of English words outside of government bodies.

The standardized language has been implemented in several ways. Most official documents are printed in standardized Irish and in English. However, other areas of official policy directed at supporting the use of Irish have tended to support the ceremonial use of Irish rather than its use for real communication. Street signs and bus scrolls, signs for public lavatories and telephone kiosks are given bilingually or in Irish alone. Stamps bear the Irish title Éire, while paper currency is bilingual. Political parties tend to use Irish in non-Gaeltacht areas for ceremonial reasons only, such as the beginnings of speeches at party congresses.

Raidió na Gaeltachta (Gaeltacht Radio) was established in 1972, and is funded by revenue from television licences. This Irish-language station is received in Gaeltacht areas on medium wave and in other areas on VHF. It broadcasts in the morning and evening for about 60 hours per week and its coverage includes news, sports, local events and music. Some Irish programmes are also carried on the two national radio channels. However, a survey by Conradh na Gaeilge in 1982 found that, over a four-week period, only 6.7 per cent of programmes on RTÉ Radio 1 and 1.2 per cent of programmes on Radio 2 were in Irish. There are two national television channels, RTÉ1 and Network 2, which broadcast approximately 130 hours per week in total. There is a news broadcast in Irish every evening, but otherwise the number of Irish programmes is low. Recent figures for television showed that in early December 1987 only about 3 per cent of broadcasts were in Irish, and these are now mainly concentrated on Network 2, whose brief is to cater for minority interest groups. There is great dissatisfaction among supporters of the language with the level of provision of Irish programmes, and some have refused to pay licence fees in protest. However, according to the Bord na Gaeilge *Action Plan for Irish 1983–1986*, it was stated that RTÉ, the national broadcasting authority, hopes to increase its Irish programmes to 20 per cent of all home-produced programmes in the medium term. More importantly, there is now a move towards the establishment of an independent Irish-language television station located in a Gaeltacht area.

The official position of the Irish language in Northern Ireland is, of course, quite different from that in the Republic. The Sweeney (1988) survey results prompted calls for government promotion of Irish in education, administration and in the media. At present, there are only 15 minutes of Irish broadcast on BBC radio in Northern Ireland each night, and there are no Irish broadcasts on television in the province. Belfast has an all-Irish 'pirate' radio station as well as a daily newspaper, *Lá*.

In the Republic of Ireland, the Irish government in 1975 established Bord na Gaeilge, whose brief was the promotion of Irish in everyday life. The Bord initiated an advertising campaign designed to portray Irish as relevant to modern lifestyles. The theme of the campaign was: 'Our language – It's part of what we are.' While this campaign was criticized as a misdirection of resources by some language supporters, it was well received by the general public. The Bord also established a language advice and information service and a distribution centre for books in Irish. Tovey (1988) argues that the Bord is placed in a dilemma in so far as it defined itself on the basis of broad public support for the language, which means that it cannot act to represent the minority of language users in ways which might threaten that public support.

The provision of Irish-language books is officially encouranged and is subsidized by the state bodies An Gúm and Bord na Leabhar Gaeilge. However, most of the Irish books bought are textbooks, and the total number of books published each year in Irish is estimated at less than a quarter of the number published in Welsh. One factor in the low levels of book sales in Irish is the fact that most Irish titles are on minority-interest subjects, for example poetry. The Fishwick (1987) survey notes that there is some evidence that books written in Irish on more popular subjects would reach higher sales than are suggested by current sales of existing materials.

The smallness of the readership for Irish language materials is again illustrated by the circulations of Irish newspapers and magazines. *Comhar*, a monthly arts and current affairs magazine, has a circulation of about 3,000 copies, while *Anois*, the only Irish Sunday newspaper, has a circulation of approximately 5,000. There are several other magazines and newspapers, some of which are directed at young people only. The national papers, *The Irish Times* and *The Irish Press*, also carry items in Irish.

The congress of voluntary Irish-language organizations, Comhdháil Náisiúnta na Gaeilge, was established in 1943 and co-ordinates the work of eighteen organizations. The largest and oldest member organization is Conradh na Gaeilge, which was established as the Gaelic League in 1893 and now has about 250 branches throughout the country. It provides language classes and other activities such as lectures, music evenings and social occasions when the language is used. It also campaigns for the rights of Irish speakers to government services in Irish, including increased use of Irish on radio, television and in the national newspapers. Ógras was founded in 1969 by Conradh na Gaeilge to cater for young people between 15 and 19 years of age and has 60 branches around the country. A major cultural festival, An Toireachtas, held under the auspices of Conradh na Gaeilge, includes competitions in literature, folk-music and singing, story-telling and acting, as well as an art exhibition. Gael-Linn organizes intensive Irish courses for adults and children, including a scholarship scheme to allow English-speaking children aged between 10 and 12 years to live with a Gaeltacht family for three months and attend a local school. Gael-Linn also organizes a national festival for young people, publishes folk-music records, and runs summer colleges. There are about 70 summer colleges which are members of the central organization, Comhchoiste Náisiúnta na gColáisti Samhraidh, and about 20,000 young people participate in their courses in Gaeltacht areas each year, spending about a month in the Gaeltacht.

There is great interest in Irish music, and Comhaltas Ceoltóir Eireann, the organization for folk-musicians, has about 400 branches around the country. Their emphasis is on music, song and dance, but they also provide contexts for Irish use. There are several Irish-language theatre groups, but the principal one is Taibhdhearc na Gaillimhe, in Galway. Some Irish-language plays are produced in Dublin in the Peacock, the smaller of the Abbey theatres, and in An Damer.

In surveying the future for Irish the report of the Advisory Planning Committee (1988) concludes that there is an urgent need to change the perception of the state role in language issues, with a greater emphasis in official policy on the promotion of language use in the public service, in state agencies interacting with the Gaeltacht and in the media. The document notes that there has been a shift in government policy away from 'revivalism' which has an implicit concern with use, to bilingualism, which requires the individual to choose to speak the language independently of state facilitation. The Advisory Planning Committee goes on to urge a far more committed attitude in the future to language planning than that of recent years, described as *laissez-faire*. The report argues that the state must take the initiative in the re-creation of an ideological basis for Irish language loyalty, the facilitation of the emergence of a popularly-based cultural movement and the extension of the usage of Irish in a bilingual society through its political and bureaucratic structures. This is based on the projection that without greater use of the language, there will be an accelerating decline in the numbers achieving competence.

Education and the reproduction of language

With the founding of the Irish state, the main burden of the revival effort was placed on the educational system, particularly the primary level, because participation in second-level education at that time was low. Irish was made compulsory for all pupils. The new state's eventual objective was the implementation of a bilingual or full immersion programme in all primary schools. While there was substantial support from teachers for the accomplishment of this aim, nevertheless there was some resentment of the government's apparent decision to revive Irish through the schools alone, and in many cases teachers were dissatisfied with the resources placed at their disposal for teaching the language. Despite the problems in implementing the policy initially, Harris (1988: 69) notes that by the 1940s, 12 per cent of all primary schools were teaching entirely through Irish, while 43 per cent were teaching at least some children (usually the youngest children) through Irish, the remainder teaching Irish as a single subject. By this time there was a supply of primary teachers who were highly competent in the language, as a result of Irish-medium Preparatory and Training Colleges.

While the main thrust of the revival policy was directed at the primary level, the second-level was not excluded. The state provided higher subsidies and capitation grants for schools teaching other subjects through Irish. These were private schools, mainly run by religious orders, and they responded positively to these incentives. Ó Gliasáin (1988) notes that by 1935, more than half of all recognized secondary schools were either Irish-medium, or taught some subjects through Irish. Teaching of the language was further supported by the necessity of obtaining a pass in the language in order to receive state certificates and by the requirement of Irish proficiency for entry into the civil service and other state agencies. Until the 1960s Irish played an important role in upward mobility, allowing access to attractive public sector employment, and this ensured its promotion by second-level schools at the time.

State activity favouring the language in the education system peaked during the 1940s and 1950s, and has declined slowly but steadily since then. Only 3 per cent of primary-level pupils in 1984–85 were taught entirely through Irish, and figures for 1980 show that only 3 per cent of second-level pupils were attending Irish-medium schools. One reason for the erosion of Irish in the education system during the 1960s and 1970s was a general concern about overall educational achievement, particularly following Macnamara's (1966) report. Another reason was that second-level education was being made accessible to larger numbers of pupils at that time and improving employment opportunities in commerce and industry led to a demand for a more modern and technologically oriented education system.

The result was a significant decline in the number of pupils in Irish-medium post-primary schools. By 1973 it was no longer necessary to obtain a pass in Irish in order to be awarded either of the two main State certificates, the Intermediate and Leaving Certificates (for students aged 16 and 18 years). The Advisory Planning Committee report (1986) on Irish in the education system notes that the effect of this change in policy was a trebling of the failure rate in Irish in the Leaving Certificate examination, from 5 to 15 per cent between 1973 and 1983, and a rise from 3 to 10 per cent in the proportions not sitting the Irish examination. Irish is still a compulsory subject (with English and Mathematics) for all students educated within the state; the rise in the number not taking Irish as part of their Leaving Certificate examinations is partly accounted for by the children of returned emigrants (students receiving part of their education elsewhere are exempt from this requirement) but is mainly due to an increasing number of students who do not present themselves for the Irish examination. A pass in Irish is still required for entry to the National University of Ireland, but compulsory Irish for entry to most public sector jobs was abolished in 1974. These changes have meant that while schools are still officially operating state policy for language maintenance and promotion, the awareness that there has been a decline in the value and status of Irish in

other areas of public life has led to frustration among teachers
and pupils and increasing marginalisation of the language.

There is some evidence of a movement among voluntary groups
to counteract this weakening of the position of Irish in the
schools. Interest has grown, mainly among middle-class groups,
in the provision of Irish-medium schools in English speaking
areas; about 50 such schools have been established since the
1970s as a result of pressure from parents. These schools are well
regarded, achieving good overall standards and high levels of language competence. There has also been significant expansion in
the numbers of Irish-speaking playgroups (naíonraí) both in the
Gaeltacht and English-speaking areas. There are now about 200
such naíonraí which cater for pre-school children who may then
go on to an Irish-medium school, if there is one in their area.

Outside the Republic, Irish is taught in Catholic primary
schools in Northern Ireland and there is an all-Irish primary
school in Belfast, as well as an all-Irish unit in a primary school
in Derry. Irish is included in the curriculum of some Catholic
second-level schools and in 1986, according to Sweeney's (1988)
survey on Irish in Northern Ireland, about 1800 students took
secondary level examinations in Irish (for comparison, about 9000
took French).

Under the new curriculum which will probably become effective for language programmes in 1991, every secondary school in
Northern Ireland must offer French, German, Italian or Spanish,
and may in addition offer Irish. Pupils must study one of these
five languages as well as English, so where their school offers it,
they may study Irish alone, or Irish in addition to one of the
continental languages. The decision not to make the study of a
continental language compulsory was hailed as a victory by language activists on the grounds that such a ruling would have
resulted in a lower status for Irish, and a decline in numbers
studying the language. One group, 'Teanga', is seeking a status
for Irish which would be comparable to the status of Welsh in
Wales, where study of the language is compulsory, in addition to
a continental language, unless the school is exempted from offering Welsh. Irish courses for adults are run by various
organizations in Northern Ireland, and there is strong interest in
them. The desire to learn the language is closely linked to
nationalistic sentiment, and Sinn Féin has been active in organizing classes. Ó hAdhmaill (1985) found seventy adult Irish
language classes operating in west Belfast, most of which were
taught by voluntary teachers. Celtic languages and literature are

also offered in Queens's University, the University of Ulster and Catholic teacher training colleges.

Past and contemporary emigration from Ireland has resulted in a substantial Irish community in Britain. Irish is taught mainly in areas where large numbers of past emigrants from Ireland settled, such as London, Birmingham and Liverpool. At present in the UK there is an upsurge of interest in learning Irish. Most of these learners appear to be second- or third-generation Irish. The periodical *Irish Studies in Britain* (No. 12, *pp* 10–11) estimates that there are currently about 40 teachers giving Irish classes in Britain, with between 1,000 and 2,000 pupils. A training programme and qualification in Irish has been jointly proposed by the Institute of Linguists and the British Association of Irish Studies, while courses in Irish studies are offered by the North London Polytechnic. The Institute of Irish Studies at the University of Liverpool has recently inaugurated BA and MA courses in Irish studies (see Buckland 1988). That institute is also involved in the preparation of GCSE syllabi in Irish and Irish studies, in order to promote the study of Ireland in British schools. In addition, Irish music and culture are frequently presented in Britain, and can be a focal point of contact for the recent immigrant and the second- or third-generation Irish. Comhaltas Ceoltóirí Éireann has thirty branches operating throughout Britain and they report that interest in Irish music there is high.

What has been the success of policies regarding the teaching of Irish in schools in the Republic? Criterion-referenced tests of the proficiency in Irish of children leaving the primary school in 1985 (see Harris 1988: 76) showed that 34 per cent of pupils on average had mastery of the objectives for their grade, while another one-third failed to make even minimal progress. The survey by Ó Riagáin and Ó Gliasáin (1984) showed that two-thirds of adults sampled agreed with the statements that 'children seldom learn enough Irish to use it after school', and 'if Irish were taught better in the schools, more people would speak it'. The change in the teaching of Irish in primary schools in the late 1960s with the introduction of audio-visual methods raised expectations regarding achievement levels which many feel have been disappointed. Harris (1988: 83) compared the achievement levels of pupils from ordinary schools (where Irish is taught as a single subject) with those of pupils with a greater exposure to Irish, either in their homes or in school. He concluded that the expectations embodied in the Irish courses (*Nuachúrsai*) are unrealistic for pupils in ordinary schools learning the language as a single subject.

It is difficult to evaluate the results of the Irish system without comparing it with a similar primary-level second-language programme. However, the Irish programme in ordinary schools is unusual in that it aims to establish speaking proficiency by teaching the language as a single subject from the beginning of primary level, usually without the support of the wider community in using the language for real communication. The fact that the expectations of the *Nuachúrsaí* are set unrealistically high for a language being taught as a single subject perpetuates the unrealistic expectations of parents and teachers and leads to disaffection from the teaching of the language, rather than a desire to change the fundamental programmes. Harris (1988: 84) concludes that higher levels of proficiency cannot be achieved without a significant increase in the time allotted to the language and the best way to achieve this is by increasing the use of Irish as the medium of instruction, at least for one or two other subjects.

Ó Riagáin (1988: 43) notes that, if the task of the educational system is judged only to be the maintenance of the present 5–10 per cent level of usage of the language in the general community, then it is accomplishing that objective. He points out that the maintenance of fairly stable rates of bilingualism over recent decades is mainly the result of the production of enough competent bilinguals by the educational system to replace those who, for a variety of reasons, are lost from the Irish-speaking networks. In order to maintain even that low level of use, the educational system needs to produce quite high numbers of competent bilinguals, since these are then distributed fairly randomly in English-speaking areas. The report on education by the Advisory Planning Committee (1986: 8) notes that students taking the academically most demanding Irish syllabus make up only about 15 per cent of their age cohorts (according to figures for 1983) and it is mainly from this group of high-ability speakers that active bilinguals emerge.

The distribution of these high levels of competence in Irish is uneven across the social classes. The highest concentration of ability is found in the higher social classes, who are more likely to have reached third-level education, especially university education. The requirements until the mid-1970s that a pass in Irish be attained in order to be awarded the Leaving Certificate, or to be appointed to a post in the state sector, and the continuing requirement of Irish for entry to the National University of Ireland, means that Irish was, and is still, though to a lesser degree, an important asset. This resulted in a patchy distribution of Irish ability, with the highest representation among upper-middle-class public sector employees. Ó Riagáin (1987: 14) notes that some 60 per cent of the respondents in the 1984 survey who reported either native-speaker ability or ability to understand most conversations were employed in the public sector. The private sector, where Anglo-American models dominate (and where, until recent decades according to Ó Riagáin (1988), inherited economic capital was a more important entry requirement than cultural capital) contains far fewer speakers of high ability. Ó Gliasáin (1988) claims that the private sector will tend in the future to attract the most highly qualified to workplaces where Irish will have no place or value. This, he argues, will lead to changes in the schools as they respond to the different priorities of their pupils, so that the position of Irish will continue to be eroded.

According to the CLAR (1975) report and the more recent Ó Riagáin and Ó Gliasáin survey (1984), there are high levels of support for Irish in the country, but low levels of use of the language, and apparently little optimism about its future. Edwards (1985: 51) comments that it is quite possible for favourable cultural attitudes to coexist with language shift based on practical considerations. Projections from current trends (see the report of the Advisory Planning Committee 1988) suggest that it is likely that ideological support for the language will remain high and stable, but the pool of speakers is likely to contract. The accelerated pace of social change in Ireland in the last thirty years has encouraged the adoption of Anglo-American models by new high-status groups, and Irish identity and culture are not valued in these models. There has been a swing to instrumental education, and strong political backing has been given to the teaching of modern languages, which, it is suggested, will facilitate job creation in the future. This orientation carries with it the danger that Irish is viewed as a cultural nicety, a luxury which the hard facts of modern economics cannot support.

It is clear that the concept of Irish group identity is evolving. The widening of economic, political and cultural contacts has led to changes in the judgements of what constitutes essential Irishness. Edwards (1985: 48) argued that group identity is not indissolubly linked to a given marker, including language; the erosion of an original language does not necessarily mean the erosion of identity. He claimed that the Irish as a group have not lost their national identity, but have enshrined it in English. The Advisory Planning Committee document *The Irish Language in a Changing Society* (1988) notes that there is now a lack of a consensus on how Irish people assert their group identity. There appears to be a movement towards a recentring of that identity around cultural factors other than the Irish language. This is what underlies the movement to replace the teaching of the language in schools by 'Irish studies', covering music, folklore and customs.

Despite these trends, there can still be a future for Irish in Ireland. Public goodwill towards the language is strong, and the numbers with moderate to high competence are substantial. However, for that future to be realized, it is necessary that current policies should be reassessed in light of the present economic climate and the rapid social change of the last thirty years. If the failure to achieve idealistic objectives is used as the reason for abandoning the language, then the more moderate successes achieved through the efforts of several generations will be thrown away. This is a crucial time for Irish, and the policy decisions made or not made in the next few years will decide its fate.

Acknowledgements

The author wishes to thank Eoghan Mac Áogáin, Director of ITÉ, Prof. Pádraig Ó Riagáin and Dr John Harris for their comments on an earlier draft of this paper, and Mícheál Ó Gliasáin and Íosold Ó Deirg for their help. The usual disclaimer of course applies.

References

Advisory Planning Committee/Coiste Comhairleach Pleanála (1986) *Irish and the Education System: An Analysis of Examination Results.* Dublin: Bord na Gaeilge.

Advisory Planning Committee/Coiste Comhairleach Pleanála (1988) *The Irish Language in a Changing Society: Shaping the Future.* Dublin: Bord na Gaeilge.

BLISS, A. (1972) 'Languages in contact: some problems of Hiberno-English', *Proceedings of the Royal Irish Academy* 72, 63–82.

BLISS, A. (1976) *The English Language in Ireland.* Dublin: Clodhanna Teoranta.

BLISS, A. (1984) 'English in the south of Ireland'. In P. Trudgill (ed.) *Language in the British Isles*, pp. 135–151. Cambridge: Cambridge University Press.

BORD NA GAEILGE (1983) *Action Plan for Irish 1983–1986.* Dublin: Bord na Gaeilge.

BUCKLAND, P. (1988) 'Irish breakthrough in Liverpool', *Irish Studies in Britain* 12: 9.

COMMINS, P. (1988) 'Socioeconomic development and language maintenance in the Gaeltacht', *International Journal of the Sociology of Language* **70**, 11–28.

Commission of the European Communities (1986) *Linguistic Minorities in Countries Belonging to the European Community*. Luxemburg: Office for Official Publications of the European Communities.

Committee on Irish Language Attitudes Research (CLAR) (1975) *Report*. Dublin: (Government) Stationery Office.

CONRADH NA GAEILGE (1982) 'Survey of Irish in broadcasting in 1982'. Unpublished manuscript. Conradh na Gaeilge, Dublin.

CONRADH NA GAEILGE (1987) 'Survey of Irish in broadcasting in 1987'. Unpublished manuscript. Conradh na Gaeilge, Dublin.

EDWARDS, J. (1985) *Language, Society and Identity*. Oxford: Blackwell.

FISHWICK, F. (1987) *The Market for Books in the Republic of Ireland*. Dublin: Irish Book Marketing Group.

FITZGERALD, G. (1984) 'Estimates for baronies of minimum level of Irish speaking amongst successive decennial cohorts: 1771–1781 to 1861–1871', *Proceedings of the Royal Irish Academy* **84**, C, (3).

GREENE, D. (1966) *The Irish Language: An Ghaeilge*. Cork: Mercier.

HARRIS, J. (1985). 'The Hiberno-English "I've it eaten" construction: What is it and where does it come from?' In D. Ó Baoill (ed.) *Papers on Irish English*, pp. 36–52. Dublin: Irish Association for Applied Linguistics.

HARRIS, J., LITTLE, D. and SINGLETON, D. (1986) *Perspectives on the English Language in Ireland*. Proceedings of the First Symposium on Hiberno-English. Dublin: University of Dublin.

HARRIS, J. (1988) 'Spoken Irish in the primary school system', *International Journal of the Sociology of Language* **70**, 69–88.

HILLIARD, E. (1982) *Migration History and Language Usage among Mothers of Gaeltacht Primary School Entrants*. Dublin: Bord na Gaeilge

KALLEN, J. (1985) 'A global view of the English language in Ireland'. In D. Ó Baoill (ed.) *Papers on Irish English*, pp. 63–78. Dublin: Irish Association for Applied Linguistics.

KALLEN, J. (1988) 'The English language in Ireland', *International Journal of the Sociology of Language* **70**, 127–42.

MACNAMARA, J. (1966) *Bilingualism in Primary Education: A study of Irish Experience*. Edinburgh: Edinburgh University Press.

Ó BAOILL, D. (ed.) (1985) *Papers on Irish English*. Dublin: Irish Association for Applied Linguistics.

Ó BAOILL, D. (1988) 'Language planning in Ireland: the standardization of Irish', *International Journal of the Sociology of Language* **70**, 109–27.

Ó GLAISNE, R. (1981) 'Irish and the Protestant tradition', *The Crane Bag* **5**, 33–44.

GLIASÁIN, M. (1988) 'Bilingual secondary schools in Dublin 1969–1980', *International Journal of the Sociology of Language* **70**, 89–108.

Ó HADHMAILL, F. (1985) *Report of a Survey of the Irish Language in West Belfast*. Department of Social Administration, University of Ulster.

Ó MUIRITHE, D. (ed.) (1977) *The English Language in Ireland*. Cork: Mercier.

Ó RAHILLY, T. (1932) *Irish Dialects Past and Present*. Dublin: Dublin Institute for Advanced Studies.

Ó RIAGÁIN, P. (1988) 'Bilingualism in Ireland 1973–1983: an overview of national sociolinguistic surveys', *International Journal of the Sociology of Language* **70**, 29–52

Ó RIAGÁIN (1987) 'Social class, education and Irish', *Teangeolas* (Journal of Institiúid Teangeolaíochta Éireann **23**, 13–14.

Ó RIAGÁIN, P. and Ó GLIASÁIN, M. (1984) *The Irish Language in the Republic of Ireland* 1983: Preliminary Report of a National Survey. Dublin: Institiúid Teangeolaiochta Éireann, the Linguistics Institute of Ireland.

SWEENEY, P. (1988) *The Irish Language in Northern Ireland*. Occasional Paper No. 17, Policy, Planning and Research Unit, Northern Ireland Office.

TOVEY, H. (1988) 'The state and the Irish language: the role of Bord na Gaeilge', *International Journal of the Sociology of Language* **70**, 53–68.

WALL, M. (1969) 'The decline of the Irish language'. In B. Ó Cuív (ed.) *A View of the Irish Language*, pp. 81–90. Dublin: Government Stationery Office.

Chapter 5

The Romani speech community

Ian Hancock

Varesave foki nai-len pengi nogi chib, si kokoro posh foki
A people without their own language is only half a people.
(BRITISH ROMANI SAYING)

Amari chib si amari zor
Our language is our strength.
(HUNGARIAN ROMANI SAYING)

British Romani might, with some justification, have been placed in the section on South Asian speech communities, since its ultimate origin, like that of Hindi, Gujarati, Panjabi and other neo-Indic languages is traceable directly to Sanskrit, in India. However, it was not until the arrival of its speakers in south-eastern Europe in the early medieval period that we date the actual crystallization of the language (much like the dating of English only from its arrival in Britain in the fifth century). All modern European dialects of Romani, including the British, descend from one earlier ancestor language whose speakers subsequently spread out over Europe; today, there are some sixty such dialects, though the original Romani from which they descend is itself no longer spoken.

Although in the eyes of European society the identity of the Roma ('Gypsies') has traditionally been viewed as somewhat mysterious, the reasons for this are not to be sought in linguistics or history; the academic community has been aware of the Indian origins of the language for over two centuries. Since the Indian connection was made in 1763,[1] sporadic, though sustained scholarship has continued up until the present time, and the body of scientific literature on the linguistic and racial affiliations of the Romani populations numbers in the thousands of titles.

Very many suggestions have been made over the centuries about who and what Gypsies are; most have by now been dismissed as fanciful and unscientific, but the question has not been entirely resolved even today. While the Indian affiliation of the language and the gene pool has now been established beyond question, determining the time and circumstances of the move out of India still leaves room for debate. It was thought for many years that the story of the Romani exodus was preserved in the epic *Shah Namah*, which tells of 10,000 Luri coming from India to serve as entertainers in the Persian court in AD 439, but evidence that the people referred to in that poem had anything to do with the present-day Roma is inconclusive, and in any case, if it were substantiated it would apply to the Nuri (Nawari) people of the Middle East rather than to the Roma of Europe, whose historical and social connection with the former population is questionable. For almost as long, it has been accepted that the ethnonym *Rom* is cognate with the Indian word *Dom*, the name given to members of an Indian social class consisting of jugglers, entertainers, slaughterers and so on, and that it was here that the origins of the Roma were to be sought. More recently, however, research by Kochanowski (1968), Rishi (1975) and others (summarized in Hancock 1988a) suggests a multiple ethnic origin for the first identifiable Gypsy population, and an exodus out of that part of the world at the time of the Rajput incursions against the Ghaznavids in the tenth and eleventh centuries. The Rajputs themselves were 'welded out of different non-Aryan material into a martial society of interrelated families, and rewarded with kshatriya status and certificates of descent from the sun and the moon' (Watson 1981:88).[2] These high-caste warriors, together with their camp followers of the Sudra, or lowest of the four castes (to which the actual *Dom* belonged), moved further and further west, reaching the Byzantine Empire by perhaps AD 1050, and the Balkans in southern Europe by perhaps AD 1250. Such reconstruction must be pieced together from vague historical references to population movements, and from the evidence inherent in the Romani language itself. Once in Europe, the Roma were confused with the Islamic invaders who were probably the cause of their being there in the first place, and were called by a variety of names reflecting this: Tatars, Saracens, Egyptians (hence ''gypsies') and so on; such names still persist today. Christian reaction to the Muslim occupation of the Holy Land and of their trade routes to the East led to the Crusades during this period, and to an increasing persecution of the Roma, who were seen as interlopers, spies for the Turks, carriers of disease, and a danger to Christendom. Anti-Gypsy legislation was soon everywhere in effect, and has scarcely abated in the present day. In southern Europe, Gypsies were enslaved by the Church and the nobility, a condition which lasted for over 500 years. During the period of Nazi domination in this century, Gypsies were being put into camps beginning in the 1920s and selected for sterilization from the very year that Hitler came to power. Contemporary scholarship in Germany is now indicating that perhaps as many as 1.5 million Gypsies had been murdered by 1945 (Hancock 1988b), though practically no war crimes reparations have been paid to the survivors since then. It is the continuing oppression of the population in Britain which, to some extent, has ensured the perpetuation of the Romani language.

The Roma in the British Isles

While parallels exist elsewhere, in Britain in particular the issue of the identity of the Romani population remains contentious. This is because wherever Roma have migrated, they have encountered, and have sometimes formed permanent alliances with, other, non-Romani, peoples. This has given rise to newer, syncretic populations which, because of the pervasiveness of the core culture and language, have remained essentially Romani in terms of their own perceived identity; non-Romani groups have usually adjusted to the Roma rather than the reverse, although sufficient non-Romani elements have also been incorporated to affect the broader cultural and linguistic characteristics of each individual group. Over time, this has resulted in the linguistic diversity referred to earlier, and has led to different Romani populations emerging in different parts of Europe. Roma in Australia, South Africa and the Americas have descended in turn from the various European Romani populations. In some instances, the Indic element has not been sufficient to keep the overall identity of the group Romani, so that while Romani elements are discernible in the speech of such peoples as the Jenisch in Germany or Switzerland, for example, or the Quinquis in Spain, other factors, both genetic and cultural, are insufficient either for them to think of themselves as Romani, or for them to be regarded as such by members of coexisting populations.

In Britain, at least three other peoples have interacted with, and influenced the character of, the Romani (in Britain called the *Romanichal*) population: these are the sixteenth-century outlaws, the Scottish Travellers and the Irish Travellers. The Welsh Travellers may also be counted here, though their influence has been much smaller. The emergence of these populations is only now being examined in detail, and some scholarly debate exists as to their respective ultimate origins.

Thanks to a wealth of Elizabethan documentation, most is known about the outlaws of the Renaissance period, whom the Romanichals first encountered after their arrival. These people consisted of ex-soldiers home from foreign wars, dispossessed landowners, legitimate beggars such as the maimed and sightless no longer being cared for following the dissolution of the Roman Catholic monasteries by King Henry, apprentices who had left the disintegrating guild system to work on their own, and so on.[3] These people, unable or unwilling to ally themselves with the Establishment, took to the roads in search of a livelihood, legal or otherwise. This population was not merely a sixteenth-century phenomenon; whatever the origins of such outlaw communities (*ie* communities outside the law), references to them go back at least to the early Middle Ages. The *Westour* or (unbidden) 'guests'[4] in medieval English society were apparently of both Celtic and Saxon origin, while from the seventeenth century on, Irish and Scottish itinerants, some because of famine or unemployment in their own countries, others because of war or domination by the English, or who were dispossessed following the Enclosures Acts, were found in great numbers throughout Britain. A law dated 1654 ordered the arrest of 'all wanderers, men and women, and such other Irish [. . . without] a settled course of industry' (Williams 1932:12), while between 1678 and 1685, large numbers of Scots, displaced by the Scottish Civil War, were being arrested in England, hundreds for transportation to the American plantations (Niles 1980:21–2).

The most often cited dates of the earliest appearance of Romanichals in Britain are 1505 for Scotland and 1512 for England, though neither of these refers to their actual *arrival* in those years. MacRitchie, however, lists two earlier dates: 1452 and 1470.[5] Given that the first documented appearances of Gypsies in France and the Netherlands were in 1419 and 1420 respectively, the first actual venture across the Channel was almost certainly earlier than the usually accepted dates. The presence of French-derived items in British Romani (*eg fuzhara* (fern), and *povera* (poor), from Fr. *fougière* and *pauvre*) suggest arrival in England from France, though those reaching Scotland first probably did so via Scandinavia. The actual branch of Romani to which the British dialect belongs is Northern, connecting it most closely with those spoken in Germany and Scandinavia.

Upon arrival, the groups of Romanichals trickling in found themselves in an environment which, because of their lack of a political or geographical identity, or ties to traditional British society, made them subject to the laws affecting other such elements within the population. It was a period of excessive xenophobia; Liégeois pointed out that 'Even before the arrival of Gypsies in Great Britain, an English Act of 1388 showed that wanderers were already regarded as "suspicious persons living suspiciously"' (1986:101–2), helping to explain legislation against Gypsies which emerged in subsequent years: by the sixteenth century ordering their deportation out of the country, and by the seventeenth century making it an offence punishable by death merely to be born a Gypsy.

It has been the ability to absorb and assimilate non-Romani elements which has from the beginning – if the connection with the Rajputs can be demonstrated – characterized Gypsy populations. In Britain, this has led to a blurring of the distinctions between the different Traveller groups from the perspective of the Establishment. Because of the nineteenth-century literary idealizing of the 'free and unspoilt' Gypsy (see especially Brown 1985, and Mayall 1985, 1988), probably as a reaction to industrialization and because of Victorian conceptions about race, the notion has become widespread that a small, pristine population of 'true Romany Gypsies' exists but that the majority of Travellers are of non-Gypsy or mixed descent. Racist notions equated the diluting of the gene pool with the diluting of culture and identity. 'Pure' Gypsies were clean and part of the rural heritage; the rest did all the mischief, gave them a bad name, and were not real Gypsies anyway. Statements reflecting this are found even at the administrative level: a certain county councillor's decision concluded that one individual, a house-dwelling Romanichal, 'has not been a man of nomadic habits and so in my judgement he is not a Gypsy'.[6] Some quite appalling statements have been made by public officials in recent years; some have even called for the extermination of the Traveller population, either by driving them into the sea[7] or, most recently, by burning them in a garbage incinerator.[8] The 1968 Caravan Sites Act empowered County Councils to move Gypsies – and only Gypsies – on, by force if necessary, if they were designated as not meeting qualifications for site occupancy. In Bradford, apartheid-like policy forbids Gypsies from entering city limits without passes. This situation may change since the 27 July 1988 Central Court of Appeal ruling that Gypsies did in fact constitute a racially determined group (*The Times* law report for 29 July 1988),[9] although this new decision applies only to Travellers of Romani descent. Irish, Scottish and other Travellers will continue to be discriminated against without protection from the law.

Classification from outside of who and who is not Gypsy has

led to confusion on the part of the general population in Britain
as to what a Gypsy actually is. It has been less of an effort for
the British public to cling to the romantic Hollywood image that
the media doggedly help to sustain, than to sort out the real situation. While the popular image presents the Gypsy as a colourful,
caravan-dwelling individual, the real population continues to en-
dure on a daily basis the kind of hardship described here, while
the ignorance about the true ethnic composition of the Traveller
population ensures that public outrage at these violations of both
civil and human rights here in Britain, remains minimal.

From the Travellers' point of view, group identity is not a problem, resting upon demonstrable family connection, and more
overtly upon linguistic and social behaviour. However, unless it,
too, can be successfully challenged, the new ruling favouring only
Romani Travellers is likely to stimulate a whole new set of problems related to ethnic identity, with families who have disclaimed
Romani ancestry now finding it to their legal advantage to
promote it if it exists. Mode of living is less of a factor; there are
more house-dwelling ethnic Gypsies in England today than those
who are permanently mobile, a point which was made in the Appeal Court to underline the fact that the word 'Gypsy' was not
synonymous with 'Traveller': 'The judges held that the United
Kingdom's 80,000 Gypsies had not lost their separate identity because, unlike Saxons and Danes, they had not merged wholly into
the general population, even though *between a half and two thirds
had abandoned a nomadic way of life*' (Shaw 1988:12; see also
Acton 1985. Emphasis added).

Furthermore, of those who are mobile, less than 5 per cent
travel in the traditional horse-drawn 'caravan'. Nor is traditional
means of livelihood as important as an ethnic determiner within
the Romani population as it seems to be for the non-Gypsy eth-
nographers. Gypsies in Britain are found in many occupations,
including those of film-maker, journalist and actor – professions
which, however, usually allow independence from a hierarchy of
authority.

Changing patterns of language use

It was not only pressure from outside which kept the Romanichals
at a distance from the settled community. Part of the Indian
legacy brought into Europe included (and continues to include)
well-instilled notions of ritual defilement, called *moxaviben*[10] or
mokadipen in earlier British Romani, and most commonly
mokadi kovels or *mokadi kuvas* today. This concept is found
everywhere, though the word for it has become lost for some

groups. It is the *magardipen* of the Hungarian Roma, the *mahrimos* of those in Serbia, the *gadnipé* of the Italian and the *maxdigar* of the Armenian Gypsies. In all of the dialects which have preserved these terms, they contrast semantically with other words which mean 'dirty (from dirt)', thus one could be spotlessly clean in a physical sense, yet still unclean ritually. The criteria for what makes a person, thing or situation *mokadi* vary from group to group throughout Europe, but generally relate to the handling and preparation of food, male interaction with females, interaction with certain animals, the washing of the body, clothing and cooking utensils, and so on. The non-Gypsy, or *gaujo*,[11] populations are seen as being *mokadi* by virtue of their personal habits, and as a result capable of defiling Gypsies through intimate contact; thus socializing beyond business relationships is minimized. Chairs, crockery and other items may be kept separately in a Romani home simply for the use of non-Gypsy visitors; implements meant for family use will be discarded if used unintentionally by outsiders, and even within the same household, certain utensils such as cups or plates will be destroyed if inadvertently employed by other family members.

The concept of *mokadi kovels* ensured not only that distance was kept from the settled population, but from the British outlaws together with whom the Romanichals were obliged to cohabit. It may well have been the desire to remain separate, in an already separate larger body, which led to the emergence of the distinct dialect of Romani spoken in England today. Having to interact with the British outlaws, a common bond was necessary; Renaissance documents depict in detail the unions between the two groups (Hancock 1984a) which led to the development of a secret, or cryptolectal, register as a means of group identity and surreptitious activity. It is likely that the Romanichal population was willing to have its language serve as a lexical reservoir for this 'canting tongue' – essentially cryptic lexemes in an English grammatical framework – but did not otherwise make available the knowledge of their own inflected native language, which they kept as insulation between themselves and the non-Gypsy world.

With the passage of time, isolation in the British Isles from Roma elsewhere in Europe, and the harsh legal and social conditions shared by Gypsy and non-Gypsy outlaw alike, led to a relaxation of the factors separating the two populations, for some families more than others. The original, inflected common Romani gradually fell into disuse, surviving only in isolated areas such as Wales[12]. Everywhere it was being replaced as the ethnic language by the newer, cryptolectal variety, called variously

Pogadi-Jib (*ie* 'Broken Language'), *Posh 'n' Posh* (*ie* 'Half and Half'), *Pikey Talk* and so on. This is referred to in linguistic descriptions as '*Angloromani*',[13] a term not used by its speakers themselves. Similar developments from inflected Romani have taken place elsewhere, though not enough research has been undertaken in the area to determine whether the social processes resulting in the emergence of such dialects have been the same in each case. The best-known restructured variety besides Angloromani is the Caló of Spain, but descriptions exist of a number of others.[14] To illustrate Angloromani as it is used today, here follow the closing lines of a letter written in 1987, as spelt: 'Mandi rokkers to the deary Devel in Romanis, because I gin that lesty gins duva jib. Fokkie akie vader at mandi like mandis divia when they shun mandi rokker. There is only one gara akie that gins it. Tuti, bitcher mandi a lil when you sas the charis, mandi is leling sudieus and it is late in the radie. This bootie that mandi is kurring makes mandi to lel sudieus durring the devis.'

In normalized spelling, this would read as follows; Angloromani items have been italicized, and those of ultimately Indic origin underlined:

> <u>*Mandi* *rok*</u>er<u>s</u> to the *diri* <u>*Devel*</u> in <u>*Romanis*</u>, because I <u>*jin*</u> that <u>*Lesti*</u> <u>*jin*</u>s <u>*duva* *jib*</u>. *Foki* <u>*akai*</u> *vader* at <u>*mandi*</u> like <u>*mandi*</u>'s <u>*divia*</u> when they <u>*shun* *mandi* *roker*</u>. There is only one *gera* <u>*akai*</u> that <u>*jin*</u>s it. <u>*Tuti*</u>, <u>*bicher* *mandi*</u> a <u>*lil*</u> when you <u>*sas*</u> the *cherus*, <u>*mandi*</u> is <u>*lel*</u>ing <u>*suti*</u>ous and it is late in the <u>*rati*</u>. This <u>*buti*</u> that <u>*mandi*</u> is <u>*ker*</u>ing makes <u>*mandi*</u> to <u>*lel* *suti*</u>ous during the <u>*dives*</u> (<u>*mandi*</u> 'I, me', *roker* 'speak', *diri* 'dear' [< Eng.], *Devel* 'God', *Romanis* 'Romani language', *jin* 'know', *Lesti* 'He, Him', *duva* 'that', *jib* 'language, tongue', *foki* 'people' [< Eng.], *akai* 'here', *vader* 'look' [< Polari], *divia* 'crazy', [< Slavic], *shun* 'hear, listen', *gera* 'man, person' [?< Slavic], *tuti* 'you', *bicher* 'send', *lil* 'letter, paper, book', *sas* 'have, be', *cherus* 'time' [< Greek], *suti*(ous) 'sleep(y)', *rati* 'night', *buti* 'work', *ker* 'do, make', *dives* 'day').

An examination of the dialect gives the impression of its being something like the Nadsat in Anthony Burgess's *Clockwork Orange* (1963), though the actual linguistic processes which have yielded it may or may not have been the same. Nadsat is English into which Anglicized Russian items have been introduced; if Angloromani began as an earlier non-Gypsy Cant which was subsequently supplemented with Romani-derived lexemes following the arrival of the Romanichals in Britain, then a parallel could be drawn; but there are arguments against this. First of all, there are very few items of Cant origin in Angloromani, even though Cant continues to coexist with it in Britain as the major component of the cryptolect of the Scottish Travellers, and Angloromani speakers are able to identify those which do exist in their own speech. Secondly, Angloromani includes grammatical, as well as lexical, items of Romani origin, and these – *eg* pronouns and prepositions – are far less likely to be adopted in Nadsat-like registers of a language. Lastly, and perhaps most significant, recent work done on the similar development out of inflected Romani, the Caló spoken in Spain, questions, on the basis of lexicostatistical analysis, 'the productivity of arguments that explain away Caló as a "Gypsified" version of Castilian. While clearly influenced by Castilian, Caló has an apparent combinatorial pattern of its own' (Dietz and Mulcahy 1988:15). Indications are that the same will hold true for Angloromani, and work is planned in this area to test the hypothesis.

It is true to say that the use of Angloromani is greater in some domains than in others. Overall, it will be spoken less in the course of a day among the house-dwelling Romani population than by those who travel, and even then it is likely to be heard at specific functions such as horse-fairs, weddings, funerals and the like. Angloromani is not usually the medium of casual discourse in the home environment, though individual items (*eg grai* (horse), *chavi* (child) etc.) may be adopted into Romani English very freely.

Angloromani is not learnt from earliest childhood, and must therefore be seen as an ethnic, not a native, language. It is not until children, boys in particular, reach the age of nine or ten and begin to work alongside the adults, that its acquisition proper begins. Here, it functions as an occupational register, and serves also to distinguish Romanichal from non-Romanichal Travellers. It consists of some 300 vocabulary items which everybody seems to know, and perhaps twice that many which can be found in specific family dialects. Thus while everyone will understand and use *dik* (look) for example, only one or two families might be familiar with *basha* meaning a 'meat-skewer'. Angloromani has become something of a lingua franca, Irish, Welsh and Scottish Travellers all being familiar with its basic vocabulary, but speaking in addition their own ethnolectal dialects. Romanichals do not as a rule know more than a few common words of these.

Thomason and Kaufman have recently commented upon the persistence of Angloromani whose speech community, they say, 'exhibits a stubborn resistance to cultural assimilation so strong that its ethnic language is partially preserved functionally, though not grammatically' (1988: 103–4).

There is certainly no indication that Angloromani, with some 90,000 speakers in Britain and perhaps twice that overseas, is disappearing; indications are that its use may in fact be increasing; certainly the overall numbers of the non-sedentary Traveller population appear to be rising each year, not merely from normal internal growth but from being joined by previously sedentary Traveller families.[15]

Language, culture and community

The persistence of Angloromani as a spoken medium is a strong indication of the persistence with which Romanichal identity is maintained in Britain. Five centuries of assimilative pressure have worked upon a community isolated from the reinforcing ethnic contact with other Romani groups, which is constantly available to related populations in continental Europe. Infusions of Romani language and culture from outside have been relatively few in England during the past 500 years, while non-Gypsy factors on the other hand have been ever-present and constant in the Angloromani environment. That the recent judicial ruling (*supra*) should acknowledge that 'unlike the Saxons and Danes', Romanichals 'had not merged wholly into the population' despite half a millennium of interaction with outsiders in an isolated geographical environment, must stand as the ultimate testimony to the vitality of this particular ethnic minority.

The point has already been made that, in one sense at least, being a Rom means not being a *gaujo*. The Romanichal population in particular has to maintain a kind of 'ethnic vigilance' in order to protect its identity, and the perpetuation of the ideas of ritual uncleanliness, the *mokadi kovels* discussed above, is a prime factor in achieving this. It may be significant that both the Romanichals and the Vlax[16] Roma maintain this concept more rigorously than any other group, each having had to preserve its Romani identity in the face of extreme, albeit radically different, pressures. *Mokadipen* is more than simply the avoidance of pollution in the narrow sense; for those who maintain it, it determines many aspects of social and even business behaviour, and one's identity as a Rom. It is central to *Romanipé*, or 'Gypsiness'. In communities where external oppression has not threatened *Romanipé*, for example in Turkey (and among Turkish Gypsies in Greece), its perpetuation as a survival technique has not been crucial, and as a result its function has weakened.

For Romanichals, language is as much a factor of ethnic

identity as is the regard for *mokadi kovels*, and is therefore fostered for the same reasons. In a recent paper, Bickerton (1988:281) makes the case that languages of the Angloromani type *only* come into existence when it is necessary to insulate their speakers from the outside world:

> So far, the only attested cases of relexification, the Media Lengua and Angloromani,[17] have occurred where the speakers concerned already had a language which linguistically, if not socially, was perfectly adequate for their communicative purposes (Quechua, Romani). There thus seems to be good sociolinguistic grounds for assuming that relexification . . . only occurs when a new language is invented for social-boundary marking or similar purposes.

In the past, Angloromani has been transmitted orally from parents to children under circumstances which are still not altogether clear to us. While references to it date from the 1500s, actual samples have only been documented since the nineteenth century, so protectively has it been withheld from outside enquiry. Today, however, Angloromani serves as the medium for original literature, and an annual competition exists for the best compositions by Gypsy children. Romanichal poets such as Toni Lee, Charlie Smith and Tom Odley have successfully published their work, much of it employing the language, and the appearance of a newly compiled dictionary, and a number of sociolinguistic analyses (Acton and Kenrick 1984; Acton and Davies 1979; Kenrick 1979) all demonstrate this renewed interest.

An increase in social consciousness in the second half of this century has made Romani dissatisfaction more articulate; demands for social improvements and civil rights have become more vocal, and have led to the creation in recent years of a number of Romanichal and other Traveller organizations in Britain. The association of some of these bodies with the International Romani Union has brought about participation in events elsewhere in Europe, and the reawakening of the sense of belonging to a truly world-wide people. The traditional attitude of the British Establishment, *viz* that Gypsies (or 'gipsies', as the word most often appears in the press) do not constitute a distinct, ethnically determined population, has come to be shown as false, a deliberately fostered tool of oppression which has managed to fly in the face of two centuries of scholarship which proves otherwise, and the evidence surrounding those who attend such international functions. With the greater mid-twentieth-century volume of written and tape-recorded communication between

Romanichal communities in Britain and those overseas, in North America (Hancock 1986) and Australia in particular, Angloromani is now being used internationally. In 1988 a project was begun and funding sought, which will allow Travellers in Britain and the United States to visit each other's countries, to see how each other live and to reinforce transatlantic ties between the separate but related communities. Support for such an arrangement is enthusiastic in both countries and, if it is successful, others will surely follow.

Education and language reproduction

The situation of Angloromani both resembles, and differs from, that of other ethnic minorities in Britain; the principal dissimilarity is that for Romanichals, it is English which is the language learnt first in life, and which is the native language of the population. In this respect, the situation of Angloromani is not matched either by that of most Romani-speaking populations elsewhere in Europe, or by other linguistic minorities in Great Britain. Because of this, the argument is sometimes made that all British Romanichals speak English anyway, and that effort need therefore not be expended upon their linguistic welfare; it was, for example, an issue which was raised (though subsequently dismissed) when Gospel translations into the dialect were planned some years ago.[18] Such an attitude in any case would deny the population its rights as decreed by the United Nations Subcommittee on the Prevention of Discrimination and the Protection of Minorities, which states that: 'The protection of minorities is the protection of non-dominant groups which, while wishing, in general, for equality of treatment with the majority, wish for a measure of differential treatment, in order to preserve basic characteristics which they possess.' With the recent clarification of the ethnic and racial status of the British Romanichal population, such a statement becomes all the more relevant. Use of the Angloromani language is beyond question a major basic characteristic, and its perpetuation crucial to the overall ethnic identity.

Angloromani is learnt in an all-Gypsy environment; it has not been necessary to create special classes like those for Irish or Scottish Gaelic, or even British Panjabi; for these communities, their languages are not being transmitted with 100 per cent success to the youngest generations, and the Romanichal population must therefore be considered as being more actively determined to retain the ethnic language than some other British minorities. The fact that Angloromani is a register of English, not inflected

Romani, at first sight accounts for this; broadly speaking, learning Angloromani means learning a particular vocabulary of several hundred words and using them in the framework of Britain's national language. In fact, the situation is more complicated than that – for one thing, the English matrix into which the Romani lexicon is slotted is not the same as the English otherwise used by the same speaker; work in this area is still in progress, but it is evident that the English base of Angloromani is distinct both phonologically and lexically, and approaches regional vernacular varieties of British English to a greater degree than the non-Angloromani, non-standard dialects otherwise used by its speakers. Again, as Acton and Davies (1979) have pointed out, speaking Angloromani is not simply a matter of using as many Romani-derived items as possible; the result would sound artificial (discussed further in Hancock 1986). Nor is the dialect appropriate for all occasions; its use is determined, like any language, by social factors.

Some Romanichals, in particular those who have become involved in the national reunification movement, have suggested that it would be a good thing to teach inflected Romani to Romanichal children in Britain, as a way of regaining a part of their lost history. A number of associations working with Travellers, such as the Literacy Drop-in Centre in Sheffield, or the National Council for Travelling People in Dublin, or the Write Here organization, have indicated support for such classes, but they have yet to materialize. The choice of which inflected dialect to teach would have to be addressed; the variety now barely surviving in Wales (and described by Sampson 1926) would be logical on historical grounds, but would have local (*ie* British) relevance only. It would not be the best choice for communicating with those most closely connected with the international Romani movement, most of whom speak dialects spoken in southern Europe. This is a problem faced by all Romani-speaking populations at a distance from south-eastern Europe, and even by many non-Vlax-speaking populations who do live there; ideally, an international standard should be taught for use in addition to the home dialect, and in fact a number of groups in Yugoslavia, Bulgaria and elsewhere have acquired a knowledge of more widely spoken varieties of Romani which serve as lingua francas in their areas. The fact that Romanichals do not speak *any* kind of inflected Romani places a double burden upon them – and for those who wish to participate in Romani affairs outside of Britain, acquisition of a continental, rather than the British, inflected variety would seem essential.

At present, such considerations are academic. More pragmati-
cally, the education of Gypsy children must take priority, for until
more literate and ethnically articulate individuals exist to represent the population, the question of relearning inflected Romani
cannot be in Romani hands, and it is an intimately Romani issue.

The concept of 'education' is interpreted quite differently in a
Romani context; traditionally it has not included literacy skills,
for example. Romani parents are quick to point out that often
the values taught in the *gaujos'* classrooms are directly contrary
to those taught in a Gypsy home, and that sometimes, historical
figures presented to the pupils as heroes in *gaujo* culture, were
responsible for the deaths or persecution of the Gypsy people in
earlier times.

Teaching Gypsy children to function as Gypsies within Gypsy
society is taken care of quite adequately at home. Teaching Gypsies to function as Gypsies in non-Gypsy society on the other
hand, has not been seriously addressed until fairly recently.
Earlier attempts to 'educate' Gypsy children have simply been
attempts to de-Gypsify them, usually in a Christian context, and
to assimilate them as rapidly and completely as possible. The
nineteenth century saw a proliferation of books and articles on
the subject (discussed especially in Mayall 1988).

Today, a number of non-Gypsy organizations exist to deal with
the situation, and a growing sensitivity to the distinctive identity
of the Romani people is becoming evident. Reports (*eg* Liégeois
1987, 1988) have been commissioned detailing the requirements
of Gypsies and recommending pedagogical techniques which
when implemented would lead to integration rather than assimilation. It is still the case today in England that reliance upon
non-Gypsy teachers is the rule rather than the exception, however, and many such individuals come to the task inadequately
prepared. Some are attracted simply by the notion of working
with 'Gypsies', and the imagined romantic aspects attending such
a job. These individuals are quickly disabused, and tend not to
stay long. Others see such a task as simply a matter of teaching
the children of mobile families, and give too little acknowledgement to the internal values and cultural behaviour of
the pupils, or of their families with whom they also interact.

It has also been the case that too little background preparation
is given to those aspects of Romanichal life in the training sessions of such organizations as, for instance, the National
Association of Teachers of Travellers, whose several hundred
employees, all non-Gypsy, deal with Romanichal children on a
daily basis. Parents have told me that some teachers come into

their homes demonstrating no awareness whatsoever of the traditional Romani etiquette of cleanliness and propriety. Such instances have included sitting on the edge of a table, eating a cheese sandwich after having had the hand licked by a dog, asking whether the wife were expecting a baby, and loudly announcing a desire to visit the lavatory. Only with time and carefully planned teacher training courses will such problems be overcome, but the indications are promising, and it is evident that there is a growing awareness in Britain of who and what the Romani people really are.

As the protection of group identity and way of life is increasingly threatened by the homogenizing pressures of today's society, linguistic distinctiveness will continue both to shield and help identify the British Romanichal population. And as educational opportunities, made available in an ethnically sensitive context, lead to more and more members of the Romani community emerging to work and lead in both worlds, so we can expect to see more evidence of Romanichal self-determination, both politically and linguistically.

Notes

1. The frequently told story concerns one Stefan Valyi, a Hungarian student of theology at Leiden, who had learnt some Romani from Gypsies living in his home town, and was struck by its similarity to the Sanskrit being discussed by some of his fellow students from India.

2. Thus – if the current hypothesis is correct – this 'facility for assimilating foreigners' (Watson 1988:88) was already a characteristic of the earliest ancestors of the Roma. A remnant of the symbolic association of 'tribes' with the sun and the moon, as well as with the stars, is found among some central European Romani groups today (Chatard and Bernard 1959:93–4; Clébert 1963:127, based on the former source; Sutherland 1975: 125).

3. This period is documented in more detail in Hancock (1984a, b).

4. This plural form is from Welsh *Gwestwr* (in Modern Welsh *gwesteion*, singular *gwestai*) – which is itself an adoption from Middle English, suggesting association with a specifically Celtic population. Wilde (1889:306) believes that Saxons displaced as a result of the Norman takeover of their lands also came to constitute part of this phenomenon. Serfs fleeing feudal oppression probably also added to their numbers.

5 MacRitchie's sources state respectively that in Scotland '. . . a Company of Saracens or Gipsies from Ireland infested the country of Galloway' (1894:20), and that 'Johnny Faa, captain of a gang of gipsies' was engaged as a courier (1894:27).

6. The *Essex Courier* for Friday 15 February 1974, *p* 21.

7. The *Dover Express and East Kent News*, Friday 24 May 1974, *p* 5. See also Hancock (1987: Ch. 13).

8. Councillor Frank Millar of the Belfast City Council called for the disposal of Gypsies in the Duncrue Street rubbish incinerator in April 1988. A document circulated by the Council dated 2 May 1988, condemned his statement as 'an insult to the victims of the Holocaust'.

9. This ruling overturned the earlier Court of Westminster decision by Judge Harris that Travellers were not an ethnically identifiable population, and that signs refusing service to them were therefore not in violation of the Race Relations Act.

10. In this Romani orthography, /x/ represents a voiceless uvular fricative like the 'ch' in German *Achtung*.

11. This is usually spelt 'gorgio' in the literature, thanks probably to George Borrow, and is pronounced ['gɔːdžou] or ['gɔːdžə] (but ['gɔrdžər] in the dialect of the North American Romanichals). It is derived from the common Romani *gadžo* 'non-Gypsy', which is masculine singular, the feminine singular being *gadži*, and their plurals *gadže* and *gadžia* respectively in the subject case. Such grammatical distinctions do not apply to the word *gaujo*, however, which follows English rules of morphology. The same grammatical distinctions must apply to the noun *Rom* 'Gypsy' in the inflected dialects, thus possible forms include *Romni*, *Roma* and *Romnia*. The adjectival forms are *gadžikano* and *Romano*, also subject to change in inflected common Romani. Historically, *Romanichal* applied only to men and boys, but is now often used to apply to women as well. In the inflected British Romani of the Welsh Roma, the word refers only to the English Gypsies, not to themselves. Their self-designation is *Kalé* (a plural form, from *kalo* 'black').

12. Romani migration into Britain was not confined to the fifteenth and sixteenth centuries, and later arrivals from the Continent have helped perpetuate the existence of inflected Romani in Britain. The ancestors of the speakers of the remnant surviving in Wales came there from Somerset in the 1700s, while Francis Brown includes references to eighteenth-century Gypsies in England who were unfamiliar with English.

13. *Angloromani* refers to the dialect dealt with here. This is not the same as *Anglo-Romani*, a term which has been used in the *Journal of the Gypsy Lore Society* in the past to refer to the surviving remnants of the inflected language in England.

14. For Caló, see Jung (1972) and Tudela (1985); for a Scandinavian variety see Iversen (1944, 1945, 1950), and for a Greek variety see Triandaphyllidis (1923–24). Examples of a Bosnian variety called 'Tent Gypsy' are found in Uhlik (1941–43).

15. The term 'Traveller' need not imply that those so designated actually travel. Romani families which have been house-dwelling for many years are also called Travellers.

16. A Vlax or Vlach is a Romance-speaking inhabitant of Romania.

17. Shelta would probably qualify here as well (see Hancock 1984c).

18. Some of these translations into Angloromani, and other materials published in, and on, the language are available from Romanestan Publications (See useful addresses, p. 268).

References

Acton, Thomas (1985) 'Gypsies in Great Britain: a report for the Council of Europe'. Unpublished first draft.

Acton, Thomas and Davies, G. (1979) 'Educational policy and language use among English Romanies and Irish Travellers in England and Wales'. In Hancock, *Romani Sociolinguistics, pp.* 91–110.

Acton, Thomas and Kenrick, Donald (eds) (1984) *Romani Rokkeripen Todivvus.* London: Romanestan Publications.

Bickerton, Derek (1988) 'Relexification', *The Journal of Pidgin and Creole Languages* 3(2): 277–82.

Brown, Frances (1986) *Fairfield Folk: A History of the British Fairground and its People.* Upton-upon-Severn: Malvern Publishing Co.

Brown, Marilyn (1985) *Gypsies and Other Bohemians.* Ann Arbor: UMI Research Press.

Burgess, Anthony (1963) *A Clockwork Orange.* New York: Norton & Co.

Chatard, R. P. and Bernard, Michel (1959) *Zanko, chef tribal.* Paris: Vieux Colombier.

Clébert, Jean-Paul (1963) *The Gypsies.* London: Vista Books.

DeSilva, Cara, Grumet, J. and Nemeth, David (eds) (1988) *Papers from the Eighth and Ninth Annual Meetings*, Gypsy Lore Society, North American Chapter. New York: GLS(NAC).

Dietz, Henry G. and Mulcahy, David (1988) 'Romani of a third place: a statistical analysis of nineteenth century Caló and Castilian'. In De-Silva, Grumet and Nemeth, op. cit., *pp* 1–17.

Hancock, Ian (ed.) (1979) 'Romani sociolinguistics', *International Journal of the Sociology of Language* 19. The Hague: Mouton.

Hancock, Ian (1984a) 'The social and linguistic development of Angloromani'. In Acton and Kenrick, op. cit., *pp* 89–122.

Hancock, Ian (1984b) 'Romani and Angloromani'. In Trudgill, P. (1984) *Language in the British Isles.* Cambridge: Cambridge University Press pp. 367–83.

Hancock, Ian (1984c) 'Shelta and Polari'. In Trudgill, P. (1984) *Language in the British Isles.* Cambridge: Cambridge University Press pp. 384–403.

Hancock, Ian (1986) 'The cryptolectal speech of the American roads: Traveler Cant and American Angloromani', *American Speech* 61(3): 206–20.

Hancock, Ian (1987) *The Pariah Syndrome: An Account of Gypsy Slavery and Persecution.* Ann Arbor: Karoma Publishers.

Hancock, Ian (1988a) 'The development of Romani linguistics'. In Jazyery and Winter, op. cit., *pp* 183–223.

Hancock, Ian (1988b) 'Uniqueness of the victims: Gypsies, Jews and the Holocaust', *Without Prejudice: International Review of Racial Discrimination* 1(2): 25–50.

Iversen, Ragnvald (1944, 1945, 1950) *The Secret Languages of Norway.* Oslo: Dybwad.

Jazyery, A. and Winter, Werner (eds) (1988) *Papers in Honor of Edgar C. Polomé*. The Hague: Mouton.

Jung, Christof (1972) *Wortliste des Dialekts der spanischen Zigeuner, mit kurze Grammatik*. Mainz: Flamenco Studio Verlag.

Kenrick, Donald (1979) 'Romani English'. In Hancock, *Romani Sociolinguistics*, *International Journal of the Sociology of Language* **19**: 111–24.

Kochanowski, Vanya da Gila (1968) 'Black Gypsies, white Gypsies', *Diogenes* **63**: 27–47.

Liégeois, Jean-Pierre (1986) *Gypsies: An Illustrated History*. London: Al-Saqi Books.

Liégeois, Jean-Pierre (1987). *School Provision for Gypsy and Traveller Children: A Synthesis Report*. Commission of the European Communities. Luxemburg: Official Publications Office.

Liégeois, Jean-Pierre (1988). *School Provision for Gypsy and Traveller Children*. Manchester: Traveller Education Service.

MacRitchie, David (1894) *Scottish Gypsies under the Stewarts*. Edinburgh.

Mayall, David (1985) 'Lorist, reformist and romanticist: the 19th century response to Gypsy-Travellers', *Immigrants and Minorities* **4**(3): 53–67.

Mayall, David (1988) *Gypsy-Travellers in 19th Century Society*. Cambridge: Cambridge University Press.

Niles, Norma (1980) 'Provincial English dialects and Barbadian English.' Unpublished doctoral dissertation, University of Michigan.

Rishi, W. R. (1975) *Roma: The Punjabi Emigrants in Europe, Central and Middle Asia, the USSR and Americas*. Patiala: The Punjabi Press.

Sampson, John (1926) *The Dialect of the Gypsies of Wales*. Oxford: The University Press.

Shaw, Terence (1988). 'Gipsies win race relations protection after ruling on ban from public house', *The Daily Telegraph*, 28 July, p 12.

Sutherland, Anne (1975) *Gypsies, the hidden Americans*. New York: Macmillan.

Thomason, S. G. and Kaufman, T. (1988) *Language Contact, Creolization and Genetic Linguistics*. Berkeley: California University Press.

Triandaphyllidis, M. A. (1923–24) 'Eine zigeunerisches-griechische Geheimsprache', *Zeitschrift für Vergleichende Sprachforschung* **52**: 1–42.

Tudela, Jean-Louis (1985). *Trejini a Caló: Cours de Caló*. Montferrand: Chez l'Auteur.

Uhlik, Rade (1941–43). 'Bosnian Romani', *Journal of the Gypsy Lore Society* **20**: 78–84, 100–40; **21**: 24–55, 110–41; **22**: 38–47, 107–19. Translated by Frederick Ackerley.

Watson, Francis (1981) *A Concise History of India*. London: Thames & Hudson.

Wilde, W. C. (1889) 'Some words of thief talk', *Journal of American Folklore* **2**(7): 301–6.

Williams, J. J. (1932) *Whence the 'Black Irish' of Jamaica?* New York: Dial Press.

Chapter 6

The Welsh speech community

Viv Edwards

Dy iaith ar ein hysgwyddau megis pwn
(Your language (*ie* English) on our shoulders like a burden)
                                                    GWENALLT
Heb iaith, heb genedl
(No language, no nation)
                            (PROVERB)

The Brythonic branch of Celtic began to separate into independent languages in the middle of the sixth century. The first
written records in Welsh date back to the eighth century but it
was not until the Middle Welsh period (approximately 1150–
1400) that a standardized language had emerged from the pens
of the bardic poets who had been especially trained to 'guard' the
form and content of the language under the patronage of the aristocracy (Lewis 1987). The extent to which this language could be
considered a national standard, however, is questionable. On the
one hand there was a very high degree of agreement as to usage
among bardic poets from different parts of Wales. On the other
hand, this usage was limited to the gentry and aristocracy.

The democratization, or nationalization, of the language was
only achieved with the translation of the Bible in 1588. Although there was a great deal of dialect diversity among speakers
from different parts of the country, there now existed not only a
literary standard accessible to all those who could read but a
uniform oral standard. This oral standard was based on the
speech of preachers which was heavily influenced by the Bible.
The Bible, in its turn, owed much to the language of the bardic
poets. Welsh has thus remained a remarkably conservative
language and medieval literary classics like the *Mabinogion* pose
no problems for the present-day reader.

There are two major dialect continua in Wales – the northern and the southern – with an extensive transition area where northern and southern forms overlap (Thomas 1987). Both southern and northern continua are further divided into western and eastern continua with nuclei at the four corners of the country. There is thus a close relationship between the physical and dialect geography of Wales. The northern continuum is a good deal more homogeneous than the southern and is more conservative in pronunciation, morphology and syntax. The south-eastern continuum is structurally furthest from standard Welsh.

Welsh has no 'standard accent' comparable to Received Pronunciation in British English. Nor are dialect forms stigmatized (cf for instance Ch. 13). The absence of significant social class variation can no doubt be explained because access to the chapel which was the primary agent in language reproduction was not determined on the basis of social class.

While the focus for the present chapter is Welsh, some mention should be made of the distinctively Welsh varieties of English, sometimes known as Anglo-Welsh, which differ systematically from the standard in various aspects of phonology, grammar and lexis (Hughes and Trudgill 1979; Trudgill and Hannah 1985; Wells 1982). Two quite distinct dialects can be discerned: a southern dialect which has strong affinities with the speech of the west Midlands and the south-west of England and a northern dialect which is influenced to some extent by the speech of the north-west English counties. However, whereas the influence of Welsh on the southern dialects is largely substratal, it is a living influence in the north where there is a relatively high proportion of bilingual speakers (cf Thomas 1984).

The geographical distribution of the Welsh speech community

The distribution of Welsh speakers is extremely uneven. The most mportant Welsh-speaking areas are in Dyfed and Gwynedd and, to a lesser extent, Clwyd and Powys. In contrast, there is no ward in either Gwent or South Glamorgan which contains more than 1 in 10 Welsh speakers (see Fig. 6.1).

The high concentrations of Welsh speakers in Gwynedd and, to a lesser extent, Dyfed have given birth in recent years to the notion of y Fro Gymraeg (the Welsh heartland) (cf the Gàidhealtachd in Scotland and the Gaeltacht in Ireland) which has gained support from academics and political pressure groups alike. Bowen (1959) first defined areas where over 80 per cent of the inhabitants spoke Welsh as heartland areas. Subsequently, Bowen and Carter (1974), using 70 per cent density of Welsh speakers as the boundary line, showed two major heartland areas: Gwynedd and Dyfed. By 1981, however, although Gwynedd remained largely intact, Dyfed had not only shrunk but had become fragmented (C. Williams 1982).

The idea of a Welsh heartland has also attracted considerable political attention (Baker 1985). Arguments for concentrating efforts on the maintenance of Welsh in y Fro Gymraeg have been made, for instance, by the pressure group, Mudiad Adfer (Recovery), although it is questionable whether this idea would ever win widespread public support. The blanket notion of a

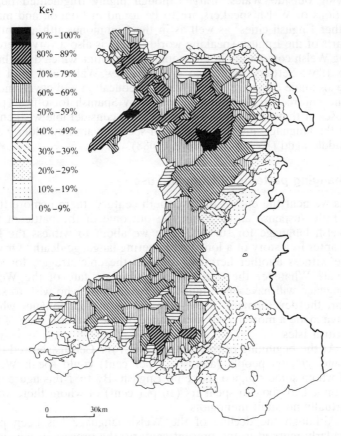

Key

90% – 100%
80% – 89%
70% – 79%
60% – 69%
50% – 59%
40% – 49%
30% – 39%
20% – 29%
10% – 19%
0% – 9%

0   30km

FIGURE 6.1 The Distribution of Welsh Speakers, 1981 Census (Baker, 1985:12)

heartland also needs to be interpreted with caution, since it is not always the case that the most active communities in linguistic and cultural terms will fall within this area. Ambrose and Williams (1981), for instance, have shown that the Welsh language is thriving in certain sub-zones in areas of apparent decline; and that, even in the heartland, it is important to take into account speakers' potential for frequent use of the language. They therefore conclude that the language is not necessarily safe in locations where over 80 per cent of the population speak Welsh, nor is it necessarily dying in areas where only 10 per cent of people are Welsh speakers.

Nor should we forget the large numbers of Welsh speakers living outside Wales. Large, though highly fragmented populations of Welsh speakers are to be found in London and many other English cities, as well as in the Commonwealth and other parts of the English-speaking world. There is also a very interesting Welsh community in Patagonia in Argentina which dates back to 1865. Settlers wanted to create a new Wales and until the 1930s made exclusive use of Welsh in education and government. The enforced replacement of Welsh by Spanish for official purposes at that time has inevitably led to a considerable weakening of the language and the majority of speakers are now elderly and middle aged (Evans 1978; Jones 1988).

Changing patterns of language use

As we near the end of the twentieth century, there is more than a little suspense as we await the outcome of the battle of the Welsh language for survival. Are we about to witness the last chapter in a story of a long and lingering language death? Or will we witness another heroic episode in the epic struggle for survival? Whatever the outcome, the ultimate fate of the Welsh language will have important lessons for those who wish to support the development of the many other mother tongues which have made a more recent appearance on the linguistic map of the British Isles.

At the beginning of the century, the 1911 Census showed that some 977,400 people (almost 45 per cent) could speak Welsh of whom some 190,300 spoke no English. By 1981 this figure had dropped to 500,000 speakers (19 per cent) of whom there were virtually no adult monoglots.

Although the decline of the Welsh language has been particularly marked in the present century, the process of language shift began some 400 years earlier. The Act of Annexation of

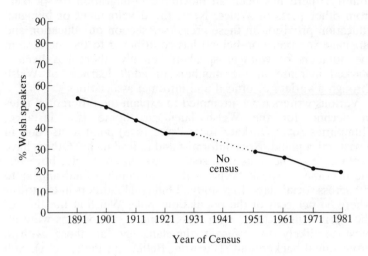

FIGURE 6.2 Welsh Speaking Population Census Figures, 1891–1981
(Baker 1985:2)

1536 attempted to integrate Wales and its language into the
English state and, from this time onwards, Welsh was restricted
to the family, the community and religion. The major pressures
for change, however, came only in the nineteenth century when
the revolutionary potential of Welsh, particularly in Nonconformist and Chartist circles, became evident and the state made
strenuous attempts to eliminate the language (G. Williams 1987).
These attempts were aided by the large-scale movements of
population both from within and outside Wales to the industrial-
ized areas, though the rate of language reproduction remained
high in rural areas until the restructuring of the economy in the
1950s.

The patterns which emerge for Welsh speakers from the 1981
Census give rise to both optimism and pessimism. On the one
hand, the majority of Welsh speakers are concentrated among the
relatively elderly. On the other hand, in Gwynedd, Clwyd and
Mid-Glamorgan there is evidence of replacement and growth in
the under twenty-five age groups.

There were also areas of overall growth in the number of Welsh
speakers in the anglicized south-east and north-east and the old
county of Radnor. Various reasons can be put forward to explain

these trends. First, as the economically strongest area of the country, there has been an inevitable in-migration of speakers from other parts of Wales. Next, the development of bilingual education provision in these areas (see section on education and language reproduction below) has contributed to the increase in the numbers of younger speakers. Finally, there has been a marked increase in the numbers of adult learners of Welsh through a variety of official and informal associations.

Various writers have attempted to explain the differential rates of decline for the Welsh language. Some (for instance, Humphries 1979; Durkacz 1983; Pryce 1978) point to its roots in a pastoral, upland, Nonconformist and radical niche. Others have explored possible links with social class. Interestingly, however, the decision to speak Welsh within the family would appear to cut across social class. In a study of bilingual mothers in ten towns where 60 per cent of the population spoke Welsh at the time of the 1971 Census, those with class 4 and 5 occupations were almost as likely to transmit the language as those with a professional background (Harrison, Bellin and Piette 1981). Still others (G. Williams 1987; C. Williams 1984, 1986) have argued that language reproduction should be analysed in terms of a changing socio-economic context. Behavioural-evaluative factors, such as the perceived usefulness of the Welsh language, can be seen to play an important role in language shift. So, too, can structural factors like the in-migration of monoglot English speakers into bilingual communities and the out-migration of Welsh speakers from rural to urban areas in Wales and beyond. Similarly, the advent of the Welfare State has played a part in the process of language shift by weakening the support functions of the chapels, traditionally a very strong agent of language reproduction.

Despite the continuing decline in the proportion of Welsh speakers, there is some reason for optimism, since both the ten-year census and survey evidence indicate that this process is neither uniform nor continuous. Extrapolation from previous censuses would have suggested an overall percentage of Welsh speakers of 14.5 for the 1981 Census. In the event, some 19 per cent of the population were recorded as Welsh speaking. Bellin (1984) sums up the situation in the following terms: 'The sting in the death metaphor is the suggestion of inevitability. If Welsh speakers maintain their commitment and the monolingual majority gain enthusiasm for measures to draw that sting, then Wales may become a stomping ground for students of language stability instead of students of language shift.'

Language, culture and community

The growing awareness that Welsh is fighting for survival has produced a sense of urgency and a great deal of activity in the attempt to reverse the pattern of rapid decline. The cultural resurgence which is following in the wake of this realization is impressive.

The Welsh Language Act 1967 gives Welsh equal validity with English. As a result it is possible to use Welsh in a court of law and to communicate with government departments in Welsh. A significant proportion of official forms from local and central government are available either in Welsh or bilingually. Many radical Welsh speakers, however, feel that this legislation has failed to bring about any improvement in the status of the language (see, for example, Council for the Welsh Language 1978a). The English version of any document is considered to be the authoritative one and decisions concerning the choice of language and the handling of translation and interpreting are relegated to individual local authorities.

It soon became clear that the Welsh Language Act was a case of what G. Williams (1987) has described in terms of 'policy as containment within democracy'. Disillusionment with legislative changes led many language campaigners to focus their energies elsewhere and, in particular, on the central role played by the media in the erosion of Welsh. The intrusion into otherwise Welsh-speaking homes of countless hours of English language broadcasts was seen as an assault on the viability of the Welsh language. The threat by Plaid Cymru Member of Parliament, Gwynfor Evans, to fast until death if the promised fourth television channel were not given over to Welsh language programmes proved particularly effective in the run-up period to a general election and Sianel Pedwar Cymru (S Pedwar C) or Welsh Channel Four, was finally introduced in late 1983. It now broadcasts 26 hours a week in Welsh, at times which include children's viewing and peak evening slots. The Schools Broadcasting Sections of the BBC and Independent Television also play an important role, with the BBC alone putting out 320 hours annually for primary schools and a further 96 hours for secondary schools. Radio Cymru has been transmitting programmes in Welsh on the VHF waveband since 1977 and the current level of Welsh-language broadcasts is about 60 hours a week (Ball, Griffiths and Jones 1988).

Although a great deal of the interest in the Welsh language is currently focused on the spoken word, both in social interaction and on radio and television, the importance of writing cannot be underestimated. The written word is clearly of paramount importance in the education process; it would also seem to be linked with language transmission. Baker (1985), for instance, points to the fact that illiteracy in Welsh is mostly to be found in wards where Welsh is spoken by the few rather than the many (*cf* also p 51).

The problems facing the Welsh publishing trade are the same as those faced by any minority language community: the small print runs make it virtually impossible to achieve financial viability (Council for the Welsh Language 1978b). In Wales, a partial solution for this problem has been found by five of the main commercial publishers who are also printers. Even so, these publisher-printers continue in business only because they receive subsidies for a large proportion of their output. Publishers who are not printers survive because all their Welsh-language publications are subsidized. There are various sources and forms of grant aid: the Welsh Books Grant, provided by the government and administered for the Welsh Office by the University of Wales Press Board; the Welsh Books Council which makes grants to authors, and provides editorial design, publicity and marketing services to publishers; the Welsh Arts Council which offers financial support to the Welsh Book Council and also administers various bursaries and prizes for authors. Equally important, the Welsh Joint Education Committee through its 'Books for Schools' scheme (see section on education and language reproduction below for fuller discussion) guarantees sufficient sales of approved books to cover at least the basic costs of book production.

In addition to a thriving publishing industry there is a wide range of local weekly newspapers (*papurau bro*), and monthly publications in Welsh (Betts 1976; Bellin 1984). Recent growth in the number of such publications has been greatly assisted by changes in print technology.

Various organizations and events, some recent, others of longer standing, play an equally important role in giving status to the Welsh language. In particular, Eisteddfod Genedlaethol Frenhinol Cymru, the Welsh National Eisteddfod or Competitive Festival of the Arts, is held in the first week of August. It lasts for a week and the venue alternates each year between the north and the south. Thousands attend the competitions and activities, all of which are conducted through the medium of Welsh. The focus is on music and literature and competitions range from choral events to folk dance, from prose to verse, and from modern free metre to traditional strict metre.

Urdd Gobaith Cymru (The Welsh League of Youth) also organize a national eisteddfod which is supported by children from
all over Wales. The *Urdd*, as it is commonly known, was founded
in 1932 and is currently the most active voluntary cultural organization in Wales with a membership of over 50,000. It has
branches throughout the country, many of which are school-
based. It organizes residential Welsh-language courses at Bala
and Llangrannog and is responsible for the publication of four
monthly magazines, two of which are aimed at Welsh speakers,
the other two at learners.

The dynamism and originality of contemporary Welsh youth
subculture, compared with other linguistic minorities in Europe,
are also worthy of comment (*cf* C. Williams 1987: 72). The number of performers and the range of popular music available are
totally out of proportion for the actual size of the Welsh speech
community and augur well for the health of the language.

Other organizations aimed at improving the status of Welsh include The Honourable Society of Cymmrodorion, a society which
dates back to the eighteenth century and which has frequently
provided a platform for Welsh-language issues; Merched y Wawr,
a group similar to the Women's Institute which conducts its business entirely in Welsh, Cymdaithas yr Iaith Cymraeg (the Welsh
Language Society) which has campaigned on a wide range of issues from bilingual signposts to Welsh-language television;
Cymdaithas Tai Gwynedd (Society for Gwynedd Homes), a
group which focuses on the need to ensure that empty houses are
made available to local people and not second-home buyers; and
Mudiad Adfer (Recovery), a movement which aims to develop
the Welsh heartland.

It would seem that there have been significant changes in
recent years in the symbolic value of Welsh. Some commentators
(*cf* Giles and Powesland 1975; Harrison 1980) have linked the
growth in status of Welsh with a rise in ethnic feeling. However,
the growing numbers of English migrants into Wales who show
an enthusiasm for learning the language would suggest that this
is only part of the story. Bellin (1984) suggests that the favourable
attitudes towards Welsh are linked with the current cultural
vitality of Welsh and that this represents an important change
from the association with economic failure which was the
hallmark of earlier decades.

Education and language reproduction

The role of Welsh in education has had a long and chequered

history. The disintegration of the bardic schools in the Stuart period marked the beginning of a fallow period for the Welsh language in education. The early grammar schools established in the Tudor period and later were modelled entirely on the English system and afforded no time or status to either the Welsh language or Welsh culture. During the Reformation and Counter-Reformation, however, the Society for Promoting Christian Knowledge (SPCK) was responsible for the creation of a large number of schools where Welsh was tolerated, for utilitarian purposes, as the medium of instruction.

By the eighteenth century, the limited resources of the SPCK had led to many school closures and their missionary role was taken over by the circulating schools, a movement largely inspired by the work of one man, Griffith Jones, the vicar of Llanddowror. Staying in any one place only long enough to make sure that a school was well established, he set out to teach both adults and children to read the Bible and Prayer Book in Welsh. In their brief life the circulating schools taught thousands of people to read. In due course, their work was taken over by the equally influential Sunday schools which continued to play an important role in the teaching of literacy throughout the eighteenth and nineteenth centuries.

The positive attitudes towards the use of Welsh in the circulating and Sunday schools stand in stark contrast to those of the day schools which came into existence in the nineteenth century. The notorious 1847 Report of the Commissioners, known popularly as the *Llyfrau Gleision* (the Blue Books) for instance, leaves no room for doubt as to the strength of opposition to Welsh: 'The Welsh language is a vast drawback to Wales, and a manifold barrier to the moral progress and commercial prosperity of the people. . . It dissevers the people from intercourse which would greatly advance their civilization, and bars the access of improving knowledge to their minds' (quoted in Evans 1978: 14).

The influence of the Blue Books was far-reaching. With the 1870 Education Act and the advent of a state system of elementary education, it was inconceivable that Welsh language and literature should find a place in the curriculum. Attitudes towards the use of Welsh by children in these schools were draconian: any child heard speaking the language was forced to place the 'Welsh not', a wooden halter, over his or her shoulders. This was then transferred to the next child to use the mother tongue and whoever was found wearing the halter at the end of the day received a caning (*cf* also Ch. 2 in relation to punitive attitudes towards signing).

The Code for Wales issued by the Welsh Department at the Board of Education in 1907 gave some grudging recognition to the principle of bilingualism. The first notable signs of official movement in this direction, however, did not come until the appearance of the Report of the Departmental Committee on Welsh in the Educational System in Wales in 1927. Various developments within the country were creating a different climate of opinion: the appointment of Sir O. M. Edwards, a Welsh scholar of note who had personally experienced the indignities of the Welsh not; the cultural renaissance marked by the founding of the University of Wales and the National Eisteddfod; a growing sense of national confidence witnessed by the formation of Undeb Cymru Fydd (The New Wales Union) and the adoption of Home Rule policies by both Liberal and Labour parties. The 1927 Report recognized for the first time the legitimacy of bilingualism in Welsh education, recommending that the mother tongue should be the sole medium of instruction in the early years of school and establishing a case for designated 'Welsh schools'.

For many years there was a scattering of primary schools in the Welsh heartland where Welsh was used as the medium of instruction, largely at the whim of the headteacher (Edwards 1984). However, the first school to adopt a definite policy of Welsh-medium education was a voluntary school established by Urdd Gobaith Cymru in Aberystwyth in 1939 which was later adopted by the local authority. Progress in the post-war years was slow but, by 1960 there were twenty-eight such schools established in the most Anglicized areas of Wales. All subjects are taught through the medium of Welsh to the age of seven, at which point English is introduced as a subject and possibly as a medium of instruction in one or two subject areas.

Throughout this period, however, little thought was given either to what effective bilingualism meant or to how it should be achieved (Rawkins 1987). An important turning-point came with the publication of the Gittins' Report (1967) on *Primary Education in Wales* which argued not only for the early introduction of Welsh but for its use wherever possible as a medium of instruction. Its aim was to ensure that Welsh was a part of the core curriculum rather than an optional extra. The Secretary of State for Wales welcomed the main thrust of the report and invited local authorities to review and publish their language policies.

Government support for this principle has continued, at least on a rhetorical level, to the present with the acceptance of Welsh, along with English, as part of the core curriculum in discussions of the National Curriculum. With more positive official backing and the growth of nationalist sentiment from the mid-1960s, progress on the education front was rapid. By 1987 the number of designated bilingual schools had increased to sixty-seven.

It should also be mentioned that Ysgol Gymraeg Llundain, The London Welsh School, which grew from Saturday morning Welsh classes based at the Welsh chapel in Islington, has been offering a Welsh-medium education to children in the capital since 1963. Based in Willesden Green, it currently has a staff of 4 teaching some 25 full-time pupils between the ages of 4 and 11, and a further 15 part-time pupils attending the nursery and playgroup.

There has been a marked change in the language background of parents who choose to educate their children bilingually. Until the 1960s the aim had been to provide a mother tongue education for the rapidly diminishing numbers of Welsh-speaking children and one local authority even operated a 4+ examination which ensured that children could understand and express themselves adequately in Welsh (Evans 1978). Increasingly, however, English-speaking parents have grown in confidence that their children's general education will not suffer as a result of Welsh-medium instruction and are now allowed free access to bilingual schooling. In many cases, a large proportion of the children come from homes where only one parent speaks Welsh; and, in some cases, the entire school population is drawn from families where neither parent speaks the language.

One response to the largely monolingual English intake of children to Welsh schools is the development of Mudiad Ysgolion Meithrin (The Welsh Nursery School Movement). At its inception at the National Eisteddfod in 1971, seventy playgroups were set up to prepare children for Welsh-medium primary education. By the mid-1980s this number had risen to about 550 providing for some 6,000 children in the Welsh heartland and anglicized areas alike (Baker 1985). The *ysgolion meithrin* receive a grant from the Welsh Office but are funded primarily by voluntary donations. In view of the important foundations for Welsh-medium education laid by this movement, it is easy to appreciate the arguments put forward for greater government resourcing.

The widely acknowledged achievements of the designated bilingual primary schools have led education authorities in the less anglicized areas of Wales to persuade headteachers of conventional schools to give greater prominence to Welsh in the curriculum (Edwards 1984). A wide range of teaching configurations exists: classes where Welsh is the sole or main medium of instruction; classes of first- and second-language pupils where some of

TABLE 6.1 Number of primary schools, by proportion of fluent Welsh speakers and authority, 1986/87*

	Clwyd	Dyfed	Gwent	Gwynedd	Mid Glam-organ	Powys	South Glam-organ	West Glam-organ	Wales
Percentage of Welsh speakers:									
Under 20	199	123	235	31	286	96	149	154	1,273
20–49	12	79	3	29	7	11	—	3	144
50–79	20	9	—	57	8	5	2	8	191
80 and over	20	30	—	8	11	3	5	4	154
Total	251	323	238	198	312	115	156	169	1762

* Data From Welsh Office (1988: 41).

the teaching is through the medium of Welsh; classes of second-language pupils where some of the teaching is through the medium of Welsh; and classes where Welsh is taught as a second language but not used as a teaching medium. The situation in 1987 is displayed in Table 6.1.

Progress in the secondary sector has been noticeably slower but is finally showing signs of the same encouraging growth. The first designated bilingual secondary school was opened in Rhyl in 1956 and by 1987 this number stood at 16. A further 53 schools offered Welsh as a medium of instruction in one or more subjects. There has been a gradual increase in both the number of subjects offered in public examinations and the number of students taking advantage of this option. In 1987 there were, 1,830 entries for 28 subjects at CSE; 6,526 entries for 40 subjects at O level and 583 entries for 20 subjects at A level (Welsh Office 1988).

On the level of language planning and pedagogy, an ongoing problem for Welsh educators is the question of the variety of Welsh which should be taught to second-language learners. Three booklets bearing the title *Cymraeg Byw* (Living Welsh) were published between 1964 and 1970 with the aim of helping teachers to bridge the gap between the literary and the spoken language. It was argued that the introduction of a simplified prototype language would establish a 'platform' from which the learners would ultimately be able to acquire the full linguistic repertoire of the community in which they live. The debate which followed in the wake of *Cymraeg Byw* has sometimes been both heated and acrimonious (see Davies 1988). Most teachers would now agree, however, that the advantages of the *Cymraeg Byw* approach outweigh its disadvantages and that it is a useful tool in the early stages of learning.

The growing numbers of secondary bilinguals who acquire Welsh through formal education are possibly contributing to the process of language change (Thomas 1987). It would seem, for instance, that, while formal speech corresponds closely with the literary standard in all cases, younger bilinguals approximate to the literary standard to a lesser degree than older bilinguals in private domains. It remains to be seen whether these differences are an indication of language change in progress or whether they are a reflection of language learners approximating only gradually to the adult native-speaker model.

Advances in Welsh-medium education have by no means been achieved without a struggle. There has sometimes been marked polarization between those parents seeking Welsh and those who want an English-medium education for their children (Rawkins 1987; Roberts 1987). It has also been pointed out that the responsibility which is being laid on the shoulders of schools and teachers for the reproduction of Welsh is an unrealistically heavy one. Where Welsh is no longer the language of the home, which is increasingly the case, learners are likely to need continuing social and, indeed, economic motivation if they are to choose to continue speaking Welsh after they have left school. There is evidence to suggest (see, for instance, Roberts and Williams 1980) that reliance on any one kind of institution for maintenance results in less use of Welsh and less favourable attitudes to the language than when several institutions work in concert to provide mutual reinforcement.

The fact remains, however, that the distribution of Welsh-medium education is extremely uneven and local authorities vary considerably in their commitment to initiatives in this area. In order to co-ordinate developments across the different LEAs in Wales, Pwyllgor Datblygu Addysg Gymraeg (The Welsh Language Education Development Committee) was set up by the Welsh Office in 1987 with a brief to establish a forum for discussion of policies by those responsible for providing Welsh-medium education and to co-ordinate activities in the field of Welsh education so as to ensure the best possible use of the available resources. The formation of such a body is clearly a step in the right direction. While local authority policy is undisputedly of great importance, there is equally a need for a coherent long-term central government policy which removes the need for piecemeal reactive decisions (cf Rawkins 1979, 1987; Baker 1985).

The possibilities in higher education are also expanding. There is special provision for the training of teachers through the medium of Welsh at Trinity College, Carmarthen, and Bangor Normal, and, at university level, Welsh-medium education is concentrated in two of the five University Colleges, at Aberystwyth and Bangor, where courses offered either wholly or partly in Welsh up to degree level include education, drama, history, Welsh history, philosophy, French, geography, theology, music, politics and social administration. There has been some agitation for the creation of a single Welsh-medium University College (Evans 1978; Edwards 1984), but this idea has been resisted on the grounds that the rest of the University would be deprived of much of its Welshness.

The dramatic expansion of Welsh-medium education clearly has enormous resource implications. There have been two main approaches to curriculum development in Wales. The first centred on teams of experts centrally producing materials or programmes which are then disseminated to schools and has included projects such as the Schools Council Bilingual Project and *Cyfres y Ddraig* (a Welsh-language reading scheme) and the Bangor project (see Baker 1985, for a review of these projects). This approach has been complemented more recently by teacher-based developments which respond to local conditions and personal needs.

A recurring problem concerns the supply of appropriate reading and textbooks. The small target population had long since made the publication of books commercially unviable. Since 1966, however, the Welsh Joint Education Committee (WJEC) has overcome this problem by guaranteeing purchase of a sample copy for each school of every general reader approved by a specialist panel of teachers, language advisers, college lecturers and librarians from the Schools Library Service. A further specialist panel was established in 1969 to advise the WJEC on the publication of textbooks for schools where Welsh is a medium of instruction.

The Welsh National Language Unit has been producing materials for the teaching of Welsh as a second language since 1968 and is also involved in in-service training of teachers and the development of materials for adult learners. Residential summer courses for adults are organized by a large number of bodies, including the Welsh National Language Unit, the University of Wales, Coleg Harlech, Urdd Gobaith Cymru, Merched y Wewr (Welsh Women's Institute) and Cymdeithas yr Iaith Cymraeg. Welsh continues to be an extremely popular subject for adults in evening classes.

Research efforts in the area of education and language reproduction have tended to be piecemeal and underfunded. Wales lacks, for instance, a counterpart of the Scottish Council for Research in Education which has played an important part in the formulation of educational policy in Scotland for over sixty years (*cf* Baker 1985). None the less, the individual and uncoordinated research efforts of the last thirty years which have focused on the Welsh speech community have played an important part in monitoring developments, and in interpreting trends and changes which have important policy implications. The importance of continued activity in this area should not be underestimated. In particular, there is a need for research into factors that constrain or encourage the development of lifelong bilingualism and for evaluative studies of bilingual education: what makes some bilingual schools more effective than others?

There has been no shortage of discussion of the health of the Welsh language. According to the proverb, 'Peswch sych yw utgorn angau' (A dry cough is the harbinger of death), the events of recent years would suggest that the nation is suffering from debilitating backache rather than a dry cough and that, if the Welsh speech community has hopes of recovery, it would do well to actively seek the help of both conventional and alternative medicine rather than lying still and waiting to get better.

Acknowledgements

Grateful thanks to J. Wyn Thomas for information and comments on the first draft of this chapter.

References

Ambrose, J. and Williams, C. (1981) 'On the spatial definition of minority'. In E. Haugen, J. McClure and D. Thomson (eds) *Minority Languages Today*, Edinburgh: Edinburgh University Press.

Baker, C. (1985) *Aspects of Bilingualism in Wales*. Clevedon, Avon: Multilingual Matters.

Ball, M. (ed.) (1988) *The Use of Welsh*. Clevedon, Avon: Multilingual Matters.

Ball, M., Griffiths, T. and Jones, G. (1988) 'Broadcast Welsh'. In Ball, op. cit., *pp* 182–99.

Bellin, W. (1984) 'Welsh and English in Wales'. In P. Trudgill (ed.) *Language in the British Isles*. Cambridge: Cambridge University Press, *pp* 449–79.

Betts, C. (1976) *Culture in Crisis: The Future of the Welsh Language*. Upton, Merseyside: the Ffynnon Press.

Bowen, E. (1959) 'Le Pays de Galles', *Transactions of the Institute of British Geographers* **26**: 1–23.

Bowen, E and Carter, H. (1974) 'Preliminary observations of the Welsh language at the 1971 Census', *Geographical Journal* **140** (3): 432–40.

Council for the Welsh Language (1978a) *A Future for the Welsh Language*. Cardiff: HMSO.

Council for the Welsh Language (1978b) *Publishing in the Welsh Language*. Cardiff: HMSO.

Davies, C. (1988) '*Cymraeg Byw*'. In Ball, op. cit., *pp* 200–10.

Durkacz, V. (1983) *The Decline of the Celtic Languages*. Edinburgh: Donald.

Edwards, G. (1984) 'Welsh-medium education', *Journal of Multilingual and Multicultural Development* **5**(3, 4): 249–58.

Evans, E. (1978) 'Welsh'. In C. James (ed.) *The Older Mother Tongues of the United Kingdom*, London: Centre for Information on Language Teaching and Research, *pp* 7–35.

Giles, H. and Powesland, P. (1975) *Speech Style and Social Evaluation*. London: Academic Press.

Gittins' Report (1967) *Primary Education in Wales*. Cardiff: HMSO.

Harrison, G. (1980) 'Social motives in the transmission of a minority language: a Welsh study'. In H. Giles, W. P. Robinson and P. M. Smith (eds) *Language: Social Psychological Perspectives*, Oxford: Pergamon Press.

Harrison, G., Bellin, W. and Piette, A. (1981) *Bilingual Mothers in Wales and the Language of their Children*. Cardiff: University of Wales Press.

Hughes, A. and Trudgill, P. (1979) *English Accents and Dialects. An Introduction to Social and Regional Varieties of British English*. London: Edward Arnold.

Humphries, H. (1979) 'La langue galloise: une présentation', *Studi* **13/14**: 11–9114

Jones, R. (1988) 'Language variation and social stratification in progress: linguistic change in progress'. In Ball, op. cit., *pp* 289–306.

Lewis, E. G. (1987) 'Attitudes towards the planned development of Welsh', *International Journal of the Sociology of Language* **66**: 11–26.

Pryce, W. (1978) 'Welsh and English in Wales 1750–1971', *Bulletin of the Board of Celtic Studies* 28: 1–36.

Rawkins, P. (1979) *The Implementation of Language Policy in the Schools of Wales*. Centre for the Study of Public Policy, University of Strathclyde.

Rawkins, P. (1987) 'The politics of benign neglect: education, public policy and the mediation of linguistic conflict in Wales', *International Journal of the Sociology of Language* **66**: 27–48.

Roberts, C. (1987) 'Political conflict over bilingual initiatives: a case study', *Journal of Multilingual and Multicultural Development* **8**(4): 311–2214

Roberts, C. and Williams, G. (1980) 'Attitudes and ideological bases of support for Welsh as a minority language'. In H. Giles, W. Robinson and P. Smith (eds) *Language: Social Psychological Perspectives*, Oxford: Pergamon Press.

Thomas, A. (1984) 'Welsh English'. In P. Trudgill (ed.) *Language in the British Isles*, Cambridge: Cambridge University Press, *pp* 178–94.

Thomas, A. (1987) 'A spoken standard for Welsh', *International Journal of the Sociology of Language* **66**: 99–113.

Trudgill P. and Hannah, J. (1985) *International English. A Guide to Varieties of Standard English*. London: Edward Arnold.

Wells, J. (1982) *Accents of English. The British Isles*. Cambridge: Cambridge University Press.

Welsh Office (1988) *Statistics of Education in Wales: Schools*. Cardiff: Welsh Office.

Williams, C. (1982) 'The spatial analysis of Welsh culture', *Etudes Celtiques* **19**: 283–322.

Williams, C. (1984) 'Ideology and the interpretation of minority cultures', *Political Geography Quarterly* **3**: 105–25.

Williams, C. (1987) 'Location and context in Welsh language reproduction: a geographic interpretation', *International Journal of the Sociology of Language* **66**: 61–84.

Williams, G. (1987) 'Bilingualism, class dialect, and social reproduction', *International Journal of the Sociology of Language* **66**: 85–98.

Part two

Eastern Europe

Most Eastern Europeans have come to Britain in an attempt to
escape from the ravages of war, redrawn bounderies and political
turmoil: Poles, Lithuanians, Latvians, Ukrainians and Estonians,
fleeing from Soviet domination, never to return or see again the
families they left behind; dissidents escaping or choosing to leave
behind the Communist regimes in Russia, Poland, Yugoslavia and
Hungary. The plight of Yiddish-speaking Jews is perhaps more
poignant still. It is only possible to speak of a Yiddish homeland
in a metaphorical sense, since the Jews lived on Polish, Ukrainian
and Russian ethnic territories in communities which no longer
exist.

The Eastern European presence is not a recent one.
Lithuanian, Hungarian, Polish and Yiddish-speaking settlements,
for instance, can be traced back to the beginning of the century
so that the new waves of immigrants who arrived in the immediate post-war period often had the effect of enlarging existing communities rather than creating new ones. The educational and
social background and the political aspirations of earlier and more
recent settlers tended to be quite different. None the less, the
presence of compatriots greatly eased the transition to life in the
new country.

For those who have had no access to the home country – the
Lithuanians, the Latvians, the Estonians, the Yiddish-speaking
Jews and the Ukrainians – other *émigré* communities in the USA
and Europe remain useful sources of cultural and linguistic
regeneration. The problems, however, of maintaining the mother
tongue without a flow of people and ideas from the home country
are considerable. The experience of these groups would seem to
be that, although subsequent generations have a strong attach-

ment to the culture of their parents and grandparents, the task
of transmitting language becomes increasingly daunting. While
ethnic societies promoting dance, folklore and traditional skills
continue to thrive, mother tongue classes find it increasingly difficult to attract support. Recent events in the USSR and the Eastern bloc will almost certainly result in greater contact between
Eastern European Communities in Britain and the various homelands. It will be interesting to monitor the effects of this
increasing contact on attitudes towards the mother tongue.

The size of the community would also seem to have an important effect on the success of language transmission. The smaller
the community, the more difficult the task: children inevitably
marry partners from outside the community who do not always
share their commitment to preserve the mother tongue. The
small Hungarian community, for instance, would seem to have
had less success in the sphere of language maintenance than the
Poles, despite the fact that Hungarians are, in the main, more
recent arrivals in the UK.

The Polish community is, in fact, an interesting case. The substantial numbers who arrived in the post-war period joined an
already established community. They are free to travel to the
home country and to receive visits from the family they left behind. In addition, waves of political dissidents leaving the country
in the 1980s have had the effect of rejuvenating the community
and making Poles and Polishness much more of a reality for the
British-born generations. The thriving social life, cultural resources and commitment to the Polish language within the community
suggests that Poles have been exposed to optimum conditions for
long-term mother tongue maintenance.

Eastern European communities are among the longest established immigrant groups in Britain. Although the pressures to
assimilate linguistically and culturally have been enormous, they
seem to have succeeded in retaining a sense of their ethnic identity. It therefore seems likely that the experience of the Eastern
Europeans will be of considerable relevance to more recent language minority groups in the UK. The lack of research and
information in this area, however, is a matter of concern. The
Polish community has attracted the attention of a small number
of scholars; the situation of Yiddish speakers has generated a
great deal of literature on an international level but remarkably
little in a UK context. Sadly, the other Eastern European communities remain largely undocumented, a subject of neglect.

Chapter 7

The Hungarian speech community

Marika Sherwood

> *Nyelvében él a nemzet*
> The nation lives in its language.
>
> (PROVERB)

It is much more difficult, I have discovered, to write on a topic about which nothing definite is known, than to write when one has too much material, which is my usual dilemma. Hungarian and Hungarians in Britain: no biliography, no thesis index, no 'subject' card index, no abstracts reveal a single, solitary entry for Magyars in the UK; not even the Embassy has any information! When they came, how they came and why; whether they were working or middle class, monarchists, capitalists or socialists; mono-, bi- or trilingual, what language they speak in the home; whether their marriages are endogamous or exogamous, where in the UK they have settled, how the generation born here view themselves – none of this is known.

What is much clearer, however, is the sociolinguistic situation which they left behind them in Hungary. Being a central European country whose boundaries have changed with every major war, Hungary has at times encompassed almost as many people speaking German, Slav, Romanian or another mother tongue as Hungarian. (Understandably, and especially as Hungary had been part of the Austro-Hungarian Empire, many Hungarians had been bi- or trilingual.) Since the Second World War about 93 per cent of the population has Magyar as its mother tongue, the majority of the remainder are Gypsies (See Ch. 5). Hungary is attempting to assist the approximately 1.5 million Hungarians resident in what is now Romania, to retain their language and culture. There are also Hungarians in what is now

Czechoslovakia and Yugoslavia and hundreds of thousands have emigrated to other European countries, Australia and the Americas (between 1880 and 1914, 1.7 million were admitted to the USA, where the 1980 Census showed that 144,000 residents were Hungarian-born). Some say that if one counts those of Hungarian descent, there are as many Magyars living in Hungary as elsewhere (approximately 10 million).

The term 'Hungarian' derives from 'On-Ogur', meaning ten tribes in an old Turkish language. It should not be confused with the Huns who were not the people who settled in the Danube basin in what is called 'Hungary' in English. The people who migrated there from the east and the language they speak should properly be called Magyar; their country is Magyarország.

Hungarian is agglutinative; it takes suffixes and prefixes; nouns do not have gender; spelling is (mercifully) phonemic. Despite decades of study, the etymology of a considerable proportion of words remains obscure. Hungarian is a part of the Finno-Ugric language group: the 'Finno' part comprises Finnish, Lappish and Estonian while the 'Ugric' is made up of Hungarian and some languages spoken by a very small number of east and central European peoples, such as Yogul, Ostyák and Zyryan. The Finno-Ugric group may perhaps be a subdivision of Ural-Altaic.

There is a voluminous literature in Hungarian: poetry, plays, essays, novels and a genre of humorous writing which is almost unknown in English (Thurber being one exponent) are all popular. The works of the best-known writers are usually snapped up within hours of publication from the many bookshops dotted around the capital, Budapest, and the shops in every town. Though various European languages are taught in school, foreign masterpieces and even popular fiction (eg Robert Ludlum, Frederick Forsyth) are translated into Hungarian.

The Hungarian speech community in the UK

The most relevant dates of Hungarian history for emigration to the UK are the dissolution of the Austro-Hungarian Empire at the end of the First World War, which was followed by the establishment of a republic under a Communist/socialist government. Within a few months, and with Western collusion, the government was overthrown and the monarchy restored under the regency of Admiral Horthy, who became an ally of Germany during the Second World War. At the end of the war Hungary was placed under the USSR's sphere of influence; the uprising of

1956 against Stalinist repression resulted in Hungary becoming the most liberal of the 'Iron Curtain' countries.

Each of these political upheavals and the repression of Jews in the late 1930s (over 300,000 were subsequently murdered in Hitler's concentration camps) led to successive waves of emigration. The nature of each upheaval would have dictated the composition of each emigrant group: capitalists and smaller entrepreneurs fleeing the 1919 republic; left-wingers escaping from the regency; Jews, rich and poor, fleeing from Fascism; Jewish survivors, élite army officers, landholders, capitalists avoiding future persecution or the anticipated horrors of a Communist state; and, in 1956, people from all classes and groups who had suffered under the repressions, fearing Soviet reprisal for having participated in the uprising, or seizing the opportunity to seek a higher standard of living in the West. Of the approximately 200,000 who fled in 1956, about 26,000 were admitted to the UK.

Because of the lack of research in the UK, we do not know how many Hungarians came here and when. I have seen references to Hungarians in London and Manchester in the 1930s; but whether these were Jews, Catholics or Protestants, landless peasants, unskilled workers, craftsmen, professionals or entrepreneurs, we do not know. Did they come singly, or with families? Was their mother tongue Magyar, or were they from the pre-Second World War ethnic minorities? What kind of work did they do, and where?

One of the very few sources of information on Hungarians in Britain is the Inner London Education Authority Language Census, but even this source poses more questions than it answers. In 1981 there were 90 Hungarian speakers attending schools in the capital; in 1983 there were 86; in 1985 there were 83 and in 1987 there were 86. Because the numbers are so small, Hungarians are aggregated with 'other Eastern Europeans', and it is not possible to say, for instance, whether these children were also fluent English speakers or whether they had arrived more recently and were in need of language support.

Changing patterns of language use

The dearth of research in the UK leads me to fall back on my own situation. How typical is my history? Does it provide some clues as to the reasons for this dearth of information? Can we conclude that though the immigrant generation has retained its

mother tongue, marriage outside the community and other external factors have oriented their children and grandchildren to be
almost exclusively English speakers?

As a ten-year old, I emigrated to Australia in 1948 with my
parents and grandparents. Quickly learning the new language, I
easily assimilated into school life; the few Magyar friends I had
were children of my parents' friends (who were exclusively Hungarian) and I saw them rarely. Briefly I married an Australian.
However, an amorphous yearning for Europe led to remigration
to London, where I have settled and formed a circle of friends
which includes a few 'Brits' but almost no Hungarians. I return
to Hungary regularly to visit a fast-diminishing number of relatives; my Hungarian is English-accented and of the 'kitchen'
variety. My adult son, who understands a few words of my native
tongue, has a special place in his heart for Hungary. His friends
are English, as is my daughter-in-law, who is intrigued by Hungary and wants to visit, but the probability is that my
granddaughter's links with her grandmother's birthplace will be
very tenuous indeed.

So is this dearth of information due to the fragmentation of
Hungarian immigrants? To exogamy? Are we too dispersed
throughout England, too divided by class, religion and political
orientation? Or is there something in English society which encourages assimilation? There are no hyphenated nationalities
here, such as Italian-Americans, and no parades celebrating
European origins such as the Ukrainian or Greek parades in the
USA. Even more pointedly, while there is a body of research on
Hungarians (and other European immigrants) in Canada and the
USA, in the UK the word 'immigrant' refers almost exclusively
to Black people and most British research reflects this usage.

Language, culture and community

Judging by the addresses of the ten Hungarian associations I have
been able to find, Hungarians are now scattered all over England:
there are Hungarians in Bradford, Bristol, Cleveland, Croydon,
Folkestone, Ivinghoe, London, Rochdale, Wembley and Worth-
ing. I only succeeded in contacting seven of these associations[1];
interestingly, only three are survivors from the 1950s and one
was formed as recently as 1987. The secretary of one survivor
association reported a membership slowly decreasing from the
original 300 because 'most young Hungarians have become integrated into English society and do not feel the need to belong

to a Hungarian associations – (they) find the Hungarian language difficult and not very useful'.

I know that there is a Magyar bookshop in London and that Magyar newspapers published in Hungary and the USA are available from a central London newsagent and by subscription. There are Hungarian churches, both Catholic and Protestant, in London and I believe in some other English cities. The Hungarian Embassy offers financial assistance to nine of the associations I mentioned, the exception being the British Hungarian Fellowship in London which conducts its meetings in English. (The Fellowship was established in 1951; in the past 20 years the membership has dropped from 150 to about 75.) Of the three associations formed between 1965 and 1971 one reports a loss in membership in the past five years from 100 to 80; one grew from 50 to 70 and another from 250 to 360, from an original membership of 120; the club formed in 1987 has 35 members and hopes to start language classes in 1989. The membership of one association is aged over 45, while the others' members range in age from 18 to 85. In one area the Hungarian 'community' comprises only 'fifty sixers', as 'earlier immigrants have either died or moved away'; in two areas the 'community' includes earlier groups of immigrants. What is not known is the proportion of those of Hungarian descent in any geographical area who belong to an association and if membership is homologous with 'community'.

It is thought that perhaps the revitalization of some of the associations is due to visits 'home' and the easing of the political situation in Hungary awakening or reawakening an interest in 'roots'. Because of the extent of the Hungarian diaspora, and also undoubtedly because of economic interests, Hungary has for some years attempted to foster Hungarian and a 'knowledge of Hungary' among the 'children of Hungarian descent living abroad' by running summer camps for 7 – 14-year-olds in 3 locations in Hungary. For the summer of 1988 8 camps are scheduled of either 10 or 14 days' duration. As the information brochure quotes prices only in US dollars, it is perhaps reasonable to assume that more Hungarian-American than British children of Magyar descent attend these.

Education and language reproduction

Given the low ethno-linguistic vitality of the Hungarian speech community, and the rapid shift from Hungarian to English which, it would appear, has taken place in the second and subsequent generations, it is not altogether surprising to note that mother tongue teaching does not seem to be generally demanded by those of Magyar descent.

Marriage to non-Hungarians seemingly consolidates assimilation for some while others attempt to integrate their partners into existing Hungarian circles; some partners and children attend language classes especially to enable them to converse with relatives when visiting Hungary or when relatives visit here. Three of the five associations mentioned hold language classes; students' ages range from 8 to 45 and one group even helps with 'preparation for O and A level exams in Hungarian'. In Inner London, ILEA funds Hungarian-as-a-foreign-language classes in Pimlico and there is a new Saturday morning class in Highbury for young children. At this class, as well as in the social clubs, folk-dance is also taught; the clubs also show films, hold dances and other social functions; Hungarian historical events are commemorated and traditional crafts such as embroidery taught; some groups participate in the annual Hungarian Cultural Festival. In London it is possible to take O and A level examinations in Hungarian and the School of Slavonic and East European Studies at the University of London offers a course in Hungarian.

As I indicated earlier, there are questions but little information. What about us, the Hungarian-born? Why are those of us now in academe not reflecting our origins in our research interests? Why is it that, though clubs and associations flourished after the 26,000 of us were admitted following the Hungarian revolution of 1956, few have survived? In the summer of 1988, only eight students entered for the University of London School Examination Board's A level in Hungarian, compared with eighty entries for Polish. Even allowing for the fact that the Polish community is much larger than the Hungarian, the number of entries for Hungarian is disproportionately small. Why should this be the case? I have no answers: all I can do is ask what seem to be pertinent questions.

The British myopia regarding immigration has prevented researchers recognizing that some more general questions regarding the absorption or assimilation of immigrants have to be answered before we can begin to understand reactions to Black immigrants or the responses of Black peoples to such host reactions. We need to know the ramifications of meaning behind the lack of hyphenated Britons. We need to know if there are pressures to lose one's 'foreignness' and how these pressures operate. We need to know what the indicators are of this 'foreignness' and which indicators the natives find least tolerable – and why. When we know more we might be able to deal more successfully with some aspects of the racism which greeted and continues to oppress Black immigrants.

Note

1. My thanks to those who completed my questionnaires or gave their time in lengthy telephone conversations.

Further reading on Hungary

CSÁSZÁR, E. (1978) *Decision in Vienna: the Czechoslovak – Hungarian Border Dispute of 1983*. Astor, Florida: Danubian Press.

CZIGÁNY, I. (1984) *The Oxford History of Hungarian Literature*. Oxford: Clarendon Press.

ENYÉDI, G. (1976) *Hungarian. An Economic Geography*. Colorado: Westview Press.

HAJDU, P. (1975) *Finno-Ugrian Languages and People*. London: André Deutsch.

HEINRICH, H-G. (1986) *Hungary (Politics, Economics and Society)*. London: Frances Pinter.

KABDEBÓ, T. (1980) *Hungary (a Bibliography)*. Oxford: Clio Press.

PAMLÉNYI, E. ED (1975) *A History of Hungary*. London: Collet's.

PÁNKI, G. (1984) *Hungarian History – World History*. Budapest: Akademia Kiado.

SANBORN, A. F. and WASS DE CZEGE. (1979) *Transylvania and the Hungarian – Rumanian Problem – a Symposium*. Astor, Floria: Danubian Press.

NB: There are innumerable books on Magyar language and literature, mainly written in Hungarian; the School of Slavonic and East European Studies of London University has an excellent stock and card index.

Chapter 8

The Lithuanian speech community

Josephine A. Boyd

Kas savo kalbą niekina – kitos neišmoks
Anyone who devalues their own language will not learn anyone else's

Language and society are inseparable. For this reason, if society ceases to operate in a mode of the language or, indeed, in the language itself, then the skills related to the language or that part which is no longer used, become obsolete. Such is essentially the situation in Britain with regard to the languages of the Baltic states – Lithuanian, Estonian and Latvian. The present chapter will concentrate on one of these languages, Lithuanian, although it is very likely that the development of the other two has followed a very similar course.

The sociolinguistic situation in Lithuania

The current population of Lithuania (*ie* the Lithuanian Soviet Socialist Republic) is 3,570,000 and of these, 2,750,000 are speakers of Lithuanian. Approximately 80 per cent of the population are Lithuanian and the bulk of the remainder are Polish or Russian. The Russian language is widely used and indeed demanded because of Lithuania's incorporation within the Soviet Union. In the 1940s, Russian became a compulsory element in the state school system, to the detriment of Lithuanian, because of its widespread use in the realms of officialdom. However, Lithuanian predominates socially and culturally and is now officially recognized as the state language.

Lithuanian is considered part of the Balto-Slavonic branch of the Indo-European family (cf Simpson 1979). It carries with it the distinction of being closest in relationship with the original Indo-European and currently this remains unchanged. Within its vocabulary are many words which are identical to those in Sanskrit, *eg sunus* (son); *avis* (sheep). It is equally possible that some words in Lithuanian are even older in origin, but unfortunately, there exists no written evidence before the fifteenth century to substantiate this (Zeidonis *et al.* 1972).

The alphabet in use is Roman and composed of thirty-two letters, using a variety of diacritic marks, eg *c, s* and *z* (pronounced *ch, sh* and *zh* respectively) and the vowels ą, ę, į, ų, ė and ū. The Baltic states (Lithuania, Estonia and Latvia) are unique within the Soviet Union in that they continue to use Roman script.

Both Russian and Lithuanian are taught in state schools of which there are two basic types – those which offer both languages and those where tuition is in Russian only. This pattern would tend to indicate that the role of Lithuanian is secondary. There are currently four major educational institutions in Lithuania, including an Institute of Linguistics and a University at Vilnius. This does not compare favourably with statistics published by the Committee for the Liberation of Lithuania which claims that, during the academic year 1939–40, there were two universities (Kaunas and Vilnius) and eight institutions of higher education. The reduced importance of higher education in Lithuania in the immediate post-war period would appear to be supported by the claims of the now defunct Lithuanian Council of Great Britain that, in the initial purges within Lithuania, 15 per cent of the student population, the bulk of whom were at the University of Kaunas, were either arrested or deported. This expulsion extended to 70 per cent of the teaching population in secondary schools in towns like Alytus, as well as 20 per cent of the staff of institutions of higher education. Until very recently the popular press was confined to Soviet publications like *Pravda*. Now, with *glasnost*, many other publications are starting to emerge.

It is little wonder then that relatively little literature has emanated from Lithuania itself since the 1940s. However, this is not to say that Lithuanian literature does not abound abroad, though regrettably not in Great Britain. In the handbook compiled for Lietuviu Literatura Svetur (Lithuanian Literature Abroad; Laisve 1968), it is claimed that, from the Second World War to the end of 1971, publications in Lithuanian were of the order of 213 collections of verse, 253 volumes of fiction and 37 books of plays. Bearing in mind that the total immigrant population to the West in the mid-1940s was only in the range of 62,000, the quantity of literature produced has not been inconsiderable, though the bulk of this work was produced in the United States.

Lithuanians in Britain

There were two influxes of immigrants from Lithuania and these two groups were very different in composition. The first group arrived between 1900 and 1910. They were essentially illiterate, coming from mainly peasant backgrounds and migrating to Britain for economic reasons. The second group, who arrived in the 1940s, came from divergent social groups and, for the most part, were better educated. As political refugees, they came through necessity rather than choice. The communities established by the first group in places like London, Manchester, Nottingham, Glasgow and parts of Lanarkshire in Scotland, acted as hosts to the second group. However, since the new wave of immigrants was chronologically in parallel with the adult offspring of first-generation *émigrés*, the two factions, separated by very different experiences, were not entirely compatible and the Lithuanian community in Britain was by no means homogeneous.

The linguistic difficulties perceived by the first group on arrival in the UK were considerable and left them at the mercy of their new environment. Most had very little education and many were illiterate even in their mother tongue. The burden of language fell to the few who had some knowledge of English and a certain level of education. These people acted as scribes, interpreters, sources of information, financial advisers, social advisers and so on. The early immigrants encountered the most basic problems. The Lithuanian community abounds with stories of newcomers who could not ask for directions, find methods of transport and cope with fares or timetables. Restrictions such as these further compounded the need to live and operate as a closed community. In this way, the common problems experienced by the community held it together.

The second group were able to make use of the existing Lithuanian community and rapidly adjusted to their new environment. The early settlers who had little education were obliged to accept menial occupations in the mills, mines and factories because they were uneducated. The next wave, however, was made up of people whose education was somewhat better from the outset. A higher proportion of the post-war influx tended to make their way into white-collar occupations such as nursing, clerical work and middle management and, in many cases, overtook the indigenous second-generation Lithuanians.

Changing patterns of language use

While the Lithuanian language in Britain is by no means dead, we have witnessed the gradual and irreversible shift over three or four generations to English. In the homes of the early immigrant community, when the family were together, only Lithuanian was spoken even where children of immigrants were attending school and learning English to the extent that they were bilingual. The children then adopted the role of interpreter removing the need for parents to develop their competence beyond 'survival English'.

The immigrants of the early twentieth century are now dead and within the present-day community we can see a complete range of language competence. At the one extreme are the elderly first-generation immigrants of the 1940s, for whom Lithuanian remains the dominant language, and the children of the earlier wave of immigrants who, in the main, have retained the ability to speak Lithuanian. At the other extreme are the third and fourth generations of British Lithuanians whose knowledge of the mother tongue is limited to the odd word or expression. Between these extremes are individuals with varying degrees of fluency in Lithuanian which depend, no doubt, on factors such as whether one or both parents came from the Lithuanian community, exposure to Lithuanian in contexts outside the home and degree of identification with Lithuanian culture.

Separation from and lack of contact with the mother country has been a major factor in the loss of Lithuanian in Britain. The geographical dispersal of the community and the small numbers of people involved led, among other things, to marriage outside the community, and has accelerated the process of language decay. The passing of the Lithuanian language, however, in no way diminishes the interest expressed by current generations in their heritage from the Amber Coast.

Language, culture and community

Contact beyond personal correspondence with the mother country has long presented difficulties for both groups of Lithuanians in the UK, because of the Soviet Union's isolationist stance. This isolation has inevitably contributed to the obsolescence of the language within Britain.

Lithuanian language and culture are therefore dependent on the efforts of the British and, to a lesser extent, the international Lithuanian community. Within this framework, the Church has over the years provided valuable support. In addition to the Lithuanian Roman Catholic Church in London, a number of priests are based in areas of Lithuanian settlement, including

Manchester, Nottingham and Motherwell, and have played a vital role in the life of the community. A religious periodical in Lithuanian, *Šaltinis* (The Spring) is produced in Nottingham.

Lithuanian House in London serves as a focus for cultural and political activities both in the capital and nationally. Like the other clubs scattered over the country, it offers a range of social and cultural activities. It also publishes a Lithuanian language newspaper *Europos Lietuvis* (Lithuanian in Europe) which has an international circulation, and a variety of books. The Lithuanian Country Club in Hampshire is another important focus. It serves as a social centre and also a retirement home for Lithuanians.

In the 'heyday' of the clubs, Lithuanian was very much alive and these establishments became focal points for the social activity of the community, permitting such things as the wearing of national costume, the performance of amateur drama, poetry readings and choral societies, first using the meagre materials brought with them and, later, materials imported from areas like the United States. Today, however, while features like dance and folklore remain, the Lithuanian language plays a decreasingly important role and the clubs are basically British with Lithuanian overtones.

Education and language reproduction

The level of interest in minority languages in Britain reported in this volume and elsewhere (*eg* Linguistic Minorities Project 1985) has regrettably come too late for Lithuanian. There is no doubt that its preservation within Britain is still a concern to those like the Lithuanian Association in Great Britain who propagate the cause of freedom for the Baltic states. However, no educational facilities existed during the two immigrant influxes which would have permitted the teaching of Lithuanian in mainstream schools. Interestingly, Lithuanian was available at an academic level in universities such as Glasgow and Cambridge, which boasted a Chair of Ancient European Languages held by the late Professor Jopson of St John's College.

Some tuition takes place within the clubs, though on a very limited basis. Currently the mother tongue is taught at Lithuanian House in London and also in the Lithuanian clubs in Nottingham and Motherwell. Teaching materials from the USA, where the language still flourishes, are freely available and there is no shortage of grammers (*eg* Zobarskas 1948; Schmalsteig 1967), dictionaries, poetry and plays available from the United States. In Britain, however, it is possible to argue that the main linguistic issue related to Lithuania is the fact that the language and culture associated with it are likely to be lost to future generations, unless the political situation changes and there is freer interchange between the homeland and Britain.

A number of conclusions can be drawn from the experience of Lithuanians in Britain. First, incoming communities can operate adequately at a survival level within the minority community with their language and culture relatively unaffected. However, integration into the larger community requires the adoption of the indigenous language and this provokes an inevitable shift from the mother tongue to the indigenous language. In the case of a language like Lithuanian, which is spoken by small numbers of geographically dispersed people who have little contact with the country of origin, it is inevitable that the mother tongue should be completely replaced in the course of three or fourth generations by English.

The Lithuanian experience is an interesting one from which we can learn a great deal. Why, for instance, have the Polish community and, to a lesser extent, the Ukrainian community survived so much better than the Lithuanian, Estonian or Latvian communities? For a language to exist in a state of stable bilingualism certain conditions clearly need to be fulfilled. Continuing contact with the country of origin – in the form of visits or new arrivals – would seem to be a prerequisite. The strong ongoing links with Poland, for instance, have contributed a great deal to the ethnolinguistic vitality of the British Polish community (see Ch. 9). It would also seem that large communities in geographically limited areas have a better chance of linguistic and cultural survival than smaller, dispersed groups. In this respect, the Ukrainian and Yiddish communities seem to have had a better chance of success than the Baltic state communities. Determination of purpose on the part of the first and even second generations is not enough if a linguistic minority is to avoid becoming a silent minority.

Acknowledgements

Thanks to Aleksas Vilcinskas and the Lithuanian Association in Great Britain for comments on earlier drafts of this paper.

References

LAISVĘ, I. (ed.) (1968) *Lietuvių Literatūra Svetur* (Lithuanian Literature Abroad). Chicago: Chicago University Press.

Linguistic Minorities Project (LMP) (1985) *The Other Languages of England*. London: Routledge & Kegan Paul.

SCHMALSTEIG, W. R. (1967) *Lithuanian Reader for Self-Instruction*. Brooklyn, NY: Franciscan Fathers' Press.

SIMPSON, J. M. Y. (1979) *A First Course in Linguistics*. Edinburgh: Edinburgh University Press.

ZEIDONIS JR, A., PUHVEL, J., SILBAJORIS, R. and VALGEMAE, M. (1972) *Baltic Literature and Linguistics*. Columbus: Ohio State University.

ZOBARSKAS, S. (1948) *Aušrele-Elementorius* (Daybreak – an Elementary Reader). New York: Voyagers' Press.

Chapter 9

The Polish speech community

Elizabeth Muir

Do Mlodziezy Polskiej	To the Young Polish
Ucz sie ojcow twych jezyka	Learn your fathers' mother tongue
On mysl kazda wydac zdolny	It is able to express every thought,
Gnie sie dzwieczy, grzmi,	It is flexible, it sounds, thunders,
przenika,	penetrates,
Jasny, smialy, bo jest wolny.	Bright, courageous as it's free.

JAN N. KAMINSKI (1777–1855)

The Polish language is spoken in a variety of places all over the world. The Polish community in Britain, however, the third in respect of its size after the United States and Canada, represents a totally different entity in comparison to other Polish communities. It has been shaped by several waves of Polish immigrations to Britain but its unique character has been determined specifically by 1940–50 'wartime *Emigracja*'.

The sociolinguistic situation in Poland

Polish is an Indo-European language belonging to the West Slavic branch and is closely related to Czech, Slovak and the Sorbian language of East Germany. It contains a great number of words borrowed from Latin, Czech, German, Belorussian and Ukrainian and also some words from Italian, French and English.

Polish is spoken by about 40 million native speakers, including the present population of Poland (35 million). The modern literary language, written in the Roman alphabet, dates from the sixteenth century and was originally based on the dialects of the area around Poznan, in western Poland. The main Polish dialects are Great Polish (in the north-west), Little Polish (in the south-east), Silesian and Mazovian. This last dialect shares some features with Kashubian. There are about 200,000 native speakers of Kashubian remaining in Poland on the left bank of the Lower Vistula River. Kashubian, although classified as one of the dialects, is historically a separate language.

The language used in Poland for official/national and educational purposes is a standard Polish. It is the language children learn in all schools throughout the country. Standard Polish displays a variety of styles depending on the speaker and the purpose of the speech. Klemensiewicz (1953), for instance, divides standard Polish into colloquial and literary languages. He further separates colloquial Polish into conversational and monologue, and literary Polish into artistic, scientific and didactic.

The linguistic resources of Polish immigrants to Britain basically represent standard Polish with traces of regional and dialectal influences, so that, for instance, Poles from the eastern part of Poland (now Soviet territory) speak with Lvovian and Vilenski accents. There are also social class differences in language, middle-class speakers approximating more closely than working-class speakers to the standard.

Poles in Britain

According to the 1981 Census, there were 93,721 Poles living in Britain (59,374 males and 34,347 females). Stowarzyszenie Polskich Kombatantow (SPK) (Polish Ex-combatants' Association) puts this figure at approximately 120,000 while Zebrowska (1986:70) estimates that there are 135,000 Poles in the UK, about one-third of whom make up the younger generations. Census and other statistics concerned with birthplace and nationality can, of course, give a relatively inaccurate picture of the size and characteristics of the Polish and other ethnic minority communities in Britain. This is due both to the difficulty in making a distinction between ethnic affiliation and nationality, and also to the absence of published data on the increasing numbers of British-born children of parents who have come to Britain from Poland.

The Polish community in Britain is a result of four waves of immigration which correspond with the period up to 1940; the decade 1940–50, known as 'wartime *Emigracja*'; post-1950; and the 1980 immigration. The first wave of immigration was in 1772 when Poland was partitioned by Austria, Prussia and Russia. Political insurrections in 1795, 1832 and 1863 brought more refugees seeking asylum in Britain. Soon these refugees were joined by other Poles migrating to America for economic reasons. Lack of finance, however, meant that many were unable to complete their journey and therefore decided to stay in Britain. By the end of the nineteenth century, three main Polish centres in Britain had emerged: London, Lanarkshire in Scotland and neighbouring districts in Lancashire and Cheshire. By 1931 there were 4,500 Poles, mainly Christian, the majority of whom were labourers and artisans (Zubrzycki 1956).

The second wave of immigration, 'wartime *Emigracja*', brought the biggest influx of Poles to Britain. Patterson (1977) estimates that some 165,000 Poles arrived during this period, though numbers had decreased to 130,000 by 1960 through emigration to other countries and repatriation to Poland. The Polish exile community was made up of members of the Polish Armed Forces with their families and dependants, political prisoners from concentration camps in Germany and Russia, Polish refugees from East Africa and the Middle East and Polish civilians from the displaced persons' camps of Europe. These political exiles formed the core of the Polish community in Britain.

The exile population fell into three main occupational groups. The first included those with professional qualifications which could be used in the new country. (The 1951 Census shows 504 Polish-born registered general practitioners and 35 dental practitioners. By 1958, Patterson (1977) reports 600 Polish doctors and 80 Polish dentists, approximately 2,000 engineers and technicians, 6 barristers and 10 solicitors.) The second was a small group of civil servants, entrepreneurs, journalists and artists who found employment within the exile community. Finally, a rather larger group of the disabled and elderly entered the postwar British economy as unskilled labourers regardless of their education or occupational background. Many ambitious Poles with lesser qualifications set up small businesses. Some became house-owners and small-scale landlords. As early as 1954, Zweig (1954) gave the number of Polish-owned business establishments at about 1,000.

The location of Polish forces during the war largely determined the areas where Polish immigrants gravitated. Airmen settled in Nottingham, Leicester and Blackpool, while naval personnel and seamen tended to move to Portsmouth, Cardiff and other ports. The relatively small number of Poles settled in Scotland is, however, surprising considering the fact that this was the main location of the Polish Army in the West during the war. London, as home of the government in exile, became the largest Polish resettlement area, accommodating one-quarter of the community (30,000–35,000). Next came Birmingham, Manchester (4,000–5,000 each), Bradford (3,000), and Leeds, Sheffield, Coventry and Slough (1,500–3,000 each). In London, the main districts of Polish resettlement were in the Polish parishes of Islington, Brompton, Clapham, Lewisham, Brockley, Highgate, Ealing, Croydon and Willesden.

Since the wartime immigration, there have been two further small waves of Poles arriving in the UK. According to the 1971 Census 13,470 persons (75 per cent of whom were women) settled in this country between 1950 and 1971, some of whom were more or less traditional anti-Communists. After 1980, some 2,000 entered the UK from post-Solidarity Poland. It is hard to tell, however, to what extent the latter influxes of Poles have influenced the already well-established Polish community in Britain. These more recent arrivals are reflected in the figures reported in the ILEA census (Table 9.1).

TABLE 9.1 Data on Polish pupils from ILEA *Language Census* (1981–87)

Year	Number
1981	589
1983	547
1985	533
1987	582

Changing patterns of language use

As mentioned above, the first-generation Polish exiles who found themselves in Britain during or after the Second World War, lived in the constant hope of returning to their homeland. This was a strong enough motive to force them to make every possible effort actively to cultivate their Polish heritage and the Polish language. The first-generation exiles show a wide range of social and geographical variation in their language use.

Poles vary a great deal in their attitudes towards Anglicization. Those who display great care for purity of Polish, sometimes preface the borrowing with a comment in English like 'as one would say it in English'. Others will switch to the English word or phrase without much hesitation. Often, however, the English loan word undergoes some modification, retaining Polish morphosyntactic features, such as those which mark case and gender (Hofman 1981). Examples include *dastbiniarz*, derived from the English word 'dustbin' by the attachment of Polish *-arz; nersa* (nurse) formed by adding the ending *-a* to an English stem, thereby automatically attributing gender; *zadragowany* in which the Polish prefix *za* + 'drug' + the suffix *-owany* are used to create a new word which means under the influence of drugs. Some calques, such as *pocztowe ordery* (literally, 'postal orders'), are a direct translation from English and result in a different meaning in Polish, in this case 'postal medals'. Muir (1986) mentions similar examples of the influence of English on the Polish speech of third-generation children in Britain.

In many ways the Polish of the second generation shows traces of the language of the parents. It is, after all, the language taught at home. There are, however, certain noticeable characteristics in the speech of second-generation Poles which occur neither in the Polish repertoire of the first generation nor in that of the native speakers of Poland (A. Zebrowska, personal communication). Such features, one might suspect, are symptoms of the lack of native-speaker intuition for the Polish language. Other characteristics of second-generation Polish include code-mixing and code-switching. There seems to be a strong tendency to shift to English in conversations or discussions on difficult topics which involve the expression of abstract concepts.

The Linguistic Minorities Project (LMP) (1985) Survey of Adult Language Use provides corroborative evidence for the shift to English (see Table 9.2). In Coventry and Bradford, the Polish language skills of the adult respondents were, predictably, very high. However, the reported level of fluency in Polish for members of respondents' households as a whole – which is likely to include a high proportion of British-born children – was significantly lower.

TABLE 9.2 Language data on the Polish community, extrapolated from LMP (1985)

		Polish	English
% of respondents who speak and understand the language fairly well or very well	Coventry (*N*=168)	92	82
	Bradford (*N*=155)	92	83
% of people (including the respondents) reported as knowing the language fairly well or very well	Coventry (*N*=465)	71	93
	Bradford (*N*=401)	79	83

Some 91 per cent of the respondents in Coventry and 69 per cent of those in Bradford also reported that English was used only or mostly between children. It is noticeable, for instance, that third-generation children speak English among themselves in Polish Saturday schools. While the first-generation Poles are uniform in their strong desire to maintain the mother tongue, second-generation Poles show attitudes ranging from no interest in Polish matters, through support for the maintenance of Polishness and the Polish language to very active participation in promoting Polish language and heritage (Zebrowska 1986).

The Polish of the second generation is a mainly interfamilial experience, consequently, it lacks contemporary expressions which have entered the Polish language over recent years. Meetings held by Duszpasterswo Akademickie (a religious students association), for example, represent an opportunity to right this balance as they provide, among other things, linguistic exchange between students from Poland and young Poles born in Britain. There is in fact widespread community support for any initiative which brings together British-born and native Poles.

The initiative of language revival is also supported by the first-generation Poles. It is manifested by the desire to create new associations which would gather Poles of younger generations and those who came from Poland recently. Although there has undoubtedly been a shift from Polish to English, the enormous emotional attachment to Polishness among Poles in Britain augers well for the longer-term maintenance of Polish.

Language, culture and community

It was the wartime *Emigracja* which determined the shape and character of the life of the Polish community in Britain. It was an exile community which arrived with an organizational network of various military, civilian and religious institutions, and welfare associations like the Polish Red Cross, the Polish Young Men's Christian Association (YMCA), servicemen's clubs, and the Polish press.

Factors such as patriotism, the social and educational declassing of a considerable proportion of exiles and the negative attitude of the host government towards Polish immigrants ensured a high level of community participation, strengthening the need for ethnic identification and compensatory status, reinforcing minority group solidarity and building the community into a social entity. These conditions defined the ethnic vitality of the community, giving shape to its social, religious, economic and political life and

allowing it to meet every need of Polish immigrants in Britain.
Wilk (1970:20) states: 'The Pole can buy Polish food from Polish
shops, eat in Polish restaurants, sleep in Polish hotels or digs,
with a Polish landlady, entertain friends in Polish clubs, attend a
Polish doctor (over 500 are practising in Britain) or dentist (80
Polish dental surgeries), have a Polish priest and be buried by a
Polish undertaker.'

This picture is supported by the findings of the LMP (1985)
Adult Language Use Survey. Although the ethnic economy
employs only a small proportion of the community, almost half
of those consulted in Bradford and Coventry worked in a situation where there was at least one other Pole and it would appear
that Polish is used relatively often in the workplace (see Table
9.3).

TABLE 9.3 Language use in the workplace, extrapolated from LMP
(1985)

% of working respondents where at least one fellow worker can speak Polish	Coventry 47 Bradford 48
% of working respondents where all fellow workers can speak Polish	Coventry 2 Bradford 7
% of working respondents (who work for someone else) where the boss can speak Polish	Coventry 1 Bradford 8
% of working respondents who used only or mainly English with workmates	Coventry 62 Bradford 65

Coventry: $N=115$
Bradford: $N=94$

A picture also emerges of Polish being used in a wide range of
situations outside the workplace. Although the community is relatively dispersed, most Poles maintain a network of friends with
whom they use the mother tongue. It is also possible to do shopping and even to consult a doctor in Polish (see Table 9.4).

Polish institutional life in Britain consists of various ex-
combatants' associations, welfare, social, professional, educational and religious organizations, Polish libraries, bookshops, publishers, travel agencies, transport of parcels to Poland
and Polish radio, clubs, etc. Unfortunately, space permits discussion of only a minute fraction of them. However, full information

TABLE 9.4 Data on Polish in a wide range of situations, extrapolated from LMP (1985)

% of respondents who spoke Polish with the first person they mentioned as somebody they spent free time with	Coventry 39 Bradford 54
% of respondents who said most or all of their neighbours could speak Polish	Coventry 1 Bradford 3
% of respondents who said they had seen a film or video in Polish in the last 4 weeks	Coventry 4 Bradford 6
% of respondents who said they sometimes visited a shop where Polish was spoken by the shopkeeper or assistants	Coventry 89 Bradford 96
% of respondents who had a doctor who could speak Polish	Coventry 12 Bradford 48

Coventry: $N=168$
Bradford: $N=155$

on Polish life and institutions can be found in the *Ex-combatants' Calendar* (see addresses section at the end of this volume).

For forty years SPK has provided financial and legal assistance, cultural facilities and social activities to its members. Preservation of Polishness in new generations is one of its objectives and it gives support to initiatives such as Polish Saturday schools and the Polish Scout Movement.

The Polish YMCA, founded in 1949, is a very dynamic organization responsible for the promotion of Polish history and cultural heritage not only within the Polish and British communities but all over the world through exhibitions of Polish art, folklore and the publication of Polish song, music, etc. It has its own dance company, Mazury, which has built up a reputation in the field of Polish folk, national dance and music. The YMCA offers accommodation and information to Polish refugees. It also runs summer camps for young Polish people in Western Europe.

In 1964 a new institution, POSK (The Polish Social and Cultural Association) was set up in Hammersmith, London, with the objective of providing a centre for present and future generations to fulfil the social and cultural need of the Polish community in Britain. It comprises two theatres for adults (ZASP and ProArt) and one for children (Syrena), a Polish Library, a Central Circulating Library, a Polish youth club, and a social club (POSKlub), the Polish University Abroad (PUNO), and a Polish restaurant with a public bar. The centre provides facilities for exhibitions, lectures, public meetings, dances and receptions. It also publishes its own bi-monthly bulletin in Polish *(Biuletyn – POSK)* and distributes 4,000 copies to the Polish community in the UK. The theatre caters for Polish and English audiences. It welcomes members from the theatrical world in Poland who come here by private invitation.

The Polish Library, founded in 1942, is presently based in POSK. It contains a collection of 100,000 books, periodicals, music, manuscripts, photographs and a special collection of books on the Polish-born Joseph Conrad Korzeniowski. The library provides information on Polish matters to universities, institutions, government establishments and the press. It provides a free service to students and researchers of all nationalities. It organizes discussions and meetings in Polish and English. The Central Circulating Library organizes the distribution of Polish books to public libraries throughout Britain. Over 10,000 volumes are supplied annually to more than 100 libraries.

The Church is an integral part of Polish community life in Britain. While there might be a decline in other areas of Polish life, *eg* the number of Saturday schools or the circulation of Polish publications, the parish network appears to be strengthening. The pulpit provides information on all social events in the community and helps to promote the national language and Polish customs and traditions.

The emergence of new associations, *eg* Polskie Duszpasterstwo Akademickie (a religious association of students) and, more recently, The Club of the Polish Catholic Intelligentsia, and the Committee of New Generations, is a welcome development among the first and subsequent generations of Poles in Britain. These organizations unite younger-generation Poles with those who have come more recently to Britain. Such gatherings lead to ideological and linguistic exchange among people of different backgrounds who are none the less united by the same religious faith. The Committee of New Generations is in the process of establishing itself. Among its aims is the promotion of Polish culture among Britons who are friends or relatives of second-generation or native Poles.

The Polish-language press is a vital part of Polish community life in Britain. According to Zubrzycki (1956: 135) there were 202 periodicals published in Britain between 1939 and 1949. This number had shrunk to 33 titles by 1960. By 1976 the number had remained much the same: it comprised one daily, three weeklies, one fortnightly, several monthlies, two or three bi-monthlies, nine quarterlies, and eight annuals and biannuals (Patterson 1977). Periodicals of the 'new emigration' – the quarterly *Aneks*, published by younger left-wing Polish dissidents, the monthly *Voice of Solidarity* and the literary quarterly *Puls* – have been added in the 1980s to the already extensive list of publications. The most important publications are *Dziennik Polski* (The Polish Daily), a daily newspaper with a current circulation estimated at about 10,000, and *Tydzien Polski* (Polish Weekly) with a circulation of 11,000. *Tydzien Polski* is distributed throughout the world. The role of the Polish press should not be underestimated. It not only perpetuates the national language and a sense of national identity but also strengthens the cohesiveness of a geographically scattered community.

There is hardly anyone of Polish origin in Britain who does not maintain some sort of contact with Poland. Such contacts include visits to and from relatives in Poland and various forms of assistance to relatives and friends in Poland. There are numerous transport firms which offer a regular service of parcels to Poland once or twice a month. Anglo-Polish firms are beginning to emerge. There is also a very close link between the Church in Poland and the Polish community in the UK.

There can be little doubt of the need for more information on Polish matters not only for Poles in Britain but also for the British authorities. There are public libraries in London (*eg* in the borough of Lambeth) which have attempted to enlarge and enrich their present collection of Polish books, but lack basic information on the Polish Circulating Library in London. There is also a need to promote co-operation between the Polish Educational Society Abroad (Polska Macierz Szkolna Za Granica) (see below) and various British bodies such as the local education authorities, and individuals such as multicultural advisers. Fortunately, the formation of a centre for information on Polish matters in Britain is under way in POSK in Hammersmith, London.

Education and language reproduction

The importance of community-run schools is not only that children receive their first formal education in the language but that the process of socializing children into the community is thereby taken out of the family context for the first time. The Polish Educational Society Abroad (Polska Macierz Szkolna Za Granica) was established in 1953. The main aim of this organization was to give financial support and assistance to Polish voluntary schools in order to maintain Polishness by educating children of Polish parents and prepare them for their return to Poland. The society is presently based at POSK, in Hammersmith, and its responsibilities include raising funds from voluntary donations for the maintenance of Polish education in Britain and the supply and the distribution of teaching materials to the various Polish Saturday schools in the UK. The society also publishes a periodical for parents, pupils and teachers, *Slowo Ojczyste* (Word of the Homeland), a quarterly for children (5–11 years old), *Dziatwa* (Young Folk) and a bi-monthly for youngsters (12–16 years old), *Razem Mlodzi Przyjaciele* (Together Young Friends).

The beginning of the Polish schools in Britain goes back to the 1950s when Polish parents began to be seriously concerned about the maintenance of Polishness in their children. The underlying motive was the return to the homeland. At first the schools were located in private houses, but later on, they moved to the halls of Polish parishes throughout the country. When the numbers of pupils increased and could not be accommodated in church halls, more space had to be hired in state schools. Patterson (1977) estimates that in 1975 there were 88 such schools with over 5,000 pupils. This number rose to about 7,000 in 1976. Since then some of the schools have had to close due to lack of funds and a decrease in numbers of pupils. According to sources at the Polish Educational Society Abroad, there are approximately 60 Polish Saturday schools at the present time with an estimated 4,500 pupils. Attendance at schools fluctuates from year to year but generally speaking it appears to correlate with demographic trends. The election of the Polish Pope led to an increase in the number of pupils because some second-generation Poles, influenced by the local priest, decided to send their children to Polish schools (Gabrielczyk, B. personal communication). However, this was a development only in those schools which are attached to strong church communities with a charismatic or influential local priest.

The Polish Saturday schools vary in respect of size (the attendance varies from 81 to 500 pupils), teaching syllabus and methods of teaching. The larger accumulation of Polish Saturday schools is in London with a total of 9 centres among which the biggest school is in Ealing (380 pupils) (J. Glaze, personal communication). At present some schools rely solely on voluntary donations by the Polish community, while others (*eg* borough of Islington, borough of Hounslow) are sponsored partially by the

local authorities. Any development within the community schooling, however, is dependent on an increased level of funding.

About 50 per cent of schools have nurseries and the majority
teach the pupils up to A level. In the summer of 1988, for instance, there were over 200 entries for the Joint Matriculation
Board and the London East Anglian Group GCSE and 80 entries
for the University of London Examination Board A level in
Polish. Teachers vary in their attitudes towards the extent of use
of Polish by the pupils studying for exams. The majority adopt
the attitude that the literature should be read in Polish but any
discussions in it should be in English. There are, however, some
who encourage pupils to use Polish in both cases (D. Podolska,
personal communication).

The standard of education is very uneven and varies from
school to school. This is due to a combination of factors, *eg*
qualifications of teachers, motivation of children and attitudes of
parents which vary from relative lack of interest to active participation in teaching at school (some parents are voluntary
teachers) and cultivation of Polishness at home. The methods are
traditional and need updating in the light of the modern developments in language teaching. There is clearly a need for Polish
teachers to update their information on language teaching methodology. In addition to the possibilities for professional development in Britain, there are also conferences, seminars and training
courses for teachers of Polish as a foreign language, in Poland.
Such courses are organized in the summer months by Polonijne
Centrum Kulturalno-Oswiatowe (Maria Sklodowska Curie University, Lublin) and the Association Polonia. They offer an
opportunity for the exchange of experience in teaching Polish as
a foreign language among teachers from all over the world.

The teachers and headteachers are responsible for preparation
of the school curriculum. Classes cover every aspect of the Polish
heritage. They include not only the Polish language but also
Polish history, geography, Polish culture and religion. They also
try to cultivate children's awareness of Polish songs, folk-dances
and costumes. Teachers rely mainly on the materials available in
Britain which are generally felt to be inadequate. New teaching
materials are currently available in Poland, together with useful
suggestions for modern methods of teaching which cater for
specific needs for students (Krakowiak 1981; J. Michowicz, personal communication). Such materials can be usefully adapted to
the British situation.

An important organization which helps to reinforce the work

of Saturday schools is the highly nationalistic exile Polish Scout and Guide Movement centred in London with an organizational network in over twenty countries. There are 1,500 Polish boy scouts and 1,000 girls guides in Britain; there are also some 400 Rovers and 600 adult members of attached groups (Patterson 1961). The organization offers an invaluable opportunity for using and developing the Polish language in a range of realistic communication settings.

At present Polish is not taught in mainstream schools. Some unsuccessful attempts were made in this direction in Stepney in 1981 (Gabrielczyk, B., personal communication). More recently, the Inner London Educational Authority approached the Polish Educational Society Abroad with a similar suggestion which also failed for various reasons, one being that Poles insist that mother tongue teaching must include other elements of Polishness apart from the Polish language (Gabrielczyk, personal communication).

In 1982 a section of Polish Studies (BA degree) was added to the School of Slavonic and East European Studies (SSEES) at the University of London. The degree studies last for three years for those with a good command of the language (at least A level) and four years for other students. The basic subjects include Polish language, Polish literature and Polish history; additional subjects are economics, politics, geography and planning. Unfortunately, due to the financial and organizational difficulties, there is no separate department of Polish Studies at any of the British universities. For those who study Russain and Slavic Languages in British universities, only Oxford and Cambridge hold lectures on Polish (Davis 1985).

The Polish Section of the SSEES, with the co-operation of the Polish Educational Society Abroad, organizes conferences for Polish teachers and pupils. It also maintains contacts with the Polish Cultural Institute in London and with Sikorski's Institute and Museum in London. It has an agreement with the Universities of Warsaw and Cracow for the exchange of tutors and students.

In brief, a number of developments both inside and outside the UK suggest a note of optimism for the Polish community. The rise of the 'new ethnicity' in Canada and the USA (*cf* also Ch. 10) is being mirrored in Britain by a revival of awareness of linguistic and cultural roots. It is certainly to be hoped that Poles, like many other minority communities, are rejecting pressures to assimilate: becoming British does not necessarily involve losing one's Polishness.

156 THE POLISH SPEECH COMMUNITY

References

DAVIS, N. (1985) 'Polskie Studia no Londynskim Universytecie' (The Polish Studies at the University of London). In *Pamietnik Literacki*, vol. 9, London: Zwiazek Pisarzy Polskich na Obcyzzyznie, *pp* 96–100.

HOFMAN, L. L. (1981) 'Spostrzezenia and jezykiem Polakow osiadlych w Angli poza Londynem (na prowincji)' (Observations on the language of Poles settled down in England, outside London). Unpublished dissertion, Polish University Abroad (PUNO), London.

Inner London Education Authority (ILEA) (1981, 1983, 1985, 1987) *Language Census*. London: ILEA Research and Statistics.

KLEMENSIEWICZ, Z. (1953) *O roznych odmianach wspolcesnej polszezyzyn* (Different Varieties of Contemporary Polish). Warsaw: Panstwowe Wydawnictwo Naukowe.

KRAKOWIAK, K. (1981) 'The exchange of experience of teachers of Polonia attending the course on methods of teaching the Polish language'. In the meeting of teachers of Polonia 1980, materials from the seminar, Warsaw 9–10 August, 1980. Lublin: Centre Polonia, Cultural and Educational University of Maria Curie-Sklodowska, *pp.* 83–104.

Linguistic Minorities Project (LMP) (1985) *The Other Languages of England*, London: Routledge and Kegan Paul.

MUIR, E. (1986) 'The strategies of language acquisition in bilingual Polish/English children'. Unpublished Ph.D. dissertation, University of Reading.

PATTERSON, S. (1961) 'The Polish exile community in Britain', *Polish Review* 6(3), 69–97.

PATTERSON, S. (1977) 'The Poles: an exile community in Britain'. In J L Watson (ed.) *Between Two Cultures*, Oxford: Basil Blackwell, *pp* 214–41.

WILK, A. M. (1970) 'The Polish community in Great Britain'. Paper presented for BSc. social sciences, University of Southampton.

ZEBROWSKA, A. (1986) 'A study of second generation Poles in England'. Unpublished doctoral dissertation, University of Surrey.

ZUBRZYCKI, J. (1956) *Polish Immigrants in Britain*. The Hague: Martinus Nijhoff.

ZWEIG, F. (1954) 'The Polish worker in England', *Kultura* 3/1977.

Chapter 10

The Ukrainian speech community

Marta Jenkala

[The Ukrainian language] has never existed,
it does not exist, it cannot exist.

COUNT PETER VALUYEV, RUSSIAN MINISTER
OF THE INTERIOR, IN AN EDICT BANNING THE
PUBLICATION OF BOOKS IN UKRAINIAN, 1863

The Ukrainian language alone is the strength
of our people, the glory of our people,
and it alone allows us to claim a place
among other nations. . . . The Ukrainian language,
and nothing else, has earned us the respect
of other nations and has laid the new
foundation of our historic life.

PANTELEIMON KULISH, UKRAINIAN WRITER, 1861

"[Рідне слово] одне становить нашу народню
силу, нашу народню славу, одне дає нам право на
дільницю між іншими народами...Слово, не що
інше як рідне слово, вернуло нам повагу між
народами й нову підвалину під нашу жизнь
історичну підкинуло."

[Ridne slovo] odne stanovyt' nashu narodnyu
sylu, nashu narodnyu slavu, odne daye nam
pravo na dil'nytsyu mizh inshymy narodamy. . . .
Slovo, ne shcho inshe yak ridne slovo, vernulo
nam povahu mizh narodamy y novu pidvalynu pid
nashu zhyzn' istorychnu pidkynulo.

Against all odds, the Ukrainian language has survived to this day, both in Ukraine and in the many countries of the Western world where there are Ukrainian *émigré* communities. Some of these, as in western Canada, will soon be celebrating the centenary of their settlement. Ukrainian is a singular example of a language which does not have, and has very rarely had in the past, normal circumstances in which to develop and yet was the single most significant factor in the formation, in the nineteenth century, of the modern Ukrainian nation. Its present growth in Ukraine is still, despite recent developments in the USSR, hampered by adverse government policies, while outside Ukraine it is subject to strong assimilatory pressures.

Most research into the linguistic characteristics and bilingualism of Ukrainian settlements has been carried out in Canada (for instance, Kuplowska 1980; Hornjatkevyč 1985; Sokolowski 1985), where approximately one-fifth of the 3 million Ukrainians in diaspora live. In Great Britain, however, where the number of Ukrainians is small (estimates range from 20,000 to 35,000), relatively little research has been done into sociological, cultural and linguistic issues (some examples are: Paraszczak 1969; Jenkala 1979; Petryshyn 1980).

The sociolinguistic situation in Ukraine

Ukrainian, one of the Eastern Slavic languages, is spoken today by about 45 million people. It traces its development back to the tenth century, although modern Ukrainian is deemed to have arisen in the early nineteenth century (Shevelov 1981). It uses the Cyrillic script, and the language in use today was standardized in the 1920s. There is a distinct written literary tradition dating back to the tenth century.

The present-day Ukrainian Soviet Socialist Republic (Ukrainian SSR), one of the constituent republics of the Soviet Union, incorporates most of the Ukrainian ethnic territory, although some areas where native speakers live are now within Poland, Romania, Czechoslovakia and the Russian Soviet Federated Socialist Republic.

The status of Ukrainian in Ukraine is unusual. Although, according to the 1979 Census, 32.5 million Ukrainians (89 per cent of the Ukrainian population) considered Ukrainian to be their native language, it is not the official language of the Ukrainian SSR, and 71.2 per cent of the total population of the

Ukrainian SSR had a fluent or native knowledge of Russian (Lewytzkyj 1984). This bilingualism is forced by measures which the central government of the USSR has implemented to broaden the use of Russian and, by the same token, to narrow the use of Ukrainian among the population.

The most significant measure taken in this direction was the 1959 school reform law in which it was decreed for the first time that the Ukrainian language should not be a compulsory subject in Russian schools in the Ukrainian SSR. This paved the way for 'parental choice' between Ukrainian-language and Russian-language schools. Since Russian is the language used in most higher-education institutes and places of work in the cities, only pupils from Russian-language schools stand a chance of gaining admission to universities and polytechnics and obtaining a good job. Where the choice is available, therefore (mainly in the towns), many parents prefer the option which gives their children better educational and career possibilities. As a result, in the 1970s, many Ukrainian-language schools converted to Russian. In 1987, the proportion of Ukrainian-language schools in the capital, Kiev, and the major cities of Ukraine was 16 per cent (Pavlychko 1987).

Other examples of the Russification of Ukrainian society are the drastic reduction in the number of Ukrainian-language scholarly publications, the sending of recruits to do their military service in multinational units where Russian has to be the language of communication, Russian immigration to Ukrainian territory (in 1979 Russians constituted 21.1 per cent of the population), the closure of higher-education faculties using Ukrainian as a medium of instruction and the increasing use of Russian in theatre and television.

This gives rise to a situation, mainly in the towns, where people use Russian in their places of education, work and entertainment, reverting to Ukrainian at home. People in rural areas still use Ukrainian (though very often not the standard) in most situations, and its use is far more widespread in Western Ukraine, which was incorporated into the USSR only during the Second World War. Literacy in Ukraine is almost 100 per cent.

In recent years a widespread movement has been initiated in defence of the Ukrainian language. New *samizdat* (underground) journals and unofficial cultural clubs have sprung up which campaign against Russification, and the campaign has been taken up by the prestigious weekly *Literaturna Ukrayina* (Literary Ukraine), official publication of the Ukrainian Writers' Union.

At the 1987 plenum of this body the language issue was widely and emotionally discussed, with Dmytro Pavlychko, one of the most highly respected Ukrainian writers, saying:

> The Ukrainian language needs a constitutional defence. It should, like Georgian, Armenian and Azerbaijani, acquire the status of official language of the Ukrainian SSR [. . .] in this matter a very detailed legal code will be necessary, which will specifically define the spheres of life in which the use of the Ukrainian language would become compulsory. (Pavlychko, 1987)

In late 1989 a draft language law was introduced, but it was widely criticized for being largely ineffective.

Ukrainian speakers in Great Britain

Before the Second World War there was only a handful of Ukrainians in Britain. During and after the war about 40,000 Ukrainians found refuge in the UK. None of them had left Ukraine of their own free will. The greatest number, mainly young adults of both sexes and including adolescents, had been forcibly displaced to Germany, during the German occupation of Ukraine, as replacement labour for German men who were at war. After the war many of these were recruited to work in Britain. Others, members of a Ukrainian unit formed under the Germans to fight the Soviet forces on the Eastern front, arrived in Britain as contract labourers via British POW camps. Others still, soldiers in the Polish army, were brought in from Italy. Many of these refugees, including the majority of those with higher education, subsequently emigrated to Canada, the USA, Australia and South America.

Today there are three generations of Ukrainians in Britain. While there are no accurate statistics, it is estimated that second- and third-generation Ukrainians comprise 45 per cent of the community. Ukrainians are settled mainly in Lancashire, Yorkshire, the East and West Midlands, Greater London and southern Scotland.

The *émigrés* who settled in Britain came mainly from the rural areas of western Ukraine, and only about 3 per cent had completed secondary or tertiary schooling. They were employed initially in relatively low-paid jobs in agriculture, the mining and textile industries, in domestic service and as ancillary personnel in hospitals. After a time they moved to better-paid jobs, the majority acquired their own homes and a few opened their own small businesses. They encouraged their children to do well at school; it is sometimes suggested that, as a result of strong family life and parents' ambitions for their children, the proportions of Ukrainian children who gain academic success at the various educational levels are greater than the national averages (Swann 1985). The Ukrainians who settled here were predominantly young, male and single. Only about 10 per cent were women, and Ukrainian men had to look outside the community for marriage partners, mainly Italian, Austrian and Irish women. Later, about 2,000 women from Ukrainian settlements in Poland and Yugoslavia came to this country.

Changing patterns of language use

Ukrainians in Great Britain belong to three distinct generations. Those who originally came to this country are now elderly or in late middle age (a small number of these came with parents, who often learnt only a little English and most of whom are no longer living). Many of the children of the original *émigrés* have children of their own.

Of the first, predominantly male, *émigrés*, about 40 per cent did not marry, and a large percentage of the rest, maybe half, married non-Ukrainian women. Although many second-generation Ukrainians consciously look for Ukrainian marriage partners, a large proportion marry out of the community.

The majority of first-generation Ukrainians hoped at first that they would be able to return to Ukraine (many still do so, even if subconsciously, as demonstrated by the fact that they have not applied for naturalization). Most, however, learnt some English in their places of work. Those who married Ukrainian partners use Ukrainian when speaking with them and, in most cases, with their children. A minority considered that speaking Ukrainian to their children would be detrimental to their education at school, and consciously avoided using the language in the home. In mixed marriages, a small number of non-Ukrainian partners, mainly women, learnt excellent Ukrainian and introduced and maintained it as the language of the home. The majority of those with non-Ukrainian partners, however, used and still use a language other than Ukrainian, and speak Ukrainian with their children only on rare occasions or never.

Past experience has shown that, despite the efforts of Saturday schools and educational organizations, if a child does not start learning Ukrainian in the home, there is limited likelihood that it will do so later. Even in families where first-generation marriage partners spoke Ukrainian to each other and to their children, if parents were not very vigilant, English was brought into the home by the first child who went to school, and became the language of communication among siblings and, naturally, among peers outside the family. This often hindered the development of Ukrainian and has given rise to the situation in which many second-generation parents are used to speaking to each other and to their friends in English but to their children (the third generation) in Ukrainian, requiring the children also to use Ukrainian. Although the parents reinforce this use both inside the home (by reading with the children, for instance) and outside (by participation in community education and events), the children do not have a Ukrainian-speaking role-model to follow, and their motivation to speak Ukrainian is weakened. Television also has to be mentioned as a factor which introduces English even into a totally Ukrainophone home.

The only source of data on language shift in the Ukrainian community is the LMP's (1985) Adult Language Use Survey (ALUS). The replies of the adults who took part in the survey would appear to point to a gradual replacement of Ukrainian by English but, when compared with patterns of language shift in other linguistic minority communities, the situation of Ukrainian speakers would seem to be surprisingly stable. It must be pointed out, however, that, of all the minorities examined in the survey, the Ukrainian sample was the smallest and probably the most homogeneous (forty-eight respondents in one city), and that sampling based on 'community lists', electoral registers and telephone directories could not but fail, in the Ukrainian context, to produce a biased sample. For instance, this sample probably did not encompass many Ukrainians who have lost touch with the community or have changed their names, or Ukrainian women married to non-Ukrainians, all of whom might be expected to undergo language loss. It is also possible that there was a measure of defensiveness in the answers of some respondents, leading to exaggerated statements about their, or their children's, linguistic competence. As the authors of the survey themselves say, it is not possible 'to generalise from [the] samples to the whole of a linguistic minority in a given city'. Even less, therefore, can one generalize to the whole Ukrainian linguistic minority in Great Britain.

In spite of various attempts to maintain the language, one has to talk, as far as the Ukrainian community is concerned, of quite considerable language shift. Among first-generation Ukrainians this is mainly lexical. They have adopted from English a number of terms for objects (eg fridge, hoover) and concepts which were not common in their places of origin, adding Ukrainian morphological endings to them (*eg parkuvaty* – to park), even though words for them exist in literary Ukrainian.

Kuplowska (1980), in her discussion of the Canadian Non-Official Languages Study (O'Bryan, Reitz and Kuplowska 1976), states that crucial language loss mainly takes place between the first and second generations. This is certainly true of Ukrainians in Britain, where shift is obvious at all levels of language.

Among a number of second-generation Ukrainians some of the phonetic characteristics of Ukrainian are not being maintained; for instance, there is a loss of palatalization in certain consonants, alveolarization of dental plosives and [r], difficulty with initial dark [l], assimilation of vowels to the English (Jenkala 1979), and the virtual elision of some unstressed vowels. This not only changes the sound of the language, it also influences spelling. In addition, intonation is becoming more like the English. There are problems, too, with Ukrainian morphology and syntax, especially with case endings and iterative and unidirectional forms of verbs. There is frequent substitution of English words if the Ukrainian ones are not known (but, in this generation, often without adapting them to the morphology of Ukrainian), and literal translation of idioms and turns of phrase: 'to show someone into a room' is translated, for instance, as 'pokazaty kohos' do kimnaty' rather than the Ukrainian 'zaprosyty kohos' u kimnatu' and 'flower bed' is translated as 'tsvitove lizhko' rather than 'hryadka' (Joint Matriculation Board 1985). Ukrainians of the third generation have similar problems, often in greater measure.

Associated with this shift is fairly extensive code-switching. First-generation Ukrainians use English in their places of work (and at home if married to non-Ukrainians), and Ukrainian with their children and with other members of the community, both in more formal contacts and for social occasions. Second- and third-generation Ukrainians generally use English in their places of education, work and in most places of entertainment. They use Ukrainian with their parents and older members of the community, switching to English when talking to people of their own age. They are encouraged to use Ukrainian in the Saturday schools and meetings and camps of the youth organizations and, when speaking English, often switch to short utterances in Ukrainian to describe events or experiences connected with these. This also often happens during rehearsals of choirs or dance groups, which are very popular among the second generation. In a stable linguistic community such code-switching would be regarded as a normal feature of language. In the Ukrainian community in Britain, however, which is not being regenerated by a steady flow of Ukrainian speakers from outside the community, it can be regarded only as one more symptom of language loss.

Language, community and culture

The aims of the Ukrainian community in Britain, as stated in evidence to the Swann Committee, are 'to minimise the extent to which people of Ukrainian origin lose their identity through assimilation [. . .] at the same time encouraging them to be successful members of British society'. While the second of these aims is being fulfilled, the first is encountering difficulties. A main area of concern is the lack of ethnolinguistic vitality in the community. Contacts with Ukraine are limited and, despite efforts being made by the community to preserve the language, there are fewer Ukrainian speakers in each successive generation.

Ukrainian community life revolves around the Churches (principally the Ukrainian Catholic Church and the Ukrainian Autocephalous Orthodox Church) and a variety of organizations, which cater for the community as a whole or specifically for the interests of women, young people, ex-servicemen, students, professionals, etc. The community has acquired or built a substantial number of properties, including many churches, cultural centres with premises for schools, several commercial enterprises, two summer camps for young people and two retirement homes. A weekly Ukrainian-language newspaper (*Ukrayinska Dumka*) and a variety of periodicals are published.

Until recently, there has been, because of the political situation in the USSR, little direct contact between British Ukrainians and their country of origin, with very few visits taking place in either direction, although these are on the increase. Some books, newspapers and records published in Ukraine are available in the UK. Family and personal contacts still mainly take the form of correspondence, and parcels are sent from Britain to Ukraine. Choirs and dance groups from Ukraine sometimes tour the UK, but contact with them is limited. There are practically no new immigrants from Ukraine to this country. There is freer intercourse with Ukrainians living in Poland and Yugoslavia, with many more exchange visits taking place. Apart from this, British Ukrainians of all ages travel to other countries in the West where there are Ukrainian communities, notably West Germany, Italy, France, Belgium, the USA and Canada, for summer courses, youth camps, meetings of Ukrainian organizations and conferences.

Practically all institutions and organizations established by first-generation Ukrainians support the use of the Ukrainian language, which is perceived as an essential factor in the retention of a Ukrainian identity (Swann 1985). These include the Churches, the two main community organizations (the larger Association of Ukrainians in Great Britain and the smaller Federation of Ukrainians in Great Britain), the Association of Ukrainian Teachers and Educators with its network of Saturday schools, the Ukrainian Catholic University, the Ukrainian scouts and guides (Plast) and the Ukrainian Youth Organization (SUM). Religious services in both Churches are held in Ukrainian, as are youth organization meetings and summer camps, concerts, literary and poetry evenings, commemorations of national days, public lectures, social evenings and other events. The use of the language is also supported by several Ukrainian-language periodicals published in the UK, and a number published by Ukrainian communities in other countries.

There is, none the less, a growing number of second-generation Ukrainians who do not know the language, or whose knowledge of it is limited. They consider that many of the existing forms of community activity fail to provide for their needs. As a result they are pressing for the greater use of English in community life and are organizing their own groups in which English is the main language of communication.

The Ukrainian community is mainly self-sufficient as far as linguistic resources are concerned. Its relatively small numbers do not elicit much interest or assistance from local education authorities or other local government bodies. Official literature is rarely translated into Ukrainian, and the language is not taught in mainstream schools, with one or two exceptions in the past. Some public libraries have a limited stock of Ukrainian books, and there was a short-lived Ukrainian programme on local radio in Manchester.

Education and language reproduction

Although the majority of Ukrainians in Great Britain speak a rural variety of Western Ukrainian at home, they want their children to learn standard Ukrainian, which is promoted in the community schools, publications and at various events. Most do, however, find it difficult to accept modern Ukrainian as used at present in Ukraine, because of the strong Russian influence it is subject to.

Mother tongue teaching in the community is organized primarily by the Association of Ukrainian Teachers and Educators, which at present runs 13 schools attended by 310 pupils and staffed by 61 teachers, of whom 40 are second-generation Ukrainians. Of the latter, most have professional teaching qualifications (AUGB 1986). Numbers of pupils have dropped in recent years with the fall in numbers of school-age children, and because fewer second-generation parents send their children to the schools. (For comparison, in 1966, 2473 pupils attended 43 schools run by 217 teaching staff.) The curriculum consists of Ukrainian language, literature, history, geography, religion and folklore. Pupils have two or three hours of classes a week, attend for eleven or twelve years, including nursery classes, and sit a leaving examination set by the school. Until 1988 they sat for the GCE O level, and now take the GCSE in Ukrainian.

Ukrainian language teaching is reinforced by the two organizations for young people (Plast and SUM) where, although language is not taught as such, it is used in various cultural, leisure and sporting activities. Adults who wish to learn Ukrainian may attend classes at the London College of the Ukrainian Catholic University.

Although the fall in numbers is mainly attributable to the factors already mentioned, there are other difficulties in providing mother tongue teaching in community schools. The curriculum is fairly traditional, with Ukrainian being taught in the traditional manner as a first language and other subjects separately, whereas the present linguistic state of the youngest generation requires a more integrated approach focused primarily on teaching efficient communication in the language. There is not enough emphasis on teaching Ukrainian as a second language, although some efforts are being made in that direction. Teachers from the older generation, although they have a good knowledge of the language, are not, in the majority, qualified professionals, and find it difficult to adapt to newer, more direct methods of teaching. Younger-generation teachers, while they are professionally qualified, do not always have an adequate knowledge of the language and culture. Although the Association of Teachers runs in-service training courses, these are too infrequent and are not always adapted to the present needs of teachers.

The materials available are fairly traditional, including those in widest use, which were designed specifically for the Ukrainian-language programme in Canadian mainstream schools, and do not really answer the present needs of Ukrainian schoolchildren in Great Britain. There is not, as has already been mentioned, sufficient linguistic support from parents, and pupils tend not to be very motivated, owing to the low status which they consider Ukrianian to have when compared with English. Also, the timetabling of Ukrainian lessons, usually on Saturdays, enters into competition with other events which are often perceived to be more attractive.

The only provision for the Ukrainian language in mainstream education is the existence since 1954 of a GCE Ordinary level examination in Ukrainian (and a GCSE from 1988), a CSE examination, the introduction in 1970 of Ukrainian as a subsidiary subject at the University of London and some material support provided by LEAs like Coventry for community Saturday schools. There was an attempt to establish a Ukrainian-run secondary school, but this was unsuccessful.

There are several aspects of Ukrainian children's education in the mainstream system which have given parents and the community cause for concern. The first is the considerable ignorance on the part of teachers about Ukraine and the Ukrainian community in Great Britain. Ukraine is often confused with Russia or Poland, both in informal contacts and in the curriculum; the Ukrainian Catholic and Orthodox Churches are often incorrectly called Russian Orthodox, etc. Another aspect which has perturbed parents who speak Ukrainian to their children at home is the now discredited 'withdrawal' approach to teaching English as a second language practised in some schools (cf CRE 1987). They felt they were faced with having to make the decision of whether to retain Ukrainian as the language of the home, at the expense of their children's progress in mainstream education.

In the near future the Ukrainian community will have to come to terms with the fact that many of its members will not speak Ukrainian, and will need to adapt its attitudes and activity to this. This does not mean, however, that it should no longer promote the positive aspects of learning and using Ukrainian in the community. Efforts have to be made to overcome 'the disjunction between the home and community and the LEA school' (LMP 1985), which is an important factor contributing to the low status of the language in some children's eyes. Also, a radical change will need to be made in approaches to Ukrainian language teaching; provision will be necessary both for teaching Ukrainian in an attractive way as the first language to those children who have begun to learn it at home, and as a second language to children who have no Ukrainian linguistic background. For this, greater parental support, better trained teachers and effective and attractive materials produced specifically for British Ukrainian children are essential.

If adequate provision is to be made for efficient Ukrainian

teaching, research needs to be done into all aspects of the language of Ukrainians living in Britain. It would be useful to have more accurate general statistics about the community, information about attitudes and expectations of parents and pupils of Ukrainian origin, and considerably more data about the various features of the language they speak.

Such research is essential, for, if the Canadian Ukrainian experience is any indication, it is very likely that third- and fourth-generation Ukrainians in Great Britain will wish to rediscover their origins, culture and language, and it must be the responsibility of the Ukrainian community, with the support of sociolinguists and the British educational authorities, to help them achieve this.

References

Association of Ukrainians in Great Britain (AUGB) (1986) *Annual Report*. London: AUGB.

Commission for Racial Equality (CRE) (1987) *Teaching English as a Second Language*. Report of a Formal Investigation in Calderdale Local Education. London: HMSO.

HORNJATKEVYCH, A. (1985) 'English calques in Canadian Ukrainian'. In M. R. Lupul (ed.) *Osvita Ukrainian Bilingual Education*. Edmonton: Canadian Institute of Ukrainian Studies.

JENKALA, M. (1979) 'Language as a marker of identity among Ukrainians in Great Britain'. Unpublished M. A. project, Department of Applied Linguistics, Birkbeck College, University of London.

Joint Matriculation Board (1985) *Examiner's Reports on the Examinations held in* 1972–1985 *in Ukrainian Ordinary Level General Certificate of Education*. Manchester: JMB.

KUPLOWSKA, O. M. (1980) 'Language retention patterns among Ukrainian Canadians'. In W. R. Petryshyn (ed.) *Changing Realities: Social Trends among Ukrainian Canadians*. Edmonton: Canadian Institute of Ukrainian Studies, University of Alberta.

LEWYTZKYJ, B. (1984) *Politics and Society in Soviet Ukraine* 1953–1980. Edmonton: Canadian Institute of Ukrainian Studies, University of Alberta.

Linguistic Minorities Project (1985) *The Other Languages of England*. London: Routledge & Kegan Paul.

O'BRYAN, K. G., REITZ, J. G. and KUPLOWSKA, O. M. (1976) *Non-Official Languages: A Study of Canadian Multiculturalism*. Ottawa: Ministry of Supply and Services.

PARASZCZAK, R. (1969) 'Ukrainians in Rochdale'. Unpublished dissertation, Manchester College of Education.

PAVLYCHKO, D. (1987) 'Materials of the Plenum of the Ukrainian Writers' Union', *Suchasnist* No. 9: 317, Munich.

PETRYSHYN, R. (1980) 'Britain's Ukrainian community: A Study of the political dimension in ethnic development'. Unpublished Ph.D. thesis, University of Bristol.

SHEVELOV, G. Y. (1981) 'Evolution of the Ukrainian literary language'. In I. L. Rudnytsky (ed.) *Rethinking Ukrainian History*, Edmonton: Canadian Institute of Ukrainian Studies, *pp* 224–7

SOKOLOWSKI, J. (1985) 'Ukrainian-language acquisition in the immersion classroom: findings of a preliminary study'. In M. R. Lupul (ed.) *Osvita Ukrainian Bilingual Education*, Edmonton: Canadian Institute of Ukrainian Studies.

SWANN, LORD (1985) *Education for All: The Report of the Committee of Inquiry into the Education of Children from Ethnic Minority Groups*. London: HMSO.

Chapter 11

The Yiddish speech community

Judy Keiner

ייִדיש רעד זיך

Yiddish ret sich
(Yiddish speaks itself)

Yiddish today is the mother tongue of two main groups of Jews. It is the language of relatively small but thriving fundamentalist separatist communities of eastern European Ashkenazi[1] Jewish communities whose main centres are in New York and Israel, and of which there are some 15,000 adherents in Britain. It is also the mother tongue of dwindling numbers of former immigrants, refugees and Holocaust survivors from the main historical centres of Jewish settlement in Eastern Europe. The present chapter concentrates on the Yiddish–speaking community in the UK. This community, however, can only be understood in a wider geographical and historical context.

The history and geography of Yiddish

Historically, Yiddish derives its structures from a European language, medieval German. Its vocabulary, too, comes principally from medieval German but the influence of various other languages – including Hebrew, Aramaic, the Romance languages spoken by Jews of the early Middle Ages and the Slavic languages of the main centres of Eastern European settlement – can also be clearly detected. Its orthography derives from Hebrew.

The distinctive identity of Yiddish was forged by the enforced isolation of the medieval German Jewish communities from those of their Gentile neighbours, and preserved through the great migrations eastwards that followed successive periods of expulsion of Jews from Western European communities throughout the Middle Ages and the early Renaissance.

Yiddish evolved distinct dialects from early in its history. Western Yiddish was spoken by Ashkenazi Jews in Germany; with the coming of the Enlightenment at the start of the nineteenth century, their communities were assimilated with those of the Gentiles, and their language likewise.[2] While the majority of German Jews remained faithful to their religion, Yiddish was rejected as an inferior and corrupted form of German, and Western Yiddish had all but died out by the time of the Second World War.

The Eastern Yiddish of the Jews who lived to the east of the pre-1939 German–Polish border developed three principal dialects: 'Polnisch' Yiddish, from central Poland, between the rivers Vistula and San; 'Litvak' Yiddish, from Lithuania, White Russia and north-eastern pre-1939 Poland; and 'Galitizianishe/Ukraynishe' Yiddish, spoken in eastern Galicia, the Ukraine and south-eastern pre-1939 Poland (Birnbaum 1979).

However, the stability of the dialects was already in flux before the catastrophe of the Holocaust. There was widespread migration westwards and to the USA by central European Jews from the mid-nineteenth century onwards. Sometimes this was in response to the declining economic opportunity base of the Jewish communities, but increasingly towards the end of the nineteenth century, it was prompted, particularly in Russia and Poland, by anti-Semitic legislation and attacks on Jews. Those immigrant Jews who settled in Britain and the USA and other countries frequently married across dialect communities and dialect usages became more blurred both in the countries of origin and in the countries of emigration.

There is a rich history of scholarly research on Yiddish with the best-known grammars being those of Weinreich (1949), Birnbaum (1979) and, more recently, Katz (1987). The efforts of Yiddish intellectuals to standardize the language have been charted by Fishman (1981b,c). A great deal of attention has been paid, for instance, to the standardization of orthography. The first effective moves in this direction were established at the first World Congress of Yiddish at Czernowitz in 1908, though the orthographic conventions were finally established only in 1937. The establishment of YIVO, the Yiddish Scientific Institute, provided a world centre for Yiddish scholarship in Vilna and subsequently in New York. YIVO adopted a standard of transliteration of Yiddish into English which has become widely established, although, as Birnbaum (1979) points out, the dialect pronunciation enshrined is that of the Lithuanian dialect actually spoken by a minority of Yiddish speakers.

Two forms of script are used in Yiddish. Both are based on Hebrew. The first is the 'square' block/print script which is used in schooling and initial literacy, as well as for all typed and printed works. A cursive form is used for handwriting. Unlike Hebrew, Yiddish uses separate characters rather than diacritics to indicate vowels.

The Yiddish proverb says, 'Yiddish ret sich' (Yiddish speaks itself). Which is just as well, because it is almost unique among living languages in that the historical centres where it developed were almost entirely destroyed by the Holocaust. Those that survived were compulsorily assimilated, politically and linguistically, into the dominant secular majority ethnic culture of the post-war socialist states of the Eastern bloc.

Today, speaking Yiddish is almost invariably an act of conscious choice or at least continuing commitment to a minority culture. There is no longer a country or countries of origin. The Soviet Union, for instance, includes substantial areas of the former Jewish homelands, and recognizes Yiddish as one of its ethnic languages, as it has done since the early years after the Revolution. However, there was a long period, starting in the mid–1930s, intensifying in the period when Stalin launched purges against Communist Yiddish poets and writers towards the end of his life, and lasting to the late 1970s, when state support for officially approved Yiddish activities was run down almost to vanishing point (Erlich 1981). In any case, recent Soviet support for Yiddish has not extended to encouragement for mother tongue Yiddish or for primary schooling in Yiddish.

The largest historically continuous centre of contemporary Yiddish speaking today is in fact the USA, and New York in particular. New York was the destination of the overwhelming majority of emigrants from Eastern Europe in the peak years of the Tsarist persecutions of the 1880s, and substantial numbers of Yiddish speakers continued to settle there before and after the Second World War, including many from the fundamentalist communities. It is possible among these communities today for a child to grow up without knowing English.

A still older, but smaller historical centre of Yiddish speaking is Israel, where over hundreds of years before the rise of contemporary secular Zionism, there were small settlements of Eastern European Talmudic[3] scholars. More recently, significant numbers of those fundamentalist Jews who survived the Holocaust emigrated to Israel after the establishment of the state. These communities have grown substantially, as have their own towns and farming settlements; in these communities, children grow up speaking Yiddish, and being taught to avoid the use of modern Hebrew.

Yiddish in Britain

There is currently no readily available reliable estimate of the numbers of Yiddish speakers in Britain. The total Jewish population of the UK was estimated at 330,000 in 1985; this figure is by now likely to be lower, as it is an ageing population whose birth-rate is low, and whose numbers are being further depleted by outmarriage. There is also some evidence that a substantial proportion of the under-35 population are neither affiliating to synagogues nor to the traditional alternative Jewish organizations, such as Zionist and socialist groups and charitable organizations. Of the total number, up to 100,000 may have come, or descended from those who came as refugees, from Nazi Germany, or have emigrated from Israel, Iran, Aden and other Middle Eastern countries.

We can thus very crudely estimate that up to a quarter of a million of Britain's Jews come from families which would have been Yiddish speaking in the early years of this century. The great majority of Yiddish-speaking Jews who emigrated to the UK in response to the pogroms[4] had entered the country before 1905, when the Aliens Act, specifically designed to exclude Jews, was passed. While only a few of this group, octogenarians and above, are alive today, the vast majority of their children grew up in the Yiddish-speaking East End of London before the Second World War. A substantial proportion of their British-born children, today aged 65 and over, would have been brought up as Yiddish mother tongue speakers, although very few of them would use the language today. It is also the case that those Jews who grew up in the East End of London in any period from 1914 to 1960 would have regularly heard Yiddish spoken, most likely by a parent or grandparent. Thus, a majority of British Jews of Eastern European descent are likely to have at least some degree of listening comprehension of Yiddish.

The centres of Yiddish speaking in Britain until the early 1950s were the Whitechapel, Aldgate and Spitalfields districts of Stepney, today widely populated by Bangladeshis. In the period immediately preceding the Aliens Act in 1905, there may have been up to 90,000 Jews in these areas and surrounding East End districts. There were also substantial Yiddish-speaking immigrant communities in Manchester, Leeds and Glasgow. Today, there are some 5,000–6,000 Jews in Tower Hamlets, the larger successor borough to Stepney, most of whom are elderly former Yiddish speakers. The traditional Yiddish-speaking areas of Manchester, Glasgow and Leeds are now almost entirely devoid of Jews, and there are no longer centres of secular Yiddish-speaking in these cities.

While the fundamentalist communities had already established themselves in the Stamford Hill and Stoke Newington areas before the Second World War, it was in fact well after this time that these communities began to grow to their present size; their ranks were swelled by a significant proportion of the relatively few Holocaust survivors who were allowed to settle in Britain, and further boosted by some hundreds of Hungarian fundamentalist Jews who left Hungary after the 1956 uprising. (See Ch. 7).

Changing patterns of language use

Changes in this century in Yiddish speaking can only be understood in the context of the history of both internal and external hostility to Yiddish which was dominant until very recently. From the period of mass immigration of Yiddish speakers to Britain in the nineteenth century, until the 1970s, the mainstream communal organizations, including the main representative body, the Board of Deputies, community newspapers such as the *Jewish Chronicle*, Jewish schools and synagogues urged Jews to abandon Yiddish. It was widely regarded as a 'jargon'; certainly not a language, but as a corrupt form of German which was either corrupt through the ignorance of the speakers, or itself was a corrupting influence.

The greatest number of immigrant children and the first-generation descendants of the immigrants attended state primary schools which would not have tolerated any continuation of Yiddish, and actively urged the children and their parents to abandon it for English. The influential major Jewish school in the East End, the Jews' Free School, which had up to 5,000 pupils in its heyday in the early years of this century, saw itself as a 'citadel of anglicization' (Gartner 1960), and, again, use of or even recognition of Yiddish and Yiddish culture was out of the question.

In the first half of this century, first-generation men could look to the Yiddish-speaking Workers' Circle, a large and influential working men's club and friendly society, and to other Yiddish-speaking friendly societies, but by and large, these did not continue to recruit in any significant numbers from subsequent generations. The popular Jewish youth clubs were as much devoted to Anglicization as the schools, and these organizations were highly successful in producing a generation oriented towards sports, dancing and mainstream British leisure pursuits.

Radical socialist and Communist political organizations proved attractive to many young Jews in the 1920s and 1930s, in response to the rise of Fascism and Nazism. Communist front organizations promoted Yiddish-based socialist cultural activities, especially oriented towards building support for the Soviet Union and the British Communist Party (Waterman 1978). In contrast, Zionist groups before the Second World War, irrespective of their attitudes towards religion, promoted Hebrew and stressed their rejection of Yiddish as the product of the Diaspora (see Vol 2, Ch. 16).

It is therefore not surprising to find that a very common response on the part of first- and second-generation British Jews from the mainstream communities is to deny all knowledge of Yiddish. Of those who do acknowledge their knowledge of Yiddish, only a tiny minority would use it today.

On the other hand, among the fundamentalist communities, there now seems to be a consensus that use of Yiddish as a vernacular is on the increase, and that the decision to speak exclusively Yiddish at home is now a choice increasingly being made by the most committed young married members of these communities.

For the fundamentalist communities, it continues to be an important question as to whether the present, apparently very healthy momentum towards sustaining and even increasing Yiddish as a mother tongue in Britain will be maintained. Within the next ten to twenty years, virtually all those who came from the pre-war historical homelands of Yiddish speaking will have died. The new generation of rabbinical leaders, in most of these communities, will include a majority who are first-language English speakers. It may also be that the realities of the housing market will make it more difficult for the large, cross-generational communities of Stamford Hill, Golders Green and Hendon to be sustained in the long term. New satellite communities are likely to be set up. While, in the short term, the founders will be highly committed to making Yiddish the main vernacular, it is less clear whether this commitment would be continued by a new generation of families.

Among the majority Jewish community, too, there has been an enormous increase of interest in Yiddish in the 1980s. There is some interest in learning Yiddish as a second language, particularly among younger radicals and intellectuals. A much wider group, including some who did know or speak Yiddish as children, take part in Yiddish cultural events. But here they participate as listeners and spectators rather than as speakers and originators.

Support for Yiddish within the younger non-fundamentalist Jewish community may well be tied to perceptions and feelings about the centrality of Israel. As long as the conduct of the Israeli government increasingly alienates Diaspora youth from that country, there will be a tendency to look for another Utopian ideal, or at least a low-key version of the Jewish polity. The pursuit of Yiddish and Yiddish culture can at least satisfy those needs to the extent that it represents a way of recognizing a long and fruitful period of Jewish autonomy.

A key issue facing the non-fundamentalist communities is whether they can move from being merely transmitters of the rich Yiddish culture of the past to becoming, or helping to sponsor, originators of new Yiddish cultural artefacts. If they cannot, then they risk becoming an animated museum service. Those who learn Yiddish presently have no milieu, other than the classes or the small number of special events, for speaking it, unless they wish to engage with the fundamentalist communities (see section on language, culture and community, below). The latter would in any case have very different agendas and discursive styles. So far, there would not appear to be any evidence of parents from the non-fundamentalist groups opting to speak Yiddish as the sole home language for their children, and even if there were, there are no apparent prospects for the establishment of other new Yiddish cultural institutions.

Ironically, a vital question for the future of Yiddish in Britain arises from the striking congruencies and disjunctures between the two main groups which are promoting its use today – the radicals and the fundamentalists. Both groups share a strong resistance to the redefinition of Jewish culture as chiefly Israel and Modern-Hebrew oriented. Speaking Yiddish in the late 1980s can be a marker of some of the most hostile attitudes to Zionism within the Jewish community. However, there is an equally strong current of mutual antagonism over the gulf in the two groups' attitudes to religion. Ironically, speaking Yiddish in the late 1980s can equally be a marker for strong hostility to Judaism, or for the most intensive level of commitment to be found.

Whatever the final outcome, the Yiddish-speaking community in the UK, as elsewhere, remains for the present a bilingual community. Like stable bilingual communities in other parts of the world, their speech is commonly marked by code-switching behaviour which is often determined by the nature of the subject-matter and the relationships between the speakers. It may also be determined by the presence of non-Jewish outsiders, or, in the case of fundamentalists, by secular Jewish outsiders. It is frequently to be found in the fundamentalist communities' English-language publications, where one may find a communal notice or a discussion switching between English, Yiddish and Hebrew; the Yiddish element will frequently denote a reference to traditions of Eastern European religious culture, as well as to the familiar habits of the group. Thus the word *heimishe* (lit. 'from the homeland') will be used to denote membership from birth of a trusted community. The main community newspaper, the *Jewish Tribune*, carries mini-cab advertisements which offer the services of 'heimishe lady drivers' for women, and marriage agency adverts which state that 'heimishe men and women of all ages' are available for suitable partners.

Language, community and culture

Among the fundamentalist groups, the most important focus for the use of Yiddish outside the family and purposes of religious study is in community religious events. For example, the Melaveh Malka is a ceremonial celebration extending the conclusion of the sabbath, at which it is customary for discussions of Torah[5] to be given in Yiddish, often by a young male scholar. Yiddish songs will be sung at weddings and other family celebrations. The giving of sermons in Yiddish will be a feature of synagogue services on the sabbath and holy days. Tributes to a deceased will usually be given in Yiddish immediately following burial.

The fundamentalist communities in Britain maintain very strong contacts with the main sources of Yiddish in New York and Israel, and in other fundamentalist centres in Europe. Firstly, the rabbis who lead the communities, resident in either New York or Israel, will be visited for consultations and spiritual guidance, and frequent contacts and exchanges of personnel made between the branches of the community organization. Male students in particular may spend periods studying in a *yeshiva* or *kollel* (Talmudic College or higher-education establishment) in either the USA or Israel, and there is an increasing provision of advanced study programmes for young women students. The latter would, however, be principally in English. The communities continue to use the arranged marriage system traditional among European Jewish communities since the Middle Ages, and it is not uncommon for transnational marriages to be arranged, through the good offices of the rabbinic leader or the communal organization.

There are also widespread networks of family connections. There are particularly frequent contacts with Israeli counterparts among those groups which are ideologically supportive of religious Zionism; adherents will in any case welcome opportunities to celebrate holy days in Israel.

The fundamentalist communities publish a range of newspapers and religious literature, most of it originating in New York and Israel. The most widely distributed publication is the weekly *Der Yid* (The Jew) which is the official publication of the main umbrella organization of the American communities. The main newspaper of British fundamentalist Jews is the *Jewish Tribune*, a bilingual weekly, which carries a three-page section in Yiddish.

In the secular sphere, the growth of community arts funding directed towards ethnic minority groups has in recent years benefited the promotion of Yiddish. In the last few years, the greatest impact has been in terms of first Greater London Council (GLC) grants, and subsequently its successor, the London Boroughs Grants Association. Grants from these sources helped to add paid staff and administrative facilities to initially small Jewish voluntary community organizations, such as the London Museum of Jewish History, the Jewish Women in London Group, the Spiro Institute and the Jewish Socialists' Group. The traditional range of Jewish charitable trusts has also supported some of these ventures, though they have tended to support only applications which come from non-political and non-radical groups.

These and other institutions have contributed since the early 1980s to Yiddish film and theatre festivals and exhibitions, to the making of videos and exhibitions based on the lives of Yiddish-speaking immigrants and their children, most of which have found unexpectedly large and enthusiastic audiences.

The older-established organizations supporting Yiddish in Britain include the Friends of Yiddish and the Mame Loshen Ring; these remain the main organizations in which mother tongue secular Yiddish speakers predominate. They are small, and have kept themselves going largely without funding from either the Jewish or the wider community.

The radical Jewish Socialists' Group has made the promotion of Yiddish and Yiddish culture a key part of its programme and, with GLC fundings, has founded the Jewish Cultural and Anti-Racist Project which has a substantial Yiddish component.

Although the representative organization of British Jews, the Board of Deputies of British Jews, has recognized officers and committees connected with the promotion of Hebrew and Israel, it has no specific officer or committee with responsibility for Yiddish language or culture. Nevertheless, the Board has been represented at most of the successful Yiddish cultural events of recent years, including the 1988 World Congress of Yiddish. It also sponsors the major radio broadcast for the Jewish community, Greater London Radio's 'The Jewish World Tonight', which has a generally sympathetic attitude towards Yiddish. Yiddish records are frequently played, but there is little or no broadcasting in spoken Yiddish.

Commercial bookshops which stock Yiddish books and records are relatively few, although almost all Jewish bookshops stock books in English about Yiddish. Recently, a small specialist Jewish music distribution company has been established, and this is now importing an impressive and growing list of historical and contemporary Yiddish music on record and cassette.

Contemporary secular Yiddish writing still keeps alive a range of newspapers and periodicals in the Diaspora world. The best known of these is *Der Forverts* (The Jewish Daily Forward), published in New York, daily until relatively recently. Another major Yiddish daily newspaper, *Letste Nayes* (Latest News), is published in Israel. In addition, *Di Zukunft* (The Future) is an important literary review. There is a range of periodicals published by the Jewish Bundist movements in New York, Paris and Israel. The major publication of the official Soviet Yiddish cultural organization is *Sovietish Heimland* (Soviet Homeland). The only secular Yiddish publication now originating in Britain is the monthly *Das Yiddishe Volk* (The Jewish People).

Today, the London borough of Hackney follows the historical example of the old borough of Stepney (now part of the larger Tower Hamlets) in making information available in Yiddish. All information published by the borough about adult education, registration for voting and other community information carries sections in the main community languages, including Yiddish. As far as is known, other local authorities do not provide Yiddish-language documents.

Education and language reproduction

There has so far been little or no Yiddish teaching offered outside the fundamentalist communities to children and young people in Britain, in contrast to the United States, where, until the late 1970s, secular Yiddish schools and summer camps in New York and other major Jewish centres of settlement were widely attended by young Jewish-Americans of up to third- and fourth-generation descent (Klepfisz 1986). The most remarkable recent exception has been the institution of optional Yiddish classes at London's only state Jewish comprehensive school, the JFS School, which is a post-war reincarnation of the old East End Jews' Free School, which so strongly opposed Yiddish in the first decades of this century.

The fundamentalist communities tend not to teach Yiddish as language *per se*. Rather, it is used in the communities' private day schools as the medium of instruction for religious studies. For girls, this will consist of studies of the Pentateuch,[6] of related rabbinical commentaries, and of prayers and laws related to the conduct of family life and the home. For boys, studies of the Talmud are the core of the educational programme, and the traditional mode of study includes close study and learning by heart of the Aramaic and Hebrew texts, with translation into and commentary in Yiddish. Children will also learn some of the traditional Yiddish folklore.

The use of Yiddish in schools of this kind has sometimes been controversial. Other community schools may look with considerable interest at the outcome of an investigation undertaken by Her Majesty's Inspectorate in 1985 of a private fundamentalist boys' school in Stamford Hill belonging to the Belz community. A condemnatory report proposed closing the school down, and among the many criticisms used by HMI was the small amount of teaching given in English. The school successfully challenged DES in the courts, using the defence that the HMI and their consultant had insufficient mastery of Yiddish and of traditional Jewish methods of study to make their judgements.

In looking to the future, a key question within the fundamentalist communities may well be that of the education of girls and women, and their general status in the community. It has already been shown (Poll 1981) that girls in the US communities are more likely than their brothers to be English speakers, and the preferred language of the mother is likely to be the mother tongue of the children. Given the very large size of families (an average of five children), girls are entrusted with substantial childcare responsibilities from an early age. Their choices tend also to determine the language used among the siblings. There is a continuing wider debate within the communities about ways of enhancing the educational and community opportunities for women while also strengthening their commitment to the traditional mothering and home-making role. The extent to which Yiddish elements in the curriculum offered to girls in the fundamentalist schools have increased is unlikely of itself to strengthen the girls' commitment to Yiddish. The main form of post-school education open to girls, in seminaries, does not presently give high priority to Yiddish, and it remains to be seen whether these priorities will change.

The issue of Yiddish in education for the fundamentalist communities is further sharpened by the educational changes set in motion by the 1988 Education Reform Act. It is clear that those schools which wish to receive state funds will need to meet the requirements of the National Curriculum, and it is doubtful whether any institution which uses Yiddish as its main teaching medium could deliver on the programmes of study demanded by the Act. Those Jewish schools which do not use Yiddish as the main medium of instruction will nevertheless be under some pressure to squeeze out any provision for Yiddish as the National Curriculum, with its ambitious attainment targets for English, maths and science, begins to bite.

Apart from the case of the JFS comprehensive school cited above, there is no other known case of Yiddish being taught in a state school. It would in any case be unlikely that Yiddish would be taught in the burgeoning Jewish primary-school sector, because these schools all have a strong commitment to teaching Hebrew, (see Vol 2, Ch. 16) and there would be little support for, if not strong opposition from, parents. It also is the case that significant numbers of children at these schools are of Sephardi descent[7] – often from Israel, and there would be little justification for instituting Yiddish teaching to these groups, when their own historical community languages of Arabic and Judezmo, are not taught.

A small group of young scholars are today promoting Yiddish-language learning as the key route into Yiddish culture, largely through the organization of Yiddish classes in a number of London's adult education institutes. A more ambitious, and remarkably successful venture, has been the establishment of a Yiddish summer school, running annually since 1980 at the Oxford-based Postgraduate Hebrew Studies Institute; this runs intensive summer courses for adults of all levels from beginners to advanced, and includes associated programmes of lectures by internationally distinguished scholars. Organized Yiddish classes of this type have also attracted non-Jewish participants. The classes tend to offer tuition in the Litvak dialect as a *de facto* standard related to the dialects of the teachers, and to play down the importance of the dialect variations for learners.

There are relatively few specific materials designed for the teaching of Yiddish available in Britain today. Adult classes tend to make use of Weinreich's *College Yiddish* (Weinreich 1949), or

Goldin's *The Yiddish Teacher* (Goldin 1939). In the fundamentalist communities, traditional religious commentaries,
supplemented by informally produced teaching materials, will
tend to be used. There are elementary primers intended for
school-age learners, which teach simple structures, vocabulary
and script. Passages of continuous text usually contain some
simple moral instruction, such as explaining the need for girls to
dress modestly (Knobloch 1980; APA 1986). These primers are
usually produced in the USA and are singularly uninspiring.
There is, however, an increasingly wider array of songs and
stories available on cassette, which may be used to supplement
teaching; these are very largely produced in the USA.

Notes

1. Ashkenazi Jews are descended from those who, following the dispersal of the Jews from Palestine by the Romans, came to settle in the
   Rhineland and other areas of Germany. Following the widespread
   persecutions, murders and persecutions of Jews which began with the
   Crusades, large communities of Ashkenazis migrated to Poland, the
   Ukraine and other eastern European countries.
2. In the period following the growth of rationalist philosophies and
   politics, and particularly in the wake of the Napoleonic era in continental western Europe, many of the legal restrictions on Jews were
   repealed or neglected. These had included confinement to residence
   in specified areas, exclusion from state and professional employment,
   and exclusion from secular educational institutions. Substantial numbers of Jews from within the previously closed communities welcomed
   and embraced Gentile secular learning and culture.
3. The Talmud is the main text of rabbinical Judaism and provides commentary on legal and ritual matters as well as theological, ethical and
   folklorist issues.
4. The Tsarist government in Imperial Russia saw in its large and mostly
   unassimilated Jewish communities both a threat and a scapegoat as
   demands for democracy and more radical political change grew
   towards the end of the nineteenth century. From 1880, ferociously
   anti-Semitic laws were passed and tacit official approval given for the
   unleashing of murderous mob attacks (pogroms) on Jewish communities in Russia. Gilbert (1985) shows the extent of the attacks.
5. The Torah refers in its narrow sense to the first five books of the
   Hebrew Bible, but is also used to refer to the whole of the Hebrew
   Bible, to the oral teachings of Judaism or, in its widest sense to the
   whole of traditional Jewish law and lore.
6. The Greek-derived name for the Torah, which consists of the first
   five books of the Old Testament.
7. Sephardi Jews are those descended from the communities who settled
   in Spain and Portugal in the period following the dispersal from

ancient Palestine. Following their persecution under the Inquisition and subsequent expulsion from Spain at the end of the fifteenth century, the major Sephardi communities were established in the predominantly Arab countries bordering the Mediterranean and Persian Gulf. Jews from these countries are usually known as Mizrachi (Eastern) Sephardis. There were also substantial Sephardi communities in Holland, Greece and Italy until their virtual destruction by the Nazis in the Second World War.

References

BIRNBAUM, S. A. (1979) *Yiddish. A Survey and a Grammar*. Manchester: Manchester UP.

ERLICH, R. (1981) 'Politics and linguistics in the standardization of Soviet Yiddish'. In Fishman, *Never Say Die!* pp. 699–708.

FISHMAN, J, (ed.) (1981a) *Never Say Die! A Thousand Years of Yiddish in Jewish Life and Letters*. The Hague: Mouton.

FISHMAN, J. (1981b) 'The sociology of Yiddish: a foreword'. In Fishman, *Never Say Die!* pp. 1–97.

FISHMAN, J. (1981c) 'Attracting a following in high culture functions for a language of everyday life: the role of the Tshernovits Conference in the rise of Yiddish'. In Fishman, *Never Say Die!* pp. 369–394.

GARTNER, L. (1960) *The Jewish Immigrant in England 1870–1914*. London: Simon Books.

GILBERT, M. (1985) *Jewish History Atlas*. London: Weidenfeld & Nicolson.

GOLDIN, H. E. (1939) *The Yiddish Teacher*. New York: Hebrew Publishing Company.

KATZ, D. (1987) *Grammar of the Yiddish Language*: London: Duckworth.

KLEPFISZ, I. (1986) 'Di Rayze Aheim/the journey home'. In M. Kaye and I. Klepfisz (eds) *The Tribe of Dina. A Jewish Women's Anthology*. Special issue (nos 29 and 30), *Sinister Wisdom* 29/30.

KNOBLOCH, B. (1980) *Lernen Yiddish. Mir Kennen Schreiben*. New York: Sefer Lenoar.

POLL, S. (1981) 'The role of Yiddish in American ultra-orthodox and Hasidic communities'. In Fishman, *Never Say Die!* pp. 197–218.

UNSER JZIERUNG (1980) *Di Yiddishe Sprach*. New York.

WATERMAN, R. (1978) 'Proltet: the Yiddish speaking group of the workers' theatre movement', *History Workshop* 5, pp. 174–78.

WEINREICH, U. (1949) *College Yiddish*. New York: YIVO Institute for Jewish Research.

Part three

The Mediterranean

For the purposes of the present volume, we apply the term 'Mediterranean' selectively to three main areas: the countries of southern Europe – Spain, Portugal, Italy, Malta and Greece; North Africa, and in particular, Morocco; and countries of the eastern Mediterranean, notably Turkey and Cyprus.

Mediterranean communities form a significant proportion of Britain's linguistic minority communities. The most numerically important groups have come from Spain, Portugal, Italy and Cyprus, with smaller settlements of Moroccans, Greeks, Turks and Maltese. Although settlers from many Mediterranean countries have been present in the UK for a considerable period of time – some Italian communities, for instance, date back to the nineteenth century – the majority have arrived in the post-war period.

In the main, the Mediterranean presence post-dates Eastern European settlement. While the majority of Poles, Ukrainians, Lithuanians, Latvians and Yiddish-speaking Jews arrived between 1945 and 1950, most Italians arrived in the 1950s; most Cypriots between 1960 and 1975; most Portuguese, Spanish, Turks (other than Cypriot Turks) and Moroccans from the 1970s. The reasons for these different patterns of settlement are various. Unlike Eastern European migration, the primary motivation for Mediterranean settlement was economic and it formed a part of a much broader pattern of population movement throughout Europe and beyond. These economic forces took on a new complexion with Britain's entry into the European Community in 1973. Until this time the main source of cheap labour had been the former colonies. Now, however, migrant workers from southern Europe and North Africa who had previously chosen

France or Germany as their destination, were being faced with increasingly restrictive controls on migrant labour in these countries and began to enter Britain. In most cases, they found work only in the lowest paid and least unionized sectors of the economy: hotels and catering, cleaning and hospital domestic work.

While economic considerations have certainly played a major part in Mediterranean migration, there have none the less been occasions when political considerations have come into play. In Cyprus, for instance, the political upheaval of the 1950s played a part in many people's decision to move to Britain. Again, the Turkish invasion in 1980 and the subsequent partition of the island, saw an increase in the number of Cypriots leaving the country, as did the military take-over in Turkey in 1980. Similarly, the closing of the border with Gibraltar led to the migration of large sections of the population from La Linea in Spain.

Mediterranean communities have received a considerable degree of support from their respective governments in the question of mother tongue maintenance. In many cases funding has been made available for limited numbers of teachers from the home country, for materials and for the administrative support which is necessary to maintain a network of community language classes. The Greek and Spanish Embassies are also responsible for a school which provides a bilingual education for London-based children. Embassy help is often supplemented by other community-based organizations such as the Church, though there is a growing movement towards greater parent involvement as is witnessed, for example, by the formation of groups such as the Greek Parents' Association, and the Italian FASFA (Federation of Parents' Associations).

This pattern of provision is not without its difficulties: materials from the home country are often unsuitable for local needs; parents are agreed that the language of education should be the standard which will allow the child to integrate into the school system should the family return but, in most cases, the language of the home is a non-standard dialect; teachers who come from the home country are often inadequately prepared for the needs of children whose fluency in the mother tongue cannot be expected to match that of indigenous children.

The relationship of the embassy provision with mainstream educators is also problematic. In a small number of cases, embassy-supplied teachers have been welcomed into the mainstream. Their relationship, however, is often ill-defined. While schools are sometimes eager to accept the offer of a teacher from an outside source, they have seldom been as anxious to think through the implications for the school as a whole. The needs of speakers of community languages are quite different from those of foreign language learners, a reality which mainstream teachers have been slow to accept. There is often a feeling of malaise among embassy teachers and administrators: while embassy staff make every effort to comply with and accommodate to the demands of the mainstream, it would seem that there is very little reciprocation on the part of the mainstream, who often fail to consult or involve them in any meaningful way.

Attempts to integrate embassy teachers into the mainstream have therefore had extremely limited success. For the most part, children are still involved in spending many additional hours after school and at the weekend. However, community reservations about complete incorporation within the mainstream must also be acknowledged: the fear that the community will no longer have control over the form or content of mother tongue education is a very real one.

A more recent development is the recruitment of teachers from the various communities to offer mother tongue support to bilingual children by working alongside the classroom teachers in a team-teaching situation. This approach has much to recommend it. Support teachers are more conscious of the situation of the British-born children; their presence within the mainstream classroom also allows them to understand the demands of British classrooms better and to communicate to colleagues the needs of bilingual children. However, overseas teaching qualifications are not recognized by the Department of Education and Science and opportunities for appropriate further development for teachers trained abroad are extremely limited. Consequently, many bilingual support teachers are employed on an instructor level and therefore do not enjoy the same economic advantages or status as their colleagues. This is an issue which clearly deserves urgent attention.

While the shift from the mother tongue to English is quite clearly under way within the various Mediterranean communities, there is, none the less, a considerable vitality. Unlike many Eastern Europeans, people from the Mediterranean are free to both travel to and receive visits from the home country; the longer-established communities have thriving ethnic economies and a rich cultural life. Mediterranean peoples, like Eastern Europeans, are, for the most part, invisible minorities who, by the second and third generations, can only be distinguished by outsiders on the basis of their names. The decision to continue using the mother tongue is thus very much an individual one which will depend not only on pressures and opportunities available within the minority community itself but on the prevailing attitudes of mainstream society. Education inevitably plays an important part in this process. If bilingualism is welcomed as a resource on which to build, rather than a problem to be overcome, the prospect of language stability in minority communities are likely to be considerably enhanced.

Chapter 12

The Cypriot speech communities

A third of the population of the Mediterranean island of Cyprus currently live in the United Kingdom. The major ethnic and linguistic divisions between Greek and Turkish speakers which exist within Cyprus are, of course, reflected in the Cypriot population in Britain. Greek Cypriots are the numerically most important group of Greek speakers in the UK. However, there are also smaller numbers of speakers from Greece. Similarly, Turkish Cypriots form part of a larger Turkish speaking community which also includes small numbers of speakers from Turkey.

The Greek speech community

Evienia Papadaki d'Onofrio
Maria Roussou

Η γλώσσα κόκαλα δεν έχει και κόκαλα τσακίζει

I glóssa kókala then éhee ke kókala tsakisee

Although the tongue has no bones, it is capable of breaking bones

The Greek language is spoken by over 10 million people in Greece, Cyprus and various corners of the world in which Greek speakers have settled, including the United States, Australia and the UK. Sporadic studies have been carried out (Dowling and Edwin 1915; George and Millerson 1967; Oakley 1970, 1979;

Constantinides 1977; Anthias 1982; Roussou 1984) in an attempt to identify the locations and measure the demographic, ethnic and cultural strengths of the Greek-speaking communities in Britain. It was not until recently, however, that the issue started gaining importance as part of a broader, ongoing discussion of the cultural, ethnic and linguistic diversity which characterizes British society today.

to be seen as two distinct populations: Greeks from mainland Greece and Greeks from Cyprus. Cypriots form by far the largest Greek-speaking community in Britain today and, for this reason, will form the focus of this section.

The sociolinguistic situation of Greek in Greece and Cyprus

In order to be able to understand the linguistic behaviour of the Greek Cypriot community in the UK, we need to look at the linguistic resources which the migrants brought with them and the sociolinguistic environment in which they acquired and developed their language(s). The language used by Greek Cypriots – at least, for official/national and educational purposes – has always been influenced to a certain degree by policy decisions in mainland Greece. For instance, in the late 1970s, both countries adopted standard Modern Greek (SMG) (previously known as *demotiki* or 'common language') as the official language. The evolution of SMG has been through the oral forms of language and not the written (*katharevousa* – 'purified language') which is closely related to Ancient Greek. For many years it coexisted alongside *katharevousa* in a diglossic situation (*cf* Fasold 1985; Alexiou 1982), whereby SMG was the language variety used in normal everyday interaction and *katharevousa* was used for literary and official purposes.

In Cyprus, SMG seems to be making advances in even the most rural speech communities through the media and education. The indigenous Cypriot dialects, however, remain very strong. They have developed in predominantly rural settings and, no doubt because of their extreme isolation, remain closer to Ancient Greek than any other present-day Greek dialects. Yet while they represent a strong element in ethnic identity, like many other predominantly oral varieties (*cf* Giles and Powesland 1975) they are not held in high esteem. For this reason formal interaction usually takes place in SMG.

The majority of Greeks appear to interact in a tridialectal environment. Newton (1983), for instance, claims that the typical

Greek Cypriot villager will possess a fluent command of his or her own dialect and be able to communicate in the variety of Greek that has developed, with minor variations, in the urban centres of the island, as well as understanding and often speaking the SMG variety in the various domains in which it is used.

Greek speakers in Britain

Greeks from mainland Greece in the UK number between 10,000 and 15,000. They have mainly come as students who eventually return to Greece or as professionals and entrepreneurs based within the UK but often travelling abroad a great deal. Trade between Greece and Britain has inevitably increased since Greek entry into the European Community in 1981.

The most obvious form of contact between Greek and Greek Cypriot communities is through religious functions and intermarriage. However, Greek Cypriots form a much larger community and come from very different backgrounds. The first sizeable group arrived in the inter-war years (1920–40) and was composed of young men who came in search of education and work. Most of them were conscripted and served as British soldiers in various parts of the world. After the war, substantial numbers of Greek Cypriot men arrived, followed by their families as soon as they had found a permanent job and reasonable housing. The 1955–60 Independence struggle gave rise to further immigration to Britain, as did the civil struggles of 1963 and the invasion by Turkey in 1974. The estimated Greek Cypriot population in the UK today is approximately 200,000 (Anthias 1984). These numbers need to be seen in a total island context: one Cypriot in six lives in Britain (Walvin 1984).

Although there are small Greek communities in larger cities such as Birmingham, Glasgow and Manchester, by far the largest proportion of the Greek speech community is concentrated in London. In a national context, the numbers of Greeks are relatively small. Within the capital, however, Greeks form a

TABLE 12.1   ILEA *Languages Census* data on Greek speakers, 1981–87

Year	Number	% Phloe
1981	3,859	8.6
1983	3,410	6.8
1985	3,033	5.4
1987	2,596	4.0

PHLOE = Pupils with a home language other than or in addition to English.

significant minority. Although the overall number of Greek speakers has decreased in the 1980s, Greek children have consistently formed one of the largest bilingual groups within the ILEA (see Table 12.1).

Greek Cypriots left their homes for mainly economic reasons. Most of them came to Britain to find work and improve their standard of living. The largest section of this immigrant population came from lower socio-economic groups. They set out with high aspirations, confident in their hard-working nature, and supported by the strong feeling of solidarity which bonded them to their compatriots.

In the 1950s and 1960s Greek Cypriots worked mainly in the service sector, in catering, in the clothing and shoe manufacturing industries, in hairdressing and in grocery retailing. In the villages in Cyprus, most women's work was confined to the household and the fields. In Britain, though still undervalued and underpaid, a substantial number of women went to work in the clothing industry, either as machinists in small family-run factories, or as outworkers sewing clothes at home at piece-work rates.

From the late 1960s self-employment has become more common among Greek Cypriot men who have established a variety of small businesses – estate agencies, small building firms, travel agencies, etc – building gradually what Constantinides (1977) has called an ethnic economy. These small businesses often provide goods and services primarily for other Cypriots, although, according to Anthias (1984) there is a tendency, especially among the second and third generations, to move away from traditional employment. This change in the economic orientation of Cypriots has been well-documented by, for instance, Stavrinides (1987) who claims that the somewhat stereotypical image of the Greek Cypriot as 'unsophisticated and uneducated, although hard-working and law-abiding, is badly dated and misleading'. Their interests and abilities have moved away from the world of kebab restaurants and Mediterranean grocery shops into the more successful and highly competitive world of property development, manufacturing industry, import-export, travel and tourism, printing and publishing.

Changing patterns of language use

There have been some interesting developments in the linguistic repertoire of Greek Cypriots in the UK. Immigrants who moved from rural to the urban centres not only had to face the task of learning a foreign language but also had to create vocabulary for things which were quite alien to them in both cultural and linguistic terms (*cf* Roussou 1984). Loan words like *busso* (bus), *cooka* (cooker) and *basketa* (basket) have featured in their vocabulary since the earliest years of immigration to the UK in a form similar to that documented by Tosi (1984) in his study of the Italian community in Bedford. So, too, have sentence fillers and interjections such as 'you know', 'isn't it?'.

This has developed still further in the form of transfer of phrases, proverbs and idiomatic expressions from English into Greek:

> *ennen to kapof tinmou* – He isn't my cup of tea
> *piano to basso* – to catch the bus

Anglicisms of this kind are in everyday use and are accepted as the norm by speakers from the London and other Greek Cypriot communities. Other common strategies are code-switching (Anaxagorou 1984) and code-mixing which are reported as common features of stable bilingual communities all over the world (*cf* Hernandez-Chavez, Cohen and Beltramo 1975).

The current linguistic situation is extremely complex: some factors militate towards language maintenance, others to language shift. The fact that most immigration took place in substantial numbers over a relatively short period of time facilitated the cohesive organization of the community. The balanced sex ratio meant that the community could reproduce itself without the need to 'marry out'. This, together with a strong feeling of family belongingness and other basic values typical of Greek Cypriot culture, have bound the community tightly together.

Further, the 'myth of return' has given the first generation, at least, a strong incentive for maintaining their language. Language maintenance has been further reinforced in the case of first-generation immigrants by the isolation of the women and the aged who, because they either worked in Cypriot factories or

TABLE 12.2 Language data on the Greek community in London, extrapolated from LMP (1985)

	Greek	English
% of respondents who know language fairly well or very well (*N*=93)	94	72
% of people in respondent's household who know language fairly well or very well (*N* = 673)	66	79

stayed at home, have not needed to mix with the host community. The role of the mother and the grandparents was thus very important in transmitting the mother tongue to the second generation.

The majority of the second generation was thus brought up speaking Cypriot Greek. However, negative attitudes towards bilingualism on the part of educationalists (*cf* Wright 1980) encouraged parental anxiety and has no doubt helped to shift the emphasis from mother tongue maintenance to mastering the English language. There is definite evidence of a strong shift to English.

A comparison of the adult respondents' estimates of their own language skills and those of the entire household (which includes all but the very young British-born children) shows a marked reduction in the proportion of people reported as speaking Greek very well or fairly well and an increase in the proportion of speakers with competence in English (Table 12.2). The fact that some 82 per cent of the children in Haringey were reported as using only or mainly English when speaking to their siblings also lends support to the pattern of language shift. The ILEA (1987) *Language Census* provides still further data suggestive of language shift: some 48.4 per cent of Greek children were considered to be fluent in English, a figure significantly higher, for instance, than for Bangladeshi or Vietnamese children (though noticeably lower than for German or Italian children). In contrast, there is evidence of language stability inasmuch as Greek respondents reported that Greek was used mainly or exclusively in some 59 per cent of interactions between the bilingual members of the household.

TABLE 12.3   Language in the workplace, extrapolated from LMP (1985)

% of those working respondents where at least one fellow worker speaks Greek	66
% of working respondents where all fellow workers speak Greek	26
% of respondents (who work for someone else) where the boss speaks Greek	51
(N = 101)	

Language, culture and community

The ethnic economy to which we have already referred provides considerable support for the use of Greek. Data from ALUS (LMP 1985) set out in Table 12.3 point to the linguistic consequences of this economy in the Greek community in London.

For very many Greek Cypriots, then, the place of work offers many opportunities for the use of the mother tongue. However, the Greek language is supported not only by the economic activities of the community but a whole range of religious, social and cultural activities. The Greek Orthodox Church plays a central role in community life, with over seventy churches spread throughout the country.

Weddings, christenings and funerals are a focal point for Cypriots. Weddings, in particular, have economic and social as well as religious implications. In addition to the other presents given to the couple, there is the so-called *bloumisma* or 'money-pinning'; it is also the Greek Cypriot custom to have many *koumbaros* (best men) or *koumeras* (best women) who are expected to offer gifts of money which are often fixed in advance by the couple's families. The best men and women are expected to sign their names on a white ribbon as a means of showing not only that they have witnessed the wedding but that they have

TABLE 12.4 Language use in a range of settings, extrapolated from LMP (1985)

% of respondents speaking only Greek with the first person mentioned as someone they spent free time with	54
% of respondents who said most or all of their neighbours could speak Greek	15
% of respondents who said they had seen a video in Greek in the last 4 weeks	35
% of respondents who said they sometimes visited a shop where Greek was spoken by the shopkeeper or assistants	90
% of respondents who had a Greek doctor	35

(N = 193)

fulfilled their 'duty' to the families. Weddings also offer families valuable opportunities for matchmaking in a community anxious to promote intermarriage. Failure to attend a wedding when invited is considered to be a great social slur and is usually interpreted as an unwillingness to fulfil financial obligations or to demonstrate social solidarity.

Various community organizations fulfil a social and welfare role within the community. Very often these organizations are not simply based on a geographical area within London, but are composed of people from the same area in Cyprus. They are also responsible for promoting a wide range of cultural events, such as films, talks, concerts, dances, exhibitions and food tasting. Often internationally famous artists are brought in from both Greece and from Cyprus.

This close-knit community with its wide range of social and cultural activities thus provides many opportunities for the use of Greek. Again, corroborating evidence is supplied by the LMP's (1985) ALUS (Table 12.4).

There are also many other signs of strong ethnolinguistic vitality within the British Greek Cypriot communities. Several pirate radio stations have recently sprung up, one of which has received a licence to broadcast as an official radio station; there are a large number of video shops with Greek films imported from Greece or Cyprus; there are Greek bookshops, youth and football clubs, political associations and pressure groups and a wide range of community newspapers and newsletters are produced locally by different political and community groups. Much local government and health education information is available in Greek; school annual reports and other relevant documents are sometimes translated into Greek and local libraries are well supplied with Greek dictionaries and books.

Ethnic identity is also reinforced by strong ongoing links with Cyprus. Contact takes the form of visits; parcels with food and other gifts; regular cheques for the upkeep of elderly parents; attendance at important social and religious events such as weddings, christenings and funerals; relatives coming to Britain for medical treatment. Moreover, due to the considerable prosperity of some Cypriots in Britain, good numbers have been able to invest money in Cyprus by buying a flat or land in their home village or building on land left to them by their families. Business, government and professional links between the two countries are also strong. Cypriot newspapers and magazines are freely available and keep British Cypriots closely in touch with what is going on at home. Improvements in communication and transport have also helped to maintain contact.

Education and language reproduction

Mother tongue teaching has been provided traditionally by the Greek Orthodox Church and the twenty-three London churches currently have their own network of classes. Increasingly, however, this role is being taken over by the various parents' groups. The longest standing of these groups is the Greek Parents' Association in Haringey which dates back to the 1950s. Today, however, there are many more very active parents' associations all over London which are responsible for providing mother tongue teaching in the community. Many community members see mother tongue teaching as the key to problems of language and culture maintenance. Greek Cypriot immigrants have tried to bring up their children with a strong sense of their ethnic identity, sending them to afternoon or Saturday morning schools to learn the Greek language, history and culture. Greekness, of course, involves in most people's minds not only ethnicity but also the Orthodox faith.

Mother tongue teaching activities are inevitably concentrated in the areas of greatest Greek settlement. The first classes in Haringey, for instance, date back to 1955; by 1982 the LMP's *Mother Tongue Teaching Directory* was listing some 90 classes and some 2,700 pupils on roll. Other parts of the country slowly took their lead from London: classes in Coventry were established around 1963 and in Bradford, much later, in 1979. Children spend between 1 and 4 hours a week at these community-run classes though average attendance would seem to be in the region of 3 hours.

Both the Greek Cypriot authorities and the Greek government have, over the years, supported the community-run classes by providing a limited number of teachers, materials and other financial support. In 1988 the Cyprus High Commission provided twenty-five teachers to work in community schools; the Greek government supplied a further forty-one teachers in the same period, some of whom worked in the Greek Embassy School (for further discussion, see below), while the rest taught in community-run schools. The use of Greek-trained teachers and Greek teaching materials, however, is not without its problems and many British-trained teachers have found it essential to modify both teaching styles and content to the need of their British-born pupils. Another pressing issue is the place of Cypriot dialect. Although parents wish their children to learn to speak and read SMG, many British-trained teachers feel that the Cypriot dialect has a place both as a medium of instruction and in resource material.

More recently, local authorities have also acknowledged the work of community classes. Patterns of LEA support for community-run classes vary considerably. For instance, LMP (1985) report that the LEA provided either teachers' salaries or free accommodation for the three classes in Coventry in 1981; while neither salaries nor free accommodation were offered for the three classes in Bradford which were operating during the same period. In Haringey in 1982, the situation was more complex still: the LEA provided both salaries and free accommodation for 12 classes, either salaries or accommodation for 4 classes and no support at all for a further 74 classes. At the time of writing, ILEA offer free accommodation and a small grant to cover expenses but not teachers' salaries to all recognized voluntary groups running mother tongue classes.

Sixty per cent of the children who reported themselves as Greek speakers in the LMPs (1985) School Language Survey in Haringey also said that they were literate in Greek, although the differences between girls and boys on this question reached statistical significance, with a smaller proportion of boys reporting literacy skills. It is our experience that boys and girls attend classes in equal numbers up to the age of 10, but from this point onwards many boys seem to show less enthusiasm. This may be due to the tendency within the Greek community to exert greater control over daughters than sons, and also to the widely noted tendency in the population at large for boys to show less interest in language learning (Moys et al 1980).

In addition to these community-run classes, there are two full-time Greek-medium schools in London. The first full-time primary day Greek school was established in 1980–81 under the auspices of the Orthodox Church and was housed in the Greek Orthodox Church of Apostle Andreas in Camden Town. It then had 8 pupils, 3 of whom were the children of ex-King Constantine.

In October 1983 the Greek Socialist Goverment set up the second full-time primary day school in Holland Park, following a rift between the teaching staff, parents and management of the former school. In 1984 the Hellenic College was established in Knightsbridge attracting children of Greek-speaking entrepreneurs and diplomats. The current number of pupils on roll is 150 and it is a fee-paying establishment. The syllabus tends to put more emphasis on the teaching of English and on preparing pupils towards entry into British rather than Greek or Cypriot Higher Educational Establishments.

The Greek Embassy School, in contrast, functions under the aegis of the Greek Ministry of Education, following the exact syllabus taught at schools in Greece with a small provision for English teaching. In the late 1980's an attempt was made to set up the secondary section of the school and currently the first two years of secondary education are in place. The education here is provided free — including all text books. In 1988 the government purchased a building in West London to house the school.

Some 120 children currently attend the Greek Embassy School, 60 per cent of whom come from Greek Cypriot families and the remainder from Greek families. The school accepts children from the age of $4\frac{1}{2}$ to 14 and it is hoped to extend this provision to the age of 18 in the near future. The idea is to provide a bilingual education. The main input is in the mother tongue, following the mainland Greek pattern of education. However, as the children progress through the school, the use of Greek is supplemented increasingly with English in those areas normally associated with the British primary-school curriculum. English teachers are recruited locally and are paid by the Greek government. The aim is to enable any child who leaves the school to integrate with the minimum of difficulty either into the Greek or the British education systems. Because children come to the school from all over London, the School Parents' Association organizes a fleet of buses which pick up and drop off children at their homes.

In recent years, however, responsibility for mother tongue teaching has fallen increasingly within the sphere of interest of LEAs. Today in ILEA over twenty Greek mother tongue classes have been set up in mainstream schools, with a further thirty-five classes in the London borough of Haringey where the majority of the Greek Cypriot community is concentrated. These classes take place both within the school curriculum and outside.

A small amount of research has taken place on the role of Greek within the maintained education sector. The Mother Tongue Project, jointly sponsored by the EC, the ILEA and the Schools Council, began work in 1981. Its aim was to produce materials, initially in Greek and Bengali, which would help primary-school children develop literacy skills in the mother tongue alongside English. It was also hoped to develop strategies which would help monolingual English teachers to encourage bilingual children to make use of their full repertoire for learning purposes (see Tansley, Nowaz and Roussou 1985, for details of the materials arising from this project).

References

ALEXIOU, M. (1982) 'Diglossia in Greece'. In W. Haas (ed) *Standard Languages Spoken and Written*, Manchester: Manchester University Press, pp 156–192.

ANAXAGOROU, N. (1984) 'Code-switching: language change in two generations of Cypriot Greeks in London'. Unpublished M.Phil. thesis, University of Cambridge.

ANTHIAS, F. (1982) 'Politics, class and ethnicity with special reference to Greek Cypriots in the UK'. Unpublished Ph.D. thesis, Bedford College, University of London.

ANTHIAS, F. (1984) 'Some issues affecting Greek Cypriots in Britain: an ethnic profile'. In M. Roussou (ed) *Greek Outside Greece, a Profile of a Greek speaking Community in Contemporary Britain*, London: National Council for Mother Tongue Teaching, pp 4–8.

CONSTANTINIDES, P. (1977) 'The Greek Cypriots: factors in the maintenance of ethnic identity'. In J. Watson (ed) *Between Two Cultures*, Oxford: Basil Blackwell, pp 269–300.

DOWLING, T. and EDWIN, F. (1915) *Hellenism in England*. London: The Faith Press.

FASOLD, R. (1985) *The Sociolinguistics of Society*. Oxford: Blackwell.

GEORGE, V. and MILLERSON, G. (1967) 'The Cypriot community in London', *Race* **8**: 277–92.

GILES, H. and POWESLAND, P. (1975) *Speech Style and Social Evaluation*. London: Academic Press.

HERNANDEZ-CHAVEZ, E., COHEN, A. and BELTRAMO, A. (1975) *El Lenguaje de los Chicanos*. Arlington, Virginia: Center for Applied Linguistics.

Inner London Education Authority (ILEA) (1978, 1981, 1983, 1985, 1987) *Language Census*. London: ILEA Research and Statistics.

Linguistic Minorities Project (LMP) (1985) *The Other Languages of England*. London: Routledge & Kegan Paul.

MOYS, A., HARDING, A., PAGE, B. and PRINTON, V. S. (eds 1980) *Modern Languages Examinations At Sixteen Plus: A Critical Analysis*. London: Centre for Information on Language Teaching and Research.

NEWTON, B. (1983) 'Stylistic levels in Cypriot Greek', *Mediterranean Language Review* **1**: 55–63.

OAKLEY, R. (1970) 'The Cypriots in Britain', *Race Today* **2**: 99–102.

OAKLEY, R, (1979) 'Family, kinship and patronage: the Cypriot migration to Britain'. In V. Saifullah Khan (ed) *Minority Families in Britain*, London: Macmillan, pp 12–34.

ROUSSOU, M. (ed) (1984) *Greek Outside Greece: A Profile of a Greek speaking Community in Contemporary Britain*. Proceedings from the First National Conference for Greek, London: National Council for

Mother Tongue Teaching and Schools Council Mother Tongue Project.

STAVRINIDES, Z. (1987) 'Community life', *The Greek Review* Feb: 19

TANSLEY, P., NOWAZ, H. and ROUSSOU, M. (1985) *Working with Many Languages: A Handbook for Community Language Teachers*. London: School Curriculum Development Committee.

TOSI, A. (1984) *Immigration and Bilingual Education*. Oxford: Pergamon.

WALVIN, J.(1984) *Passage to Britain*. Harmondsworth: Penguin.

WRIGHT, J. (1980) *Bilingualism in Education*. CUES Occasional Paper No. 1, London: Centre for Urban Educational Studies.

The Turkish speech community

Aydın Mehmet Ali

Söz gümüşse suküt altındır
If words are silver, silence is golden.

Is silence and a dislike for superfluous words as deeply engrained in the community as the proverb implies? And, if so, has this been used as a convenient excuse by mainstream society for over-looking the legitimate needs of Turkish speakers? The situation of the Turkish community has been poorly documented and researched. All too often, Turkish speakers are grouped with other Europeans, thereby masking the extent of their educational underperformance. The increasing incidence of racial attacks on Turkish people, like that of various other ethnic minorities, goes largely unreported. Turkish people in Britain thus emerge not only as a silent minority, but very much as a silenced minority.

Turkish people in the UK can be divided into two main groups: an older and larger community of Turkish Cypriots and a more recent, and numerically smaller, community of migrants from Turkey. The two communities have a great deal in common; they also differ in a number of important respects. This chapter will attempt to describe these similarities and differences by tracing the social, historical and linguistic backgrounds of the communities in question.

The sociolinguistic situation in Turkey and Cyprus

Varieties of Turkish are spoken in many parts of the world from Macedonia to Siberia, but most speakers are concentrated in Turkey, Cyprus, Greece, Yugoslavia, the USSR and, more recently, in all the inner cities of the major European countries where the *Gastarbeiter*, or guest worker system, has been in operation since the early 1960s. Estimates of the numbers of Turkish speakers vary from 45 million (ILEA 1987) to 95 million (Ediskun 1985) to 150 million (Mardin 1984). It is amusing to speculate on the thought that Turkish may be on the way to becoming a European lingua franca. For the purposes of the present discussion, however, the main focus of attention will be Cyprus and Turkey, the two countries of origin of the Turkish speech community in the UK.

There is a great deal of linguistic variety within Turkey. In addition to small numbers of other Turkic languages such as Azerbaijani, Turkmen and Indo-European languages such as Armenian, Greek and Kurdish are spoken by sizeable minorities. Arabic is used by some people in the south and also by those who are joining the new religious revivial. However, the official language of Turkey is standard Turkish which is based on the Istanbul variety. All educational, cultural, political and official communications are conducted in standard Turkish and there is often considerable intolerance towards other language varieties. The existence of one of the largest linguistic minorities, the Kurds, was until recently officially denied and speaking, writing or even making reference to the language was punishable by imprisonment.

Turkish is the most important member of the Turkic group of languages which belong to the Altaic family. It has two extremely distinctive characteristics. The first is vowel harmony, whereby all the vowels in a word share certain phonological features. Thus, the plural suffix will vary according to the vowel in the noun: *ev* (house) becomes *evler*, while *at* (horse) becomes *atlar*. Turkish is also an agglutinative language which adds suffix after suffix and produces words which may be the equivalent of a whole phrase or sentence in English –

gelemeyebilirim	– I may not be able to come
gelemeyebiliriz	– we may not be able to come
gelebiliriz	– we may be able to come

Turkish was written in Arabic script from the time the Turks were converted to Islam until 1928 when President Mustafa Kemal Ataturk decreed the introduction of a slightly modified Roman alphabet consisting of 29 letters. Language reform has also taken place in other areas. Since the end of the last century there have been attempts to rid Turkish of its Ottoman elements. The *Türk Dil Kurumu* (Turkish Language Society) set up by Atatürk was particularly active in the 1970s. Many *öz türkçe* (pure Turkish) words have been introduced into the language, some with more success than others. The main effect of these changes, however, would seem to have been to increase the gap between the educated elite and the rest of the population.

These changes have sometimes been met with some amusement in Cyprus. Because of its physical separation from Turkey, Cypriot Turkish, like Cypriot Greek, has tended to remain more conservative. We have discovered with the introduction of *öz türkçe* words that the expressions which we were 'correcting' and 'modernising' in the language of our grandparents in the 1960s were, after all, a more 'pure' version of Turkish!

Cypriot Turkish has traditionally been accorded low status and has often been dismissed as 'incorrect' or as 'pidgin Turkish'. Increasingly, however, Turkish Cypriots are defending the legitimacy of their own variety. An interesting development following the invasion of the north of the island by the Turkish army in 1974 has been the active resistance to linguistic assimilation. This has led to a great deal of researching of the past, attempts to define what is 'Cypriot' as opposed to 'Turkish', and a renewed interest in oral history, songs, lullabies, *mani* (rhyming couplets), and plays written in Cypriot Turkish.

Before the invasion, Turkish was spoken by about 120,000 people. As well as their distinctive local varieties, Cypriots are also exposed to standard Istanbul Turkish through the school system, officialdom, radio, television, magazines and newspapers. The composition of the Turkish community has undergone important changes since 1974. It is estimated that between 30,000 and 60,000 settlers from Turkey have arrived on the island since this time and that, together with the Turkish army, they outnumber the original Turkish Cypriot population which recently fell below 100,000 as a result of emigration to Britain, Australia, Canada and the USA.

The original Turkish Cypriot community had a very high level of literacy which was reflected in the exceptionally high number of university graduates per capita of population. This situation has changed with the arrival of new settlers, many of whom have come from Anatolia where educational provision is poor. It is widely assumed that literacy levels amongst women are particularly low though no statistics are currently available.

The Turkish speech community in Britain

There are many difficulties in assessing the actual size of the Turkish speaking communities in Britain. Official statistics do not, for instance, distinguish between Greek and Turkish Cypriots and the Census data refers only to 'Cyprus born' people. In addition, no information is available on numbers of British born children and grandchildren of Turkish and Turkish Cypriot settlers (Mehmet Ali, 1986). It is impossible to estimate the total numbers of speakers within the UK with any degree of accuracy, but informed guesses place the figure between 80,000 and 100,000.

The vast majority of Turkish speakers are concentrated in the London area. When the ILEA first started collecting data on the language background of its pupils in 1978, Turkish speakers formed the largest linguistic minority; since that time, numbers of Bengali speaking children have increased, but Turkish children have consistently remained as the second largest group.

TABLE 12.5 Numbers of Turkish Speakers Reported in the ILEA Language Census (1981–1987)

Year	Numbers	% PHLOE
1981	4418	9.8
1983	4316	8.6
1985	4383	7.7
1987	4495	6.9

*PHLOE = Pupils with a home language other than or in addition to English

Migration from Turkey and Cyprus followed very different patterns. Cypriot settlement preceded emigration from Turkey and dates back to the 1950s when the British government was actively seeking labour. In the 1960s, the birth of the Republic of Cyprus and the subsequent fighting between Greek and Turkish communities, further encouraged migration to Britain, often in a bid to gain entry before the enactment of increasingly stringent immigration legislation. With the occupation of the northern part of the island, a further 9,000 Greek and Turkish Cypriot refugees came to England. In the majority of cases, whole families migrated, though sometimes the men arrived first to be joined within a short space of time by their families.

Migration from Turkey began in the early 1970s. Men tended to arrive first, bringing over their wives and children in the late 1970s and early 1980s. This coincided with the closing of the gates to the *Gastarbeiter* in the rest of Europe by 1975 and the military take-over in Turkey in 1980. There were two distinct groups of new arrivals: poorly educated people from the rural areas and well-educated professionals from the cities (Mehmet Ali 1989).

The initial Cypriot communities in London were established around Camden, Finsbury Park, the Angel, Islington, Stoke Newington, Deptford and Camberwell. Turkish Cypriots have now moved out to Haringey and other outer London boroughs and there are also sizeable groups scattered throughout Britain in cities such as Manchester, Birmingham, Edinburgh and Cardiff, as well as in parts of the Midlands, Kent and Essex. People from

Turkey have mainly settled around Hackney, Islington, Haringey and Southwark where they could easily find employment in the thriving Turkish Cypriot ethnic economy.

The Turkish speech community is now very much a part of the London way of life. Apart from the kebab shops, supermarkets, bakers, boutiques, video shops, insurance agencies, dry-cleaners, cafés and restaurants, there are many successful large businesses in import and export and the clothing industry. Green Lane, London, is known as 'The Ladder' or 'The Capitol' by some Cypriots. It starts at Newington Green with the predominantly Turkish communities and moves north as far as the predominantly Greek Cypriot communities of Wood Green.

Whereas most first-generation Turkish speakers are employed in the ethnic economy, the second and third generations are increasingly moving outside the traditional niches. A relatively recent development has been the policy of some councils to employ bilingual staff. While this has opened up many opportunities for younger people, it must be noted that the proportion of Turkish-speaking employees in areas where there is a large Turkish community is smaller than that of any other ethnic minority group (GLC 1986).

Changing patterns of language use

Patterns of language behaviour in the Turkish community are highly variable. The shift to English tends to be more marked in the case of Turkish Cypriots who have, in most cases, been established in the UK much longer than the more recent arrivals from Turkey. Even within these two main groups, however, there is likely to be a great deal of variation. The Cypriot group includes older people who know little English as well as the British-born generations; while the Turkish group consists both of educated professionals, who either had some knowledge of English on arrival or who have attended classes, and people with little education who came from rural areas who do not see the need to learn English when they can survive without difficulty in the community. Males report a higher level of English skills than females, no doubt because they have more contact with the English-speaking community outside the home (LMP 1985). A whole range of language behaviour is thus to be found, ranging from the monoglot Turkish speaker to British-born children and young adults whose dominant language may be English.

The only source of evidence for patterns of language use in the Turkish community is the LMP (1985) Adult Language Use

Survey (ALUS) conducted in Haringey in the early 1980s (see Table 12.5). The shift from Turkish to English becomes clear, for instance, when we consider respondents' estimates of their own language skills and those of their household as a whole. The inclusion of children results in an increased rate of reporting of English skills; reduced competence in Turkish; and an overall increase in the level of bilingualism.

Unfortunately, no information is available for Turkish children's self-reports of language use. Adult estimates, however, suggest a significant shift to English. Nearly all children have a receptive competence in Turkish and many are able to use the mother tongue in conversation with their parents and older members of the community. In the company of their siblings, however, some 61 per cent were reported as using only or mostly English. The younger generation also exercise the prerogative of the young and speak in Turkish when they do not wish to be understood by English speakers and in English when they do not want to be understood by Turkish speakers.

Irrespective of generation, the influence of English on Turkish can be clearly heard. There has been a free borrowing of words for new concepts, objects and events such as 'roundabout' and

TABLE 12.6 Data on the language skills in the Turkish community, extrapolated from LMP (1985)

	Turkish	English
% of respondents who know language fairly well or very well (N= 197)	98	75
% of people in respondent's household who know language fairly well or very well (N= 761)	87	80

'part-time' to complete the gaps in people's everyday language. This process is applied in some domains but not others. *Hükümet*, for instance, is used for a whole range of British institutions, including government, the local council, DHSS office, council housing, child benefit, social security, tax office, social services and many others. But it is also interesting to note that many easily accessible Turkish words, used in the past and in the country of origin, have been replaced by English equivalents.

Sentence construction and vowel harmony are more impervious to change:

Shopping'e gideceğim – I will go shopping
Yarın off um – Tomorrow I'm off

It is important to note that not only the younger generation but the older generation, too, adapt their language in this way, almost as a point of demonstrating their achievements in English. This would appear to be a widespread phenomenon. Gözaydın (1982), for instance, points to the way in which German words are used in a similar way in Turkish publications in Germany, thus legitimizing their use in the community.

Language, culture and community

The family clearly plays a vital part in the maintenance of the mother tongue. So, too, does the wider community. In common with other large linguistic minority groups, Turkish speakers are able to meet all their needs without having to use English. This ethnic economy to which I have already referred has important linguistic implications. Almost a quarter of the Turkish sample which took part in the LMP (1985) ALUS reported that they work in environments where all their workmates speak Turkish; almost a third worked for employers who speak Turkish; and well over half work in jobs where there is at least one other Turkish speaker.

Magazines and newspapers from Cyprus and Turkey are readily available in grocers' shops. A number of shops also sell community newspapers published in London and Turkish books. In recent years, some local authorities, including Islington, Hackney, Southwark and Haringey have set up units to translate information into Turkish and act as interpreters. The Multi-Ethnic Women's Health Project in Hackney and some law centres have also translated selected leaflets. In addition, some local authorities have appointed community development officers to liaise with the community.

There is also a wide variety of clubs and community organizations which support the use of Turkish. Every weekend there are several weddings, engagement or circumcision parties where a live band is present. Cultural evenings are also organized by various political and community groups. In all these activities, Turkish is used for speech-making, poetry reciting, songs, plays and social interaction.

The football clubs are another well-known phenomenon. Every Sunday over a hundred clubs play each other in leagues, mainly at Hackney Marshes. Football is serious business with money changing hands. Interestingly, many young men from the Afro-Caribbean community as well as a smaller number of English players take part in the Turkish clubs. Party politics also influence allegiances on the football field.

The ample opportunities for interaction both outside and inside the family with other Turkish speakers are reflected, for instance, by responses to a number of ALUS questions set out in Table 12.6.

Language maintenance is supported not only by extensive use of Turkish in the community but by the many close links with Turkey and Cyprus. People often save money to buy land and houses in Cyprus or Turkey as a preparation for retirement, for their daughters' dowries or for additional income for the family. This in turn leads to a very dynamic relationship with the home countries, especially when the relative closeness and easy accessibility of Cyprus and Turkey are taken into account. More

TABLE 12.7 Language in a range of settings, extrapolated from LMP (1985)

% speaking Turkish to the first person they mentioned as someone they spent free time with	73
% who said most or all of their neighbours could speak Turkish	45
% who said they had seen a film or video in Turkish in the last 4 weeks	64
% who said they sometimes visited a shop where Turkish was spoken by the shopkeeper or assistants	96
% who had a doctor who could speak Turkish	45
(N = 197)	

frequent visits to the home countries are helping to ensure that British-born children are more enthusiastic about wanting to learn Turkish than was the case in the 1970s and that they are speaking Turkish more fluently.

These links are not limited to family visits. The London-based Turkish Cypriot community, for instance, is now being taken seriously as a political and economic force, as witnessed by the growing numbers of visits from the Head of State, party leaders and Members of Parliament from Cyprus who come to raise funds or defend their political views. It is ironic that the poor, uneducated and, at times, despised people who left Cyprus thirty years ago have now been put on the agenda as having a political say.

Education and language reproduction

The inevitable shift towards English in the second and subsequent generations has caused a great deal of concern within the community. The assimilationist thrust of English teaching during the 1960s and 1970s (*cf* Edwards 1983; Reid 1988) meant that the mother tongues of Turkish and other bilingual children received little or no recognition. One of the consequences of these pressures was a desire to conform to English expectations as a means of resisting racism and rejection. Many Turkish-speaking children, for instance, abandoned their own names and took on English nicknames.

A number of factors, however, have resulted in children viewing their bilingualism more positively. Mother tongue classes can be traced back to 1959 when teachers were supplied by the Turkish government and Turkish Cypriot authorities in response to community pressure for their children to maintain their mother tongues. The effects of these classes, however, were double-edged. Although they were useful in placing language as an issue on the community agenda, it can also be argued that, together with the unsympathetic attitude of mainstream educators towards bilingualism, they played a part in alienating many young people from learning Turkish. Teachers used methods and materials which were not sensitive to the needs of children living in the UK and many children rejected the classes.

The Turkish government and Turkish Cypriot authorities continue to supply a small number of teachers on two-yearly contracts. Within the ILEA, premises for community language classes are provided rent free and a small grant is made to running expenses in the case of recognized voluntary bodies. Outside ILEA the situation is more variable. For instance, LMP (1985), report two classes in Haringey where either teachers' salaries or accommodation were provided by the local authority and two classes where neither teachers' salaries nor accommodation were provided.

The nature of classes varies a great deal. In some cases, emphasis is placed on bilingualism and language development. But language cannot be divorced from culture and culture is not uniform. 'Whose culture and for what purposes?' are questions which need to be answered and which preoccupy some of us in the linguistic minority communities. Religion is an important element in classes run by the mosque and the Qur'ān is also taught in Arabic.

Teaching materials continue to be a problem. A very small number of bilingual story-books have been produced commercially, but most materials are either home-made or brought from Turkey and are geared to the Turkish education system. In Germany and the Netherlands, better quality materials have been produced (eg Özhan and Binyazar 1982–85; Nederlands Bibliotheek an Lektuur Centrum 1981–86). These are more relevant to children living in Europe and have a multicultural, humanistic and universal approach. In this country, however, there has been little attempt to produce quality educational materials in Turkish.

The efforts of community activists, parents, professionals and teachers ultimately led to Turkish being introduced into state education. The first bilingual nursery in the ILEA was the Turkish Education Group Nursery set up in Hackney in 1984. Since then several other nurseries and crèches have also been established.

The ILEA and Haringey have appointed advisory teachers as well as specialist teachers of Turkish, both in the primary and in the secondary sectors. Specialist teachers of Turkish work in the same way as teachers of other community languages. They usually operate in a team-teaching situation, using Turkish to help children understand the relevant subjects. At the secondary level, greater emphasis is placed on teaching Turkish as a subject. Standard Turkish is offered by various schools as a GCSE and A level subject. For instance, there were 183 entries for the London East Anglian Group GCSE in Turkish and 120 entries at A level in summer 1988. These examinations are based on standard Turkish, although some attempts have been made to gain greater acceptance for the Cypriot variety. The option system operated by many schools also poses problems. Some children still have to choose between French and Turkish when it comes to examinations, which reinforces the argument that the schools are still operating in a tokenistic way.

The Turkish speech community has, with very few exceptions, failed to attract the attention of researchers. This is surprising in view of the fact that Turkish children constitute the second largest linguistic minority within the ILEA. It is also disturbing in view of their very low levels of educational achievement. Statistics from ILEA show that there has been more underachievement among Turkish children than in any other linguistic minority group (Mehmet Ali 1984). In 1985, for instance, a disproportionately small number of Turkish children took examinations at the age of 16. Of these, only 5 out of 268 children achieved passes in 5 or more subjects. How can a community in which literacy is widespread and higher education common in the country of origin find itself in the position of having the lowest achievement levels in British education?

I began this chapter with the reflection that 'If words are silver, silence is golden.' I would like to end by drawing on another proverb:

> Anlayana sivrisinek saz, anlamayana davul zurna az
> For those who understand, a mosquito is like a saz (the national stringed instrument); for those who don't even a davul (a large drum) and a zurna (a shrill sounding wind instrument) are not enough.

The need for research into the failure of Turkish children is an urgent priority. Any such research must take place in co-operation with the community and must be accountable to it. The mosquito may, in the end, serve another painful purpose, if people continue to ignore the sweet sound of the saz.

References

EDISKUN, H. (1985) *Türk Dilbilgisi* (Turkish Grammar). Istanbul: Remzi Kitabevi.

EDWARDS, V. (1983) *Language in Multicultural Classrooms*. London: Batsford.

GÖZAYDIN, N. (1982) Almanya 'da Calışan Türklerin Dilleri Üzerine (On the Language of Turkish People Working in Germany). Istanbul: *Bilim ve Sanat*.

Greater London Council (GLC) Equal Opportunities Unit (1986) *Head-count Information, Islington Council*. (1988) London.

Inner London Education Authority (ILEA) (1978, 1981, 1983, 1985, 1987) *Language Census*. London: ILEA Research and Statistics.

MARDIN, Y. (1984) *Colloquial Turkish*. London: Routledge & Kegan Paul.

MEHMET ALI, A. (1984) 'Why are we wasted?'. *Mult-Ethnic Education Review* 4(1): 7–12.

MEHMET ALI, A. (1989) 'The Turkish community in Britain: some comments and observations on the immigration patterns and the legal and social position', in *Language Issues* Vol. 3 No 1, pp. 19–23.

Linguistic Minorities Project (LMP) (1985) *The Other Languages of England*. London: Routledge & Kegan Paul.

Nederlands Bibliotheek an Lektuur Centrum (The Netherlands Library Service) (1981–86) *Moumouk, Alfabemizde Gezinti, Portakal Renginde Büyük Leke* (Moumouk, A Journey Through Our Alphabet, The Big

Orange Spot). The Hague, the Netherlands: Nederlands Bibliotheek an Lektuur Centrum.

OZHAN, I. and BINYAZAR, A. (1982–85) *Türçke, Dil ve Okuma Kitabı 5–10* (Turkish, Language and Reading Book 5–10). Berlin: Ararat Verlag.

REID, E. (1988) 'Linguistic minorities and language education – The English experience', *Journal of Multilingual and Multicultural Development* **9** (1 and 2): 181–92.

Further reading

The following books and articles are concerned with or refer to the Turkish speech community in Britain:

LADBURY, S. (1977) 'The Turkish Cypriots: ethnic relations in London and Cyprus'. In J. Watson (ed.) *Between Two Cultures*, Oxford: Basil Blackwell, *pp* 301–31.

MEHMET ALI, A. (1986a) 'Women and the Turkish Education Group', *Greater London Council's Women's Committee Bulletin*, No. 27: 57–8.

MEHMET ALI, A. (1986b) 'A critique of language and language education', *Multi-Ethnic Education Review* **5**(1): 9–13.

SWANN, LORD (1985) *Education for All*. London: HMSO.

TAYLOR, M. (1988) *Worlds Apart*. Windsor: Nelson for the National Foundation for Educational Research.

Chapter 13

The Italian speech community

Bruno Cervi

> Bergamo dialect: *Parla cuma ta maet* (Speak like you eat)
>
> Naples dialect: *Parla comma t'ha fatto mammate* (Speak like your mother made you)
>
> (Both sayings and many more to the same effect in different dialects, emphasize that one should speak the language of the community one belongs to)

It is estimated that some 200,000 Italian nationals live at present in the UK. They came to this country for different reasons at different times. From the middle of the nineteenth century there was a gradual build-up of an Italian presence. This presence, with very few exceptions, never became particularly conspicuous both because it developed over a long period of time and because it was not concentrated in particular areas. So much so, that until fairly recently little attention was given to the Italians as a community.

The sociolinguistic situation of Italian in Italy

Of all the Romance languages, Italian has maintained closest links with Latin. Its 60 million speakers are found not only in Italy, and in Switzerland, where Italian is one of the four official languages, but in Argentina, Australia, Brazil, Canada, Germany, the United States and the UK and various other countries where there are small but significant Italian communities.

Spoken Latin has evolved in different forms in different places under the influence of linguistic features of pre-Roman languages (substrata) and elements introduced by successive rulers (super-strata) from the fall of the Roman Empire to the unification of Italy in 1861. To number all the dialects which are spoken in Italy would be an impossible task, and the broad classification into four groups, northern, Tuscan, central and southern, with a ramification of subgroups, falls short of conveying the complexity of language diversity on Italian soil. Although mutual intelligibility between dialects might in some cases occur in areas over 100 kilometres apart, the language spoken in each village has distinctive phonological, morphological and semantic features from that spoken in the neighbouring village. To clear the ground of possible sources of misunderstanding, it must be specified that there is no geographically neutral accent in Italian equivalent to British 'Received Pronunciation'. Even among educated people, pronunciation varies locally.

In the fourteenth century, the Florentine dialect in which Dante wrote his *Divina Commedia* became the basis of a national literary language. This language, however, never became truly national and popular: it is estimated that, when the unification of Italy took place in 1861, only 2.5 per cent of the total population were able to use this form of Italian. Nearly a century later, at the time of mass emigration to England and elsewhere, a greater number of people had at least a passive knowledge of the national language. However, in rural areas the local dialect was the language of everyday transactions. Italian was normally introduced at school, as the medium of tuition. Outside school there were very few opportunities for using it: letter writing (as the dialects do not have a standardized written form); formal interaction with people outside the community; bureaucracy; and perhaps the sermon in church, on Sundays.

The interplay of dialects results in a number of varieties which are broadly categorized by Lepschy and Lepschy (1977) as: (a) standard Italian: (b) an inward-looking variety of Italian (high status regional koinê); (c) an outward-looking variety of dialect (urban dialect); and (d) local dialect. The availability of one or more varieties depends on location and socio-economic status. More often than not it was only the local varieties that the immigrants brought to this country and used in their households.

Italian speakers in Britain

The migration of Italians to the UK can be traced back to the fourteenth century. From then until around the middle of the last century it involved highly professional people from all over Italy,

but mainly from the north. The relevance of this movement was
not its size but the example it set. From the middle of the last
until the early decades of this century, migration from Italy involved two core occupational groups: itinerant hawkers and
pedlars and craftsmen and artisans, mostly from northern and
central Italy. These migrants and their descendants subsequently
developed links with the catering 'niche'. After the Second World
War, however, mass recruitment of unskilled labour drew abun-
dantly from southern Italy. In recent years, with the slackening
of demand for unskilled labour, Italian immigration is mainly
limited to highly mobile young people from all over Italy, who
have taken up temporary work, mainly in the tertiary sector.

London has received Italian migrants during all four historical
periods, whereas other areas have received Italian migrants
during certain periods and not others. Migrants who came to the
UK before the Second World War settled in different parts of the
country. Their links with the catering trade and subsequent competition encouraged dispersion. Chain migration led to the
settlement of groups coming from the same area in particular
locations (Palmer 1977).

After 1945 the destination for the mass-recruited Italian
migrants, coming almost exclusively from rural areas in southern
Italy, was towns where industrial settlements required unskilled
labour, like the brick-making industries of Bedford and Peter-
borough, or rural areas needing labour for agriculture. As Italian
migration to Britain has declined, the proportion of migrants
from the centre and north of Italy has increased at the expense
of that from south Italy (Colpi 1987).

Changing patterns of language use

The linguistic behaviour of the Italian community in Britain varies
according to the patterns of settlement, especially as far as the
first generation is concerned. Areas associated with the mass
recruitment of the 1950s have witnessed the formation of close-
knit communities of people whose history is similar, who come
from the same region or neighbouring regions, often from the
same village. The home dialects are often mutually intelligible
and therefore play a great role in community interaction. It is
often a crystallized form of dialect, that, outside its natural environment, has not followed the same evolution as the dialect
back home. Instead, these dialects are heavily loaded with
English borrowings. As Tosi (1984) suggests in his description of

the language use of the Italian community in Bedford, these borrowings, besides being sometimes used to replace items that are
different in different dialects, are a manifestation of the fact that
the vocabulary of the Italian immigrants is no longer sufficient to
express thoughts and habits in the new environment. The more
the topic is removed from the domestic domain, the heavier the
borrowings, especially when it comes to local services. But even
something as simple as a 'cup of tea' is usually offered in English,
as it represents a habit acquired in the new environment. The
resulting linguistic behaviour is code-mixing rather than code-
switching, as is shown in the following examples, quoted by Tosi
(1984):

Nun'ce stanna i _moni_, li sordi per le _olidei_.
There is no money for the holidays.

Stanno in copp'a '_basamento_, o'basement.
They are on top of the basement.

Il signor Consolo m'a data a'forma
The Consul give me the form.

L'anno passato m' suno _ritirato_.
I retired last year

In all of these cases, the underlined words either do not exist or
mean something different in Italian.

Standard Italian (or an approximation to it) is kept for interaction with Italian outsiders, not belonging to the community, or
with the Italian authorities. 'Survival English' is the language of
interaction at work and with British institutions. Gradually, the
English repertoire of the Italian immigrants expands to incor-
porate new words imported into the household by the
British-born children, but language loyalty rests with their home
dialect, which often dominates interaction between immigrant
and British-born children, in spite of their preference for and
greater proficiency in English.

The pattern of communication within the family circle is much
the same in areas with lower density and more heterogeneous
Italian communities. What may differ is the language used with
members of the community outside the family. In the absence of
a centrally oriented, homogeneous community, affiliation to a
church or a club is likely to encourage varieties closer to the
standard.

The linguistic behaviour of second-generation Italians, if we exclude those born to an inter-ethnic marriage, is very similar throughout Britain. Children are usually brought up speaking the home dialect or standard Italian, which is often the only language of the first child born to an Italian household prior to entering school (younger children are likely to interact in English with their older siblings) but the dramatic change in social network, occurring when they enter school, often results in the rejection of their first language, the use of which, however, is more or less enforced in interaction with parents.

The ILEA *Language Census* figures show a steady decline in the number of children reporting themselves as Italian speakers, set out in Table 13.1. This decline can be accounted for, partly by the drop in birth-rate and partly by the fact that second-generation Italians are now reaching school-leaving age. The learning of Italian in formal settings appears to cause children to reappraise their cultural heritage and positive values are attached both to the national language and the home dialect. From a pilot study (Cervi 1985) conducted on a sample of eighty-eight students of mother tongue Italian in mainstream schools, motivation to learn Italian appears to correlate positively with length of formal tuition. The same study shows that the subjects, regardless of their linguistic behaviour, which is unequivocally in the direction of English, evaluate Italian and their home dialect even more favourably.

Second-generation Italians are British citizens by birth, with no mark of their identity other than their names. They behave in a very similar way to their British peers and speak English with native proficiency. On the surface they could appear to be completely Anglicized; they often seem to go through a stage when they do not want to be anything but British, but this appears to be no more than a passing phase. They usually find they have to come to terms with their diverse origins. Those that become involved in language maintenance programmes, very likely at first

TABLE 13.1 Data on Italian pupils from ILEA *Language Census*, 1981–87

Year	Number	% PHLOE*
1981	2,808	63
1983	2,421	48
1985	2,102	37
1987	1,889	29

*PHLOE = Pupils with a home language other than, or in addition to English.

through parental pressure, seem gradually to foster a positive image of themselves as belonging to two different cultures.

None the less there is evidence of an inevitable shift to English. The Linguistic Minorities Project's (LMP) (1985) Adult Language Usage Survey (ALUS), for instance, shows that adult respondents reported higher levels of skill in Italian and correspondingly lower levels of skill in English for themselves than for the household as a whole (see Table 13.2). Although very young children were excluded, the household figures included their older British-born children. These data therefore give an indication of the extent of intergenerational language shift. It is also highly significant that 83 per cent of respondents in London, and 86 per cent in Coventry, reported that English was used only or mostly between children.

Language, community and culture

The myth of return is quite strong among the first-generation Italians in the UK and it is also present, albeit to a lesser extent, among the British-born children of Italian immigrants. On average, Italian families make a yearly trip to Italy. Correspondence with relations in Italy is gradually being phased out by the increasing availability of communication by telephone. This, in linguistic terms, gives more scope to the use of dialect. Italian video tapes circulate in various households and satellite television is beginning to provide direct links with Italian TV broadcasts not only to clubs but also to an increasing number of private households. Clubs and associations, often linked with the place

TABLE 13.2 Data on language skills in the Italian community, extrapolated from LMP (1985)

		Italian	English
% of respondents who speak and understand language fairly well or very well	Coventry (N = 108)	73	63
	London (N = 94)	81	69
% of people in respondents' households who speak and understand language fairly well or very well	Coventry (N = 387)	58	89
	London (N = 339)	76	86

of origin, Italian churches, parents' committees supporting at local level the extra-curricular community-run languages classes – all represent important focuses of social cohesion and provide a milieu where the use of Italian is validated.

For many Italians, the workplace provides still further opportunities to use the mother tongue. Again, the LMP (1985) ALUS provides useful information on the proportion of the community which either forms part of an ethnic community or else works alongside fellow Italians, as set out in Table 13.3. In such situations there is an inevitable shift to English, but Italian would none the less appear to continue to play an important part in interaction in the workplace.

TABLE 13.3   Italian in the workplace, extrapolated from LMP (1985)

% of working respondents where at least one fellow worker can speak Italian	Coventry London	43 65
% of working respondents where all fellow workers can speak Italian	Coventry London	6 28
% of working respondents (who work for someone else) where the boss can speak Italian	Coventry London	3 31
% of working respondents who use mostly only English to workmates	Coventry London	61 42

Coventry: $N = 81$
London: $N = 76$

Also, ALUS provides information on patterns of language use in a wide range of social settings and in the wider community. While it would appear that Italian is not spoken as widely as many other minority languages, Table 13.4 makes it clear that there are none the less many opportunities for its use outside the home.

Alongside the spontaneous forms of association, official institutions also support the use of Italian in the UK: the Italian Consulates, beside having a network of agents and correspondents in all major counties, are assisted by consultative bodies of democratically elected representatives of the community. The first poll for this institutional structure in 1986 attracted more than 8,000 voters for the constituencies of the Italian Consulate General in London alone. These figures are even more impressive in the light of the fact that the polling stations were sometimes scores of kilometres away from the prospective voter's residence.

TABLE 13.4   Data on Italian in a wide range of settings, extrapolated from LMP (1985)

% of respondents who said they spoke only Italian with the first person mentioned as someone they spent free time with	Coventy London	25 35
% of respondents who said most or all of their neighbours could speak Italian	Coventry London	8 16
% of respondents who said they had seen a film or video in Italian in the last 4 weeks	Coventry London	9 6
% of respondents who said that they sometimes visited a shop where Italian was spoken by the shopkeeper or assistants	Coventry London	75 93
% of respondents who had a doctor who could speak Italian	Coventry London	18 64

Coventry: $N=$ 108
London: $N=$ 94

Other relevant institutions are the various welfare organizations, offering Italian immigrants help in claiming benefits from the homeland (mainly pensions).

A number of periodical publications are addressed to the Italian community in the UK, including *La Voce degli Italiani*, published in London by the Scalabrini Fathers, with a circulation of 6,000 copies. *Backhill, Nuova Presenza, Londra Sera* and *Il Dialogo* are also published in London; and *Italiani in Scozia* and *Casa d'Italia Ltd*, are published in Glasgow. The Bedford community also has a radio broadcasting service.

Very little official literature, such as local government information, health education material and the like is translated into Italian. As for the reasons for this lack of concern on the part of relevant bodies, it could be true that the Italians are a particularly silent minority. Or, indeed, the need may not be registered, as second-generation children are usually in a position to understand information in English fully even if the first-generation immigrants may not always be.

Education and language reproduction

The important of language maintenance was realized by early

Italian immigrants. From the Italian School founded by G. Mazzini in 1841 until the early 1970s, classes of Italian, set up by voluntary bodies, flourished. However, in 1971 the Italian government stepped in to regulate these initiatives in all countries where a large-scale immigration of Italians had taken place (Law 3.3.1971, n. 153). This law is currently under revision as, among other shortcomings, it was not flexible enough to be adapted to different contexts in different parts of the world. Nevertheless, it is already implemented in different ways in different countries. In respect of children of school age, provisions are made available in order to; (a) facilitate access of children of Italian immigrants to the educational systems of the host countries (art. 2 Sect. a); (b) integrate the education that the children of Italian immigrants receive in the host countries with knowledge of the language and culture of the country of origin (art. 2 Sect. b).

The current interpretation of 'facilitating access to the educational systems' is teaching the language of the host countries. As this provision is generally made available by LEAs in the UK context, resources are concentrated on the latter aim. The provision is intended for pupils of mandatory school age in Italy (6–14), but it has become common practice in this country to delay the start of formal tuition in Italian by at least one year, as a number of primary-school headteachers were concerned that learning Italian would *per se* undermine achievement in English literacy. In recent years, however, increasing numbers of younger pupils have been joining Italian mother tongue classes. It has also become common practice to extend the provision up to 'A' level GCE examinations.

For the most part. community-run classes for Italian language and culture are held in rented premises – schools (only recently have some LEAs abolished rent charges for this activity), church halls or similar venues – and take place in the late afternoon/evenings or Saturdays. Pupils normally attend twice a week for $1\frac{1}{2}$ –2 hours per session, extended to 2–3 hours for A Level classes. The hostile attitude that was at one time displayed by host schools is by now a thing of the past. However, with very few exceptions, Italian teachers do not have access to the school equipment, nor are they allocated a cupboard to keep materials and equipment, which often means confining a lesson to chalk and talk practices.

Parents and authorities agree that the language to promote is the national language, the language giving social access both within the community here and back home, ensuring access to the Italian educational system in case of repatriation and enabling pupils to gain qualifications in the UK. The standard language is, however, more often than not, different from the language spoken at home and it is essential that teachers should capitalize on the interplay of the two varieties rather than promote the standard at the expense of the home dialect. The rejection of the home language may be detrimental to the child's relationship with the parents, a further reason why a foreign language approach is not suitable for the children of Italian origin.

While Catholic churches run by Italian missionaries constitute a focus of attraction for the Italian community, the Catholic religion itself does not represent a core value of Italian membership and it may only attract passing references in the community language programme. Italian culture, in contrast, is certainly one of the objectives of the provisions of the *corsi di lingua a cultura generale italian* (classes in Italian language and general culture). However, due to time constraints, the linguistic limitations of most participants and their concern with public examinations, most emphasis is placed on actual language teaching.

The ambivalent nature of these courses makes it possible to draw resources from two channels: materials for Italian as a foreign language and materials produced for use with Italian monolingual children. There are intrinsic limitations in Italian as a foreign language text – the limited market never encouraging adequate investment. These materials are, in any case, particularly unsuitable for pupils with Italian connections who are able to tackle, at least at a receptive level, more linguistically complex material.

The main drawback with material produced for use with monolingual children in Italy in relation to the needs of Italian children in this country is the discrepancy between linguistic complexity and subject-matter: what is designed for their contemporaries back home is linguistically too complex for them, and what is within their reach from a linguistic point of view does not interest them from the point of view of content.

Only recently have some Italian publishers started to produce books for *corsi integrativi di lingua a cultura generale italian all'estero* (language and general culture courses in Italian for pupils aboard). At first they consisted mainly of a collage of excerpts from books in use in Italian schools, whereas they now seem to follow more definite methodological guidelines. However, being addressed to a world-wide market, they cannot cater for the situation of the Italian pupils in the UK, and are therefore little more suitable than the material produced for use with monolingual pupils in Italy.

The teaching of a community language is a process which is not typical either of first- or of second-language aquisition. The process is complicated, in the case of Italian (as indeed it is for speakers of certain other community languages such as Panjabi/Urdu and Kachchi/Gujarati), by the fact that the target language is usually not the pupils' home language. Although this is to some extent the situation that teachers in Italy have to cope with, three major factors distinguish the two situations. First, dialect speakers in the Italian context have access to the national language through various channels and can therefore develop awareness of similarities and differences between dialect and standard and interact in the intermediate modes (see section on sociolinguistic situation in Italy, above); second, the home language of all pupils is the same dialect; and, finally, the national language they learn at school is also the medium of instruction of all other subjects.

Classes in Italian as a community language are usually made up of pupils with different home languages. There is increasing awareness among teachers that the home language should represent the starting-point for the development of competence in the national language, but the same teachers are still struggling to find a way to implement this awareness into classroom practice.

In the wake of EEC Directive No. 486/77 on the education of migrant children, the Italian authorities sought the integration of the provision offered by Legge 153 into mainstream schools. While the response of primary schools to this offer was rather limited, a number of secondary schools were quite eager to accept the offer of a teacher from the Italian authorities. The relative enthusiasm of secondary schools owes much to the well-established tradition of teaching Italian as a foreign language in mainstream schools and universities (albeit lagging behind French, German and Spanish), together with a very active Association of Teachers of Italian. Unofficial data collected personally in 1986, show that 7,635 pupils were then attending community-run classes for Italian in England and Wales. Of these, 5,849 were in extra-curricular provision, while 1,786 were learning Italian as part of their school curriculum. The last figure includes a small percentage of students from non-Italian families. London and the Home Counties contribute 50 per cent of the total number.

However, there are many problems in including the teaching of community language under the umbrella of modern languages. Such a course diverts attention from the specific needs of pupils attempting to maintain their linguistic and cultural heritage. A serious constraint also comes from the way Italian is time-tabled. When it is offered as an alternative to the more prestigious French, it often ends up by only attracting the less able children, while the brightest ones learn French at school and avail themselves of the extra-curricular provision to learn Italian, thus defeating the purpose of integrated community language classes. Other *ad hoc* arrangements – like withdrawing pupils from other lessons or setting Italian against lower-status subjects – entail different problems. The only viable solution would be to allocate the community language a place of its own within the curriculum. It should also be mentioned, however, that the integration into the mainstream is an option that does not always meet the favour of the parents who often fear that integration in mainstream institutions might entail assimilation and total loss of Italian identity.

Two European research initiatives have focused specifically on education and language reproduction in the Italian community. The first, the Bedfordshire EEC Mother tongue and Culture Project (1979–80), was essentially an experiment to determine whether Italian 5–9-year-old dialectophones could achieve, at the end of the primary cycle, a level of fluency and literacy in standard Italian approximating to that of English. It was assumed that 'the ability to develop bidialectalism (standard plus dialect) in an Italian situation through environmental exposure via natural transfer, was likely to be recreated in the classroom situation through conditions of intensive exposure to a selected repertoire of structures and vocabulary and oral practice under the teacher's guidance to "standardisation"' (Tosi 1984: 149). This structured and systematic approach would avoid the mere L2 approach and take full advantage of the children's native competence and fluency in their dialect. It was found that it was possible to encourage early literacy in standard Italian, a process which was facilitated by the relationship between writing and sound systems in Italian. The programme preserved native-like accents, which would have been lost with a later start. Not being restricted by pressure for grammatical accuracy, pupils were encouraged to produce written material.

The target population of the Bedfordshire Project was atypical in some ways of the Italian speech community as a whole. It must also be acknowledged, for instance, that the pupils involved in this experiment had fairly homogeneous dialect backgrounds and had the benefit of an early start. None the less, many of the strategies of the project are likely to have a much wider application and it is unfortunate that there has been little follow-up to the project in terms of actual practice: all too often, the natural development of the home language into standard Italian is interrupted in the name of helping with the acquisition of literacy in English.

A second European venture, the European Commission Project on Community Language in the Secondary Curriculum (1984–87) involved a team of teachers of community languages from mainstream schools. The aims of the project were to facilitate: the exploration of opportunities and constraints for the inclusion of community languages in normal curricular arrangements; the exchange of ideas on methodology (including consideration of external as well as internal examinations); and the production of materials for diverse situations and contexts, given different age/ability, group sizes, allocation of times, learning objectives.

The languages selected were Urdu, Panjabi and Italian. The association in the project with Urdu and Panjabi, which are unequivocally community languages, reinforced in the Italian teachers the awareness of the different needs of students extending their knowledge of the language of their cultural heritage from those of foreign language learners, and helped the construction of syllabi more purposeful for the participants. Unfortunately, there was not enough time to resolve all methodological questions, in particular that of catering for a variety of different home languages within the same class.

The needs of children from the Italian, and indeed other linguistic minority communities, have often been guessed rather than ascertained by means of the kind of extensive research that provides the objective evidence which can serve as a sound basis for educational policy-making. Initiatives along the lines of the Bedfordshire Project and the Community Languages in the Secondary School Project are clearly to be welcomed, though, in the current economic climate, it seems doubtful whether central government and local authorities will show the necessary commitment to act upon the recommendations which emerged from this research.

References

CERVI, BRUNO (1985) 'Language maintenance among children of Italian parentage in mainstream schools in England. A pilot study'. MA project, Birkbeck College, London.

COLPI, TERRI (1987) 'The social structure of the Italian community in Bedford, with particular reference to its places of origin and migration'. Ph.D thesis, St Catherine's College, Oxford.

Community Language in the Secondary Curriculum Project (1987) *E. C. Pilot Project: Community Language in the Secondary Curriculum. Report* 1984 – 87. University of London Institute of Education, Centre for Multicultural Education.

Inner London Education Authority (ILEA) (1981, 1983, 1985, 1987) *Language Census*. London: ILEA Research and Statistics.

LEPSCHY, A. L. and LEPSCHY, G. (1977) *The Italian Language Today*. Oxford: Pergamon Press.

Linguistic Minorities Project (1985) *The Other Languages of England*. London: Routledge and Kegan Paul.

TOSI, ARTURO (1984) *Immigration and Bilingual Education*. Oxford: Pergamon Press.

PALMER, R. (1977) 'The Italians: patterns of Migration to London'. In J. Watson (ed.) *Between Two Cultures*, Oxford, Basil Blackwell, pp. 242–68.

Chapter 14

The Portuguese speech community

Paula Santarita and Marilyn Martin-Jones

A minha patria e a lingua portuguesa
My motherland is the Portuguese language
(FERNANDO PESSOA (1982)

The Portuguese community is one of the smaller British linguistic minorities. It is a tight-knit group centred mainly on Greater London. The Portuguese are relatively recent arrivals on the British scene with most population movement taking place in the 1960s and the early 1970s. By 1975, the number of work permits granted to Portuguese nationals had been greatly reduced and the Portuguese community in Britain, at present, is predominantly middle-aged. Changes in European Community legislation planned for 1992, however, may well change both the pattern and composition of future migration and the linguistic outcomes of these developments remain to be seen.

The sociolinguistic situation in Portugal

Portuguese is a Romance language which, like all other languages in this group, developed from Latin as a result of colonization or political domination by the Roman Empire. In the Iberian Peninsula, Roman domination meant the loss of local languages and the predominance of Latin in all spheres of life. Portuguese developed mainly from 'vulgar Latin', the colloquial form of everyday Latin (at times the lingua franca in many parts of the Empire, particularly in Europe), though the influence of erudite, literary Latin can also be detected in early writing in Portuguese.

The second major influence in the development of the Portuguese language and culture was the arrival of the Arabs in the Iberian Peninsula. They stayed for eight centuries, being expelled from Portugal in 1249 and from neighbouring Spain only in 1492. The language retained its essentially Romance grammatical structure and the impact of Arabic was felt mainly in lexical borrowings for the many new technological advances introduced by the invaders. Linguistically, Portuguese is the one Iberian language variety which is closest to Gallego, the variety spoken in north-western Spain (see Ch. 15).

Because of Portugal's position as the leading European sea power in the fifteenth and sixteenth centuries, Portuguese came to be spoken in many different parts of the world. Today it is the official language not only of Portugal (including Madeira and the Azores), but also of Brazil, Mozambique, Angola, Guinea-Bissau and Cape Verde. It is estimated that by the end of this century Portuguese will be spoken by over 210 million people and, as such, will be the language with the fifth-largest number of speakers in the world (Cristovão 1987).

Portuguese is spoken by approximately 4 million emigrants settled in various countries around the world. There are, for instance, about 1 million Portuguese migrant workers in France. Numerically speaking, this makes Portuguese the second most important language after French. Some 25 per cent of the population of Luxemburg are of Portuguese origin. There is a large Portuguese community from Madeira in Venezuela and significant Portuguese settlements are also to be found in parts of North America, particularly California, Massachusetts and Toronto.

It is therefore most unfortunate that the Portuguese language should have such a low profile, not only in countries where there are considerable numbers of Portuguese settlers, but also in Portugal itself. The Portuguese government has done little more than pay lip service, until recently, to what should be done for the Portuguese language as one of the most valuable national assets, nor has it done anything of any real significance to support language planning and policies in the new Portuguese-speaking countries in Africa.

It is also important to note that English has played a significant part in Portuguese social history. After the Napoleonic Wars, British companies gained considerable control over key economic resources in Portugal, notably in the port and Madeira wine industries and in textiles. Moreover since the turn of the century, substantial interests in the tourist industry in Madeira and in southern Portugal have been controlled by British entrepreneurs.

Portuguese in Britain

The absence of reliable statistical data makes it difficult to assess the exact number of Portuguese migrants in the UK. By making projections from sources such as the 1981 Census, both the Portuguese Secretary of State for Emigration and community organizations suggest that the total number of settlers in the UK is approximately 40,000. However, official statistics do not take account of British-born children or elderly relatives who have come to join their families in Britain. The situation is also a very fluid one. A number of Portuguese workers have returned to Portugal in recent years. There are also a large number of seasonal workers in the Channel Islands who are sometimes included and sometimes excluded from official estimates. Serious consideration should be given to the possibility of including a language question in the 1991 Census. More comprehensive statistical data are needed for the development of social policies related to the welfare of migrant workers (Santarita 1983).

Approximately two-thirds of Portuguese residents live in the Greater London area. The second major concentration is in the Channel Islands where there are about 3,000 Portuguese, mainly from Madeira, and a further 5,000 seasonal workers with six-month work permits. The rest of the community is distributed between towns to the west of London, the north of England and some seaside resorts. In London, the areas of greatest concentration are Kensington and Chelsea, Lambeth, Hammersmith, Camden and Fulham, and Westminster. In Westminster, large numbers of Portuguese work as domestic staff or chauffeurs and live in tied accommodation (Santarita 1983).

The Portuguese community in London consists of two main groups: those from continental Portugal and those from Madeira. Many of the continental Portuguese settlers were skilled workers or artisans on arrival in the UK. Most migrated to Lisbon or another urban centre before leaving for Britain and therefore had access to a more standardized – or urbanized – variety of Portuguese in addition to their local or regional variety. The Madeira group is rather different. Many are from a peasant background and came directly to the UK from the mountainous rural areas of Madeira. However, there are no problems of intelligibility between the two groups and the main linguistic differences are in pronunciation. The rate of illiteracy is reputed to be higher in the Madeira group, but there are no real comparative data available to confirm or refute this assumption.

Portuguese migrants came mainly in the 1960s and early 1970s to work as cleaners, domestics, kitchen porters and assistant cooks in the National Health Service and in the hotel and catering industries. A survey conducted by the Portuguese Consulate in 1976 shows that 66 per cent of women and 55 per cent of men worked in these sectors. They were allowed into the country on work permits which were renewable every year and they were then granted permanent resident status after four years. (The migrants themselves refer to this development as *ficar livre no pais* – 'being free in the country'). During the first four years, migrants on work permits could change employers but not the type of employment, so that a person first taken on to work as a kitchen porter could work only as a kitchen porter. Restrictions of this kind have inevitably had a profound effect on the socio-economic status and mobility of the community as a whole.

The number of work permits issued has dropped significantly since 1975 and, as indicated at the beginning of this section, this has had a marked impact on the age structure of the population. The Adult Language Usage Survey (ALUS) carried out by the Linguistic Minorities Project (LMP 1985) showed that by 1981 the Portuguese community was predominantly middle aged. Most of their respondents were in the 31–55 age group. There were relatively few children in these households and those who did appear were concentrated in the 16–20 age group.

This finding would appear to be supported by the relatively low numbers of Portuguese-speaking schoolchildren reported in the ILEA language censuses (ILEA 1981–87) and set out in Table 14.1.

Changing patterns of language use

The British have always tended to meet demands for increased labour by diversifying the cultural and ethnic composition of the work-force. This was true not only in the colonies but also in the

TABLE 14.1 Data on Portuguese speakers from the ILEA *Language Census* (1981–87)

Year	Number	%PHLOE*
1981	1,858	4.1
1983	1,861	3.7
1985	1,821	3.2
1987	1,957	3.0

*PHLOE = Pupils with a home language other than or in addition to English.

'quota system' of immigration vouchers which operated in the post-war period. This type of policy has clear advantages. It diminishes the likelihood that strong unions will develop and it increases divisions between different groups in the labour market.

A labour policy of this kind has implicatons for the sociolinguistic situation of migrants. In many situations in the hotel and catering industry, for instance, the work-force will include Filipinos, Italians, Spaniards, Moroccans and Turks as well as Portuguese. Many of these workers have only a rudimentary knowledge of English. In situations such as these, a contact variety of English is used as a lingua franca. In other situations where speakers of Iberian languages are numerically dominant, the lingua franca is a mixture of Portuguese and Spanish. This mixed variety has a folklinguistic label: those who speak it refer to it as *Portunhol*.

Some Portuguese migrants have at least one fellow migrant who speaks Portuguese. As part of the ALUS carried out in London in 1981 (LMP 1985; CLE/LMP 1985), a sample of working respondents from the local Portuguese community were asked about the languages they used in the workplace. Of the workers who were interviewed, 56 per cent said that they had at least one fellow worker who spoke Portuguese, but only 12 per cent reported that all their fellow workers spoke Portuguese. Thus, for many Portuguese workers, there is only rather limited scope for the use of their community language at work.

Many first-generation Portuguese migrants work long and antisocial hours. Within the hotel and catering industry, the working week can be up to 51 hours in all. This means that opportunities for meeting and talking to English speakers outside the workplace are extremely limited. Many of these migrants are only able to learn the minimal spoken English skills necessary to carry out their daily domestic chores. Few of them have had the chance to attend formal English classes since their arrival in Britain. Few of them have had access to post-primary education in Portugal or Madeira before migrating to Britain. As a result, they tend to have considerably less confidence in their language abilities than Portuguese people who have had many years more of formal education.

A sample of men and women were asked as part of the ALUS to rate their spoken and written abilities in Portuguese and English. The effects of limited access to formal education and lack of opportunities to interact with speakers of English are clearly reflected in the survey findings. As shown in Fig. 14.1, respondents' self-ratings of their abilities in English were much

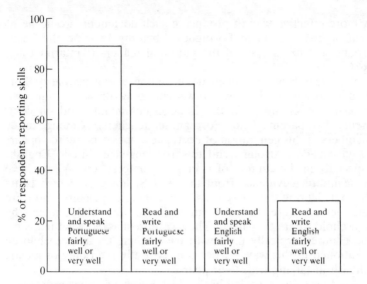

FIGURE 14.1 Language abilities of Portuguese speakers in London (CLE/LMP 1985:34)

lower than their ratings of their abilities in Portuguese. Only 50 per cent of respondents said that they understood and spoke English 'very well' or 'fairly well', and only 29 per cent reported that they could read and write English 'very well' or 'fairly well'. Moreover the ratings for both Portuguese and English literacy were lower overall than the ratings for spoken language abilities.

In response to another question asked in the survey, 65 per cent of respondents indicated that at some point since they had come to live and work in Britain, they had had to rely upon someone who could act as interpreter or translator for them. These interpreters and translators are, for the most part, friends or family members rather than trained community language interpreters and translators. They play a crucial communicative role in a wide range of situations, such as visits to the doctor, interviews related to applications for work permits, or meetings with headteachers.

A further difficulty for the first-generation migrants arises when they need to obtain information from written documents. Very few official documents or public information leaflets are written in Portuguese. When these are made available by local authorities in areas of Portuguese settlement, or by local advice centres, they are usually translated directly from the original English version.

A more effective way of producing such documents would be to write a first version in Portuguese, bearing in mind the background and experience of the potential readers (Santarita 1985, 1986).

No research has yet been done among young people of Portuguese origin in Britain so we can only draw on our own informal observations in the London community and on comments by parents and Portuguese teachers. Among many members of this generation of Portuguese speakers, there appears to have been a strong trend towards language shift to English, especially in the context of peer group interaction. We do have some indirect evidence from the ALUS, however, which bears this out. During this survey, adult Portuguese speakers who were interviewed were asked if there were any children in the household where they lived. They were then asked what language the children typically used with each other. Of all the children mentioned in this way, 74 per cent typically used only or mostly English in talking with their peers.

Another trend revealed in the ALUS was a non-reciprocal pattern of language choice in some households. As shown in Fig. 14.2, 11 per cent of the adults interviewed during the survey reported that the typical pattern of language use in their home was that some speakers would use Portuguese all or most of the time and others would use English all or most of the time. This is a common pattern in minority families, where young people often reach a stage when they refuse to answer their parents or older members of the family in the minority language. This non-reciprocal pattern of language choice begins to emerge as two main types of linguistic influence begin to be felt in a significant way in young people's lives: namely, the language of the peer group beyond the home (*eg* London English) and the dominant language of the school. Given the limited opportunities that

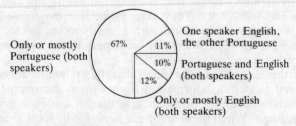

FIGURE 14.2 Household language use among Portuguese speakers in London (CLE/LMP 1985:35)

adults in the first generation have for learning and using English and the strong pattern of language loyalty to Portuguese, considerable intergenerational struggles over language tend to develop in Portuguese homes.

Over the last twenty years, the Portuguese people living in Britain have developed a distinctive way of speaking. Informal conversational language often involves quite frequent codeswitching between Portuguese and English, particularly when the topic of the conversation is related to the experience of life in Britain. Younger members of the second generation tend to codeswitch more frequently than older members of the first generation. For many of these younger people, language alternation is one of the main communicative resources through which they give symbolic expression to their bilingual and bicultural identity.

Among members of both generations, the use of English loan words and loan translations is very common. There are some English words associated with life in Britain which are typically used instead of their Portuguese equivalents. Take the following utterances for example:

Vou de bus para o trabalho
I go to work by bus

Tenho olidei em julho e agosto
I have a holiday in July and August

Vou tratar do moti
I am going to deal with the MOT

Words borrowed from English are often pronounced as if they were Portuguese words, like 'holiday' and 'MOT' above. Occasionally, examples of this kind are similar to words with quite different meanings in Portuguese. For instance, the standard Portuguese word for a 'gutter' is *goteira*. In Britain, however, 'gutter' is a common loan word, often pronounced as *gota*, which sounds similar to the feminine noun for 'cat' in Portuguese: *gata*. This can sometimes lead to misunderstandings, as in the following example:

Há um problema com a gota no telhado
There's a problem with the gutter on the roof

Loan translations from English are also a feature of informal Portuguese usage. For example, the English idiomatic phrase 'to get the sack' is translated directly into Portuguese:

O patrão deu-lhe o saco
The boss gave him the sack

The standard Portuguese equivalent would be

O patrão dispediu-o

Among both first and second-generation migrants, code-switching on single lexical items is a characteristic discourse phenomenon. These switches occur on individual noun phrases, or formulaic expressions such as greetings, or on words like 'okay' which can serve a number of different discourse functions. In the example below, 'okay' occurs in a spontaneous question/answer sequence:

Fazes isso para mim? Okay, amanhã
Will you do this for me? Okay, tomorrow

The above examples will give the reader a sense of how the use of the Portuguese language is changing in the British community. As yet, we have no systematic descriptions of the processes of linguistic convergence and change taking place in the community. These will need to be based on longitudinal sociolinguistic research in local communities. It is only when we have this kind of research evidence that it will be possible to understand the patterns of variation between the vernacular Portuguese spoken by young people at home and the standard Portuguese that they learn in their Portuguese classes.

Language, culture and community

For most people of Portuguese origin in London, Portuguese is still the language of the home. Of those people interviewed during the ALUS in 1981, 67 per cent said that they spoke Portuguese all or most of the time. This figure was high when compared with other linguistic minorities surveyed in the Greater London area. Only 12 per cent of the Portuguese respondents reported that they spoke only or mostly English at home (see Fig. 14.2).

Like other linguistic minorities in the Greater London area, few Portuguese have neighbours who speak their language. However, as we mentioned earlier, there are several focal areas of Portuguese settlement in West London and it is in these areas that community centres and activities are based. Members of the first generation spend most of the limited free time available to them with members of their family and close friends of Portuguese origin. The women and the men who were interviewed as a part of ALUS were asked to say what language they used with the person they spent most time with beyond the immediate family. As shown in Table 14.2, 71 per cent of these respondents indicated that they spoke Portuguese with this immediate companion. Besides this, a very high proportion of the respondents said that they belonged to an organization where all or most of the members could speak the minority language: 87 per cent in all. These survey findings reflect the importance of community-based activities in the day-to-day lives of the first generation of Portuguese migrants. Although the data reported in Table 14.2 relate only to the first generation, it is a reasonable assumption that such activities are also important for their British-born children.

A wide range of other situations and activities also encourages the use of Portuguese. Visits to and from Portugal are frequent and many members of the Portuguese community maintain close ties with relatives, friends, the country and the language. Many Portuguese families send money home to their families in Portugal and hope eventually to buy land or a home to which they can return.

There are also many community centres and activities which contribute to the maintenance of the Portuguese language and culture within the UK. In North Kensington, for instance, there are two Portuguese cafés, two Portuguese grocers, a community centre, several community associations and football clubs. In Camden there is a Portuguese Catholic Church which is used as a community centre. This particular centre is funded by the local council and therefore has more resources than other community facilities. It offers an advice service in Portuguese as well as recreational activities and it has a meeting room where the main daily Portuguese newspapers are on display.

TABLE 14.2 The use of Portuguese in a range of settings, extrapolated from LMP (1985)

% of respondents who said that they spoke only Portuguese with the first person mentioned as someone they spent free time with	71
% of respondents who said most or all of their neighbours could speak Portuguese	17
% of respondents who said they had seen a film or video in Portuguese within the previous 4 weeks	25
% of respondents who said they sometimes visited a shop where Portuguese was spoken	73
% of respondents who had a doctor who could speak Portuguese	42

Various other associations, shops and meeting places are to be found in other areas of London. They all play an important role in keeping individuals in touch with each other and in maintaining a vital informal network between friends and acquaintances. This is particularly important because information passes far more effectively in the Portuguese community by word of mouth than through written channels.

Education and language reproduction

Portuguese classes for children in the second generation were first organized on a small scale in the late 1960s. Classes were set up by local parent groups and community associations who provided the premises and paid for the teacher. They received no support from the Portuguese government or from LEAs in Britain.

However, the revolution that took place in Portugal in 1974 brought about significant changes in educational policy. In the same year, the Ministry of Education sent a Portuguese teacher to work in the London community. In the following year, a government department was set up with the specific brief of making provision available for the education of children of Portuguese migrant workers in different countries. This department is still known as the Serviço de Ensino Básico e Secundario no Estrangeiro. Under the auspices of an education officer based in the Portuguese Consulate in London, provision for the teaching of Portuguese gradually expanded. By 1978 there were eight Portuguese teachers working in Britain. Several new classes were opened in the London area and in Ascot and Reading. Most of them were based in local Catholic schools where a substantial proportion of pupils were of Portuguese origin. Within the ILEA area most of the classes were integrated into the regular school timetable rather than being organized after school hours.

During the decade from the mid-1970s to the mid-1980s, Portuguese teaching continued to widen in scope. By 1985 several more new classes had been established in London as well as in coastal resorts such as Brighton, Eastbourne and Jersey. By this time there were 10 Portuguese teachers working in Britain and over 1,000 children attending language classes. However, from one local area to another there was considerable variation in the form of provision: in some areas, classes were held only once a week; in other areas twice a week. Since the mid-1980s, this has been regularized. Now classes for all children aged 6 and 7 are held twice a week while all other classes are held three times a week.

Provision continues to expand. At present there are 20 Portuguese teachers working in Britain and over 1,400 children attending language classes. One significant development in recent years is that more and more learners are opting to go on to study for public examinations in Portuguese instead of just staying in the classes for an average of six years. In this way they are able to show they have an extra qualification when they leave school. There were, for instance, some seventy-eight entries for the University of London Examinations Board A level Portuguese in the summer of 1988.

It is difficult to ascertain exactly how many children are *not* yet able to benefit from provision for the teaching of Portuguese at different levels; but, according to recent informal estimates made by those most closely involved in organizing Portuguese classes, up to 52 per cent of children and young people of Portuguese origin in Britain, still do not have access to classes where they can develop their spoken and written abilities in their community language.

The future of the classes is uncertain. At the local level the demand for Portuguese classes and formal qualifications in Portuguese is clearly increasing. For the time being, the Ministry of Education in Portugal appears to have a firm commitment to continue support for the classes. Headteachers in some local authorities in Britain have shown considerable interest in classes organized in their schools. However, the far-reaching changes taking place in British education are likely to act as a brake on the continued development of provision. The most serious problem to be faced in the immediate future is the demise of the ILEA, since most of the Portuguese classes are based in schools in the area. The organization of provision will have to be renegotiated with each of the borough councils in turn. In this way, the educational planning efforts of the staff at the Portuguese Consulate will, for some time, be diverted from the central purpose of developing existing provision and resources.

References

CRISTOVÃO, F (1987) *Notícias e problemas da Pátria da Lingua*. Lisbon: Instituto de Cultura e Lingua Portuguesa.

Community Languages in Education Project/Linguistic Minorities Project (CLE/LMP) (1985) *Languages in London*. CLE/LMP Working Paper No. 12, University of London, Institute of Education.

Inner London Education Authority (ILEA) (1981, 1983, 1985, 1987) *Language Census*. London: ILEA Research and Statistics.

Linguistic Minorities Project (LMP) (1985) *The Other Languages of England*. London: Routledge & Kegan Paul.

PESSOA, F. (1982) *Livro do Desassossego*. Lisbon: Atica.

SANTARITA, P. (1983) 'The Portuguese in Kensington and Chelsea'. A report to the Kensington and Chelsea Community Relations Council. Unpublished manuscript.

SANTARITA, P. (1985) 'Migrant communities in London'. A report to the Greater London Council. Unpublished manuscript.

SANTARITA, P. (1986) 'Migrant communities in London'. A report to the London Strategic Policy Unit. Unpublished manuscript.

Chapter 15

The Spanish speech community

Salvador Estebanez

> *El silencio nos ha sido dado para expresar mejor nuestro proprio*
> *pensamiento*
> Silence is given for better hearing our thoughts
> Sor Juana de la Cruz

Spanish is the most important of the Romance languages on two
separate fronts. First, it has the largest number of speakers (estimated in the region of 225 million); second, it is spoken in
the largest number of countries (*cf* Katzner 1977). It is the official
language not only of Spain, but of every South American republic
with the exception of Brazil and Guyana; in all the republics of
Central America, in Cuba and in Mexico. Within the USA, it is
widely spoken in California, Texas, New Mexico and Arizona by
Hispanic populations of mainly Mexican descent; while New York
and Florida, respectively, have large Puerto Rican and Cuban
Spanish-speaking communities. Jews expelled from Spain in the
late fifteenth century spoke a variety of Spanish called Ladino
(see Ch. 11) which is still spoken in Turkey and Israel by their
descendants.

In a British context, the Spanish speech community has an important Latin American component. As well as students from all
over South and Central America, there is a small but significant
population of Chileans who came to Britain as political refugees
following the overthrow of President Allende in the early 1970s.
By far the largest proportion of Spanish speakers in the UK, however, come from Spain and will therefore form the focus for the
present chapter.

While Spanish is the official language of a large number of
countries, it remains, in all cases, as one language among many.

In Chile, for example, although the majority of the population speak Spanish, there are also important Italian and German communities and large numbers of speakers of indigenous Andean Equatorial languages, including Araucanian. Spain is also a linguistically diverse country in spite of the fact that it was one of the first European countries to be formed as a geopolitical entity. After eight centuries of Arab domination, Spain regained control of her territories at the beginning of the sixteenth century and under Castilian rule. Throughout the subsequent turbulent history of Spain, the language from Castile, Castellano, one of the several neo-Latin languages in Spain, established its supremacy, sometimes to the detriment of the other Spanish languages.

In post-Franco Spain (1975 onwards), the linguistic diversity of the country has been fully vindicated. Gallego and Catalan, the other two surviving neo-Latin languages, are co-official in Galicia and Cataluña respectively. Vasco, a pre-Latin language, has also become co-official in the Basque country. Valenciano and Mallorqui might be considered as two further neo-Latin languages, but their resemblance to Catalan makes them appear more like dialects of the latter. Andaluz, spoken in Andalusia, can be considered as a Castilian dialect, differing mainly in the disappearance of the /z/ phoneme and the absence of word-final consonants.

However, only the Galician language and the Andalusian dialect are relevant for discussions of Spanish immigration to the UK. The immigrants from Galicia spoke Gallego and very little Castellano. They were brought up during the Franco years and received no formal education in Gallego. Because they came from the most economically deprived rural areas, they neither regularly attended the compulsory schooling in Castellano nor did they have to use it for everyday purposes.

The Andalusian dialect is, of course, much closer to Castellano, but there are none the less linguistic difficulties. Since Andalusian differs phonetically from the very regular spelling of Castellano, there are inevitably some difficulties in spelling. However, the main obstacle to achieving standard proficiency in Castellano is the poor economic and educational background of the people concerned. The two regional groups which originally formed the core of the Spanish community in the UK were mostly illiterate in either Castellano or Gallego.

The Spanish in Britain

Throughout the twentieth century, Spanish people have

emigrated for economic and political reasons. Before 1960 the majority went to America. However, coinciding with a massive exodus from the country to the cities, the Stabilization Plan of 1959 (a deflationary economic package) resulted in 2 million Spaniards emigrating to Europe within a decade. Although a small number of Spaniards had come to the UK after the Spanish Civil War (1936–39), most arrived in the 1960s. Spanish immigration has always been on a relatively small scale. Migrants have come as individuals, making contact with prospective employers either through friends or family, rather than through government recruitment drives. As a result, the number of Spanish immigrants in the UK is comparatively low in relation to other European host countries such as France, West Germany and Switzerland.

By the early 1970s, a Spanish population of approximately 50,000 had settled in the UK. As we enter the 1990s the numbers remain little changed. The pattern of settlement of Spaniards in the UK is unique in Europe. The majority of immigrants came not only from two provinces but from small areas within these provinces: La Coruña in Galicia, and La Línea in Andalusia. Immigration from La Coruña followed the individual and family patterns already indicated. In the case of La Línea, however, it was a community emigration which took place as a result of the closure of the frontier with Gibraltar in 1969 These two geographical sources form two very distinct groups within the Spanish community. This is hardly surprising since they come from two very different regions of Spain, with separate cultural and lingistic identities.

Of the 50,000 Spaniards living in the UK, 51 per cent are men and 49 per cent women. Their geographical distribution is as shown in Table 15.1.

Table 15.1 Geographical distribution of the Spanish community in the UK

Scotland	1,000
Northern England	300
Yorkshire and Humberside	500
North west England	2,300
Midlands	1,600
Greater London	40,600
South-west England	3,400
Wales	300
Total	50,000

Of this population, 46 per cent are employed in catering services, 25 per cent in cleaning, either in private homes or in hospitals; the rest are scattered in the various other sectors of the economy. This concentration of labour in food and catering has given rise to the Spanish 'Manuel' stereotype illustrated in the comic TV series 'Fawlty Towers'.

While the number of Spaniards nationally is relatively small, they none the less form a significant minority within the capital. Thus, since the introduction of the biennial *Language Census*, Spanish-speaking children have consistently been among the five largest linguistic minorities in ILEA (Table 15.2).

Due to the high concentration of employment in the south-east and in the services sector, Spanish immigrants have not suffered the economic difficulties associated with the recession of the early 1980s. Furthermore, due to the favourable exchange rate of the sterling/peseta, they have benefited considerably since most of their savings are converted into pesetas and sent to Spain. Because they have sent their savings to Spain, even after twenty years of residence, Spaniards, unlike some members of other ethnic communities, have not set up their own businesses, and it is rather unusual to find a self-employed Spaniard in the UK.

Changing patterns of language use

The first generation was mostly illiterate in Gallego or Castellano. When they started to work in the UK they very quickly had to acquire a minimum linguistic competence in English in order to carry out their professional duties and survive. On the whole, they acquired a very rudimentary competence in English which has not improved significantly over the years. When they are with members of their own generation, they will tend to speak in Castellano or Gallego, depending on their regional origin. But even in these situations, they will borrow from the English lexicon when the Spanish equivalent term is not known to them. For in-

Table 15.2 Data on Spanish-speaking children from the ILEA *Language Census*, 1981–87

Year	Number	% PHLOE*
1981	3,436	7.6
1983	3,466	6.9
1985	3,210	5.7
1987	3,229	5.0

*PHLOE = Pupils with a home language other than or in addition to English.

stance, when they left Spain they had not seen a vacuum cleaner and so they are likely to say:

Yo estaba pasando la juva
I was hoovering

Code-mixing, resulting in a mixture of grammar and phonetics of both languages, 'Spanglish', is also common:

Me gusta la Bibici con el frich ful y la jita on
I like the BBC with a full fridge and the heater on

Most members of the second generation have lived in England all their lives and attended English state schools. Consequently, English is their dominant language. Frequently, parents talk to them in Gallego or Castellano and they respond in English. Some code-switching is observed, such as

I love my friends, *sabes*? (You know)

The shift from Spanish to English in the second generation is unmistakeable. Just over half of the Spanish children (51.4 per cent) recorded in the 1987 ILEA *Language Census* were classed as fluent English speakers, one of the highest rates for linguistic minority communities in the capital. When members of the second generation talk among themselves they prefer to do so in English. Even children who have attended Spanish nurseries in London and subsequently the Spanish Bilingual School (see section on education and language reproduction, below) use English during break times. There is no doubt that the influence of the environment is overwhelmingly more decisive than their parents and even their parents and teachers together.

As years go by, it is probable that most of the first generation will retire to Spain and will gradually lose influence over the second generation. The latter will inevitably become more Anglicized. It seems likely that the future third generation will be told about the immigration of their grandparents, probably in a glamorized way, and they may decide to take a GCSE exam in Spanish as their first foreign language, if this is an option open to them.

Language, culture and community

The Spanish community is small in number. When there has been a significant number in a particular area, such as London, Liverpool or Manchester, it has been possible to promote some socio-cultural activities, but the dispersed nature of the community has meant that many people have either remained isolated or have become assimilated into British life.

Spanish immigrants remain committed to the idea of returning to Spain. Their unsocial hours of employment in the catering services have made them very isolated. Now, more than twenty years after their arrival, they begin painfully to contemplate that they may not go back to Spain until retirement; unemployment statistics in Spain are the highest in Europe (about 19 per cent). Since 1979 the number of Spaniards returning to Spain has been approximately 500 per annum. They are being replaced by about the same number of new immigrants. The latter, however, have a higher socio-economic status and have usually chosen to come as a way of furthering their careers. This trend could change the profile of the community in the long term, but in the medium term its impact is hardly noticeable, since the numbers involved are small.

The histogram (Fig. 15.1) clearly illustrates the chronological pattern of immigration. The majority of immigrants arrived around twenty years ago and they were mostly in their twenties. They married members of their own community and, in due course, had children. There is a vacuum in the 20–30 age category; this reflects the sudden drop of new immigrants from the early 1970s onwards.

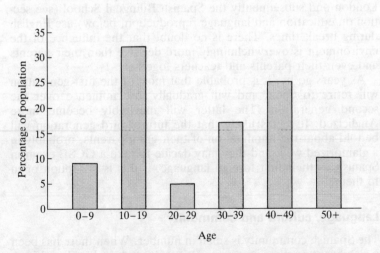

FIGURE 15.1 Age distribution of the Spanish Community in the UK (Data obtained from a survey conducted for the Spanish Embassy Labour Office in 1985 by Data-Instituto de Estudios de Mercado)

The concentration of the immigrant population around first and second generations, with very few grandparents and a vacuum between parents and children (neither younger aunts/uncles nor older cousins), may well have contributed to a widening of the generation gap. The grandparents could have provided a sense of tradition and softened the uprooting of the first generation while simultaneously fostering the acquisition of the mother tongue by the second generation. The 20–30 age group could have bridged the gap between first and second generation.

As the members of the second generation begin to decide their professional and personal futures, an unbridgeable gap between their parents and themselves becomes apparent. The older generation, many of whom have worked all hours in order to achieve the dream of returning to Spain, are confronted with children who seem more British than Spanish and who frequently cherish very different dreams. The second generation also blames the first for not giving them enough attention in their childhood; a not infrequent accusation is that their parents were too busy making money to be at home when they arrived from school.

Against this rather problematic background, the Spanish government, through the Spanish Education Office in London, has tried to provide a bridge between the two generations. The majority of the cultural activities of the community depend on the Spanish school. There are also some clubs and associations which were formed along Spanish regional lines, *eg* Centro Andaluz, Centro Gallego, Hogar Español, Centro Español in Manchester, Feña Nuestra Andalucia, etc. These clubs are subsidized by the Spanish government through the Consulate in London. They chiefly provide a place where the Spanish families can gather at weekends and have a chat over a drink. They also organize music and dancing shows from various Spanish regions.

The first generation continues to be strongly Catholic. They attend their local Catholic church where, frequently, a Spanish priest will be celebrating mass in Spanish. Once a year a religious festival is organized and it is perhaps the most popular gathering of the community. Ceremonies like baptisms, first communions and weddings are the high points on the social calendar and relatives from Spain often attend these occasions.

The annual holiday to Spain is perhaps the strongest link with the past. It provides the incentive for hard work during the rest of the year and it gives the second generation (until adolescence at least) an attractive vision of what their roots are supposed to be.

Unlike some other ethnic minority groups, the Spanish com-

munity does not tend to watch TV in Spanish, either through
videos or satellite. There is not a Spanish local radio station.
There is only one newspaper of significance, *La Región,* which
provides a summary of the main political events in Spain, focusing
particularly on those that have special relevance for immigrants.
It also devotes a few pages to each Spanish community in Europe,
commenting on any cultural activity that has taken place and in-
terviewing representatives of the community.

Institutional support from the British authorities has been non-
existent. No financial or even moral support has been given for
the educational services provided by the Spanish government.
There are no translations of information about local or national
services. Since Spanish is a foreign language taught in English
schools (it competes with German for second place after French),
Spanish students can attend these courses but no special provision
has been made for them. Due to the relatively small size of the
community and the lack of pressure on British authorities, the
Spanish community has been totally overlooked by the host
country.

Education and language reproduction

The Spanish government, through the Ministries of Education
and Science, Labour and Social Security and Foreign Affairs,
provides educational facilities for Spanish communities in various
countries, including the UK. The Education Office, based at the
Spanish Embassy with the Education Attaché at its head, has
responsibility for organizing the various services (Spanish Embassy Educational Attaché 1984). A mother tongue teaching
co-ordinator advises the Education Attaché in all matters concerning mother tongue education. There is also an advisory service
consisting of a small number of educators and psychologists which
is responsible for organizing courses for teachers and pupils,
designing materials, helping students with special needs and
providing technical advice for the Education Attaché on specific
matters. An administrative office supports the work of this staff.

A wide range of educational sevices is provided. First there are
the integrated classes: mother tongue classes taught by a Spanish
teacher in an English school during school hours. 'Integrated' is,
however, a rather ambitious label since Spanish is offered as an
alternative to physical education or religion, or is time tabled just
before or after school hours. Semi-integrated might be a more
accurate description. English pupils are welcome to attend if they
wish.

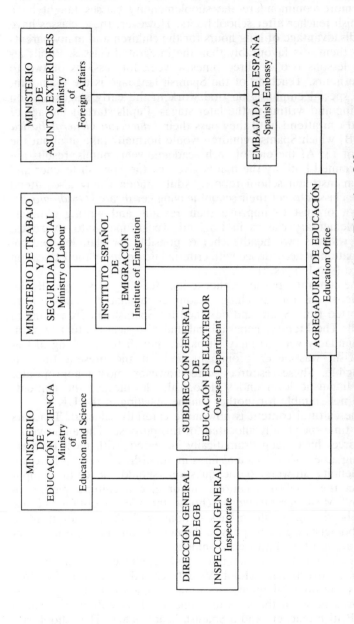

FIGURE 15.2 Educational provision co-ordinated by the Spanish Embassy Education Office

'Integrated' classes are offered by only two schools at present. Far more common are the supplementary classes taught by a Spanish teacher after school hours. However, these classes have the disadvantage of long hours for the children and many parents view them less favourably than the integrated classes. Pupils attend lessons two or three times a week for sessions of two to three hours. Teaching of the Spanish language is the main aim, with special emphasis on oral work in the early stages and on reading and writing in the later stages. Pupils start at the age of 6 and can attend until they pass their *Educación General Basica* (EGB) which Spanish children would normally take at about the age of 14. At the end of each academic year, pupils' results are determined both by the marks given by the Spanish teacher and the mainstream school report. Adult students may also attend these classes to get their school leaving certificate (*Graduado Escolar*), or just to improve their reading and writing abilities. Supplementary classes in England are grouped into six zones, each with its own headteacher responsible for planning and coordination in accordance with criteria laid down by the Education Office (see Fig. 15.2).

The cultural input in mother tongue teaching was originally dependent on the teaching resources available. These were imported from Spain and designed for Spanish children living in Spain. The literary, geographical and historical content was understandably very strongly Hispanic, though the teaching of Catholicism was never prominent and, at the present time, is negligible. These resources were, however, most inappropriate. The linguistic level and sociological relevance of the contents were not suitable for mother tongue teaching in the UK.

The cultural content is now more carefully selected. Teachers have time specifically allocated for this purpose. The audio-visual resources have been dramatically increased, with most teachers having access to videos and films in Spanish. However, there are no definite answers to the question: should the cultural input reflect the English situation, and/or give a cultural picture of Spain? Most parents would choose the second option because they believe they will go back to Spain with their children. Most psychologists would emphasize the need to build the cultural content around the child's environment.

In addition to the integrated and supplementary classes, the Spanish government school, Vicente Cañada Blanch in London, offers full-time bilingual education in Spanish and English for children between the ages of 5 and 16. It is staffed by Spanish and British teachers and a Spanish headteacher. The school tries to meet the aims of both Spanish and British education systems in one curriculum and to realize the full potential of pupils' bilingualism. Pupils are entered for both Spanish (*Graduado Escolar, Primero y Segundo de Bacgillerato Unificado Polivalente*) and GCSE examinations.

The Spanish school also offers supplementary classes similar to those already described and evening courses leading to the Spanish baccalaureant in all subjects or only in Spanish language and literature. This system is for the benefit of students following GCSE and A level courses in British schools. The results gained in the British system together with the marks given by the Spanish teacher determine whether the student has successfully completed each course. At present, however, the Spanish education authorities are tending to be less legalistic about certificates and diplomas and more concerned with designing courses specifically tailored to meet the needs of the community.

A series of tests, measuring linguistic competence in Spanish, were conducted by educational attaché staff for the whole school population in 1983. The results showed that the highest linguistic competence in Spanish was achieved by children who lived in areas where a significant number of Spanish families lived. The results were independent of the type of schooling, either bilingual, supplementary or integrated. These research findings clearly have important implications for Spanish teaching in the UK.

Until recently there has been unanimous backing for the teaching of Castellano by the various sections of the community. It is only lately that voices have been heard requesting some teaching of Gallego, though in addition to, rather than as a substitute for, Castellano. This request has not been given serious consideration. However, although it is easy to reject its implementation for practical reasons, it is harder to do so on psycholinguistic grounds (see Ch. 1).

The Spanish authorities have made co-operation with their British counterparts a priority in the formulation of their educational policies. This is witnessed, for instance, by their support for preparation for GCSE and A level examinations in Spanish; in-service teacher training activities; consultation over special educational or emotional problems faced by particular children; and the exchange of advice as regards teaching materials, resources and other facilities. There has, however, been a reluctance on the part of the LEAs even to open proper channels of communication with the Spanish authorities. In contrast, the DES have been more co-operative and have sent schools' inspectors for periodical consultations. (They insist, however, that they can only recommend and not implement policies.) One of the consequences of the present stance is that Spanish educational provision has been isolated from the mainstream and has tended to be undervalued by the English schools, a state of affairs which is deterimental to both Spanish students and staff.

The Spanish government, in the Education Law of 1987, has noticeably changed the emphasis from an educational provision mainly directed at the Spanish communities abroad to the promotion of the Spanish language and culture for Spaniards and foreigners alike. This has implications on a number of fronts. In view of the lack of interest which state schools have shown to date in Spanish as a community language, it is also to be hoped that this new policy will not result in a lower budget for the Spanish communities. The change in direction may, however, make it easier to integrate the teaching of Spanish as a mother tongue and Spanish as a modern language, though schools will clearly need to pay careful attention to the differing needs of both groups of learners. Hopefully, the promotion of the Spanish language in general may help to raise its status within mainstream education.

References

KATZNER, K. (1977) *Languages of the World*. London: Routledge & Kegan Paul.

Spanish Embassy Educational Attaché (1984) *Educational Services provided by the Spanish Government for Spanish Immigrants in the UK: General Information*. London: Spanish Embassy.

Further reading

General

BARRUTIETA SAENZ, A. (1976) *La Emigración Español: et timo del subdesarallo*. Madrid: Edicusa.

CABEZAS MORO, O. *et al.* (1979) *Emigración Española: Evolución histórica, situación actuel y problemas*. Madrid: Cabinete de Estudias y Publicaciones IEE.

CASTILLO CASTILLO, J. *et al.* (1980) *Emigrantes españoles: la hora del retorno*. Papeles de Economía Española.

CAVO, F. (1977) *Qué es ser emigrante*. Barcelona: Biblioteca Salud y Sociedad, Editorial La Graya Ciencia.

ESPIAGO, J. (1985) *Migraciones Exteriores*. Barcelona: Editorial Salvat.

IGUEIRA, J. (1976) *Los Emigrantes*. Barcelona: Plaza y Janes.

INSTITUTO ESPANOL DE EMIGRACIÓN (1958–) *Memorias del Instituto Espanol de Emigración*. Madrid: Dirección General del IEE.

INSTITUTO ESPANOL DE EMIGRACIÓN (1980–) *Agenda*.

INSTITUTO ESPANOL DE EMIGRACIÓN (1982) *Primer seminario de estudias sobre problemas educaticos de la emigración, Valle de los Caidos.* Madrid: IEE.

INSTITUTO ESPAÑOL DE EMIGRACIÓN (1985) *Interculturalismo y Educación.* Madrid: IEE

KUDAT, A. (1975) *The Comparative Study of the Reintegration Policy of Five European Labour exporting Countries.* Berlin: International Institute of Comparative Social Studies.

MINISTERIO DE EDUCACIÓN Y SCIENCIA (1976) *La educación de los hijos de los trabajadores emigrantes,* números 245–246. Madrid: Servicio del Ministerio de Educación y Sciencia.

Andalusia

GREGORY, D. (1978) *La Odisea andaluza: una emigración hacia Europa.* Madrid: Editorial Tecnos.

RAMOS, A. (1981) *Pasaporte Andaluz.* Barcelona: Planeta

Galicia

DURAN VILLA, F. R. (1985) *La Emigración Gallega al Reino Unida.* Santiaga de Compostela: Calica de Galicia.

HERNANDEZ BORGE, J. (1976) 'La Emigración Gallega a Europa 1961–1975', *Buletin de la Real Sociedad Geográfica* Volume 112.

VASQUEZ GIGIREY, E. (1979) *Crecimiento y Desamollo de los Hijos de los Emigrantes Gallegos.* Santiago de Compostela.

United Kingdom

INSTITUTO ESPANOL DE EMIGRACIÓN (1973) *Guia de Emigrante en Gran Bretaña.* Madrid: Instituto Español de Emigración.

MACDONALD, J. (1972) *The Invisible Immigrants. A Statistical Survey of Immigration into the United Kingdom of Workers and Dependants from Italy, Portugal and Spain.* London: Runnymede Industrial Unit.

Chapter 16

The Moroccan speech community

Ali Haouas

اطلب العلم من المهد إلى اللحد

Ɣutlubil Ɛilma minal mahdi Ɣilal lahdi
Seek knowledge from the cradle to the grave

Arabic is a member of the Semitic subgroup of the Afro-Asiatic or Hamito-Semitic family of languages. It is spoken across an immense geographical area by a very large number of speakers. Arabic owes its present-day world status to a history of conquest. Until the seventh century AD it was spoken only in the Arabian Peninsula. Within a few centuries, however, it had spread as far west as Spain and as far east as Afghanistan. Today it is the official language of some seventeen different states – Algeria, Bahrain, Egypt, Iraq, Jordan, Kuwait, Lebanon, Libya, Morocco, Oman, Qatar, Saudi Arabia, South Yemen, Syria, Tunisia and North Yemen. Because Arabic is the language of the Qur'ān, many millions of Muslims in other countries also have a knowledge of Arabic through Islamic studies and, since 1974, it has functioned as the sixth official language of the United Nations.

The Classical variety of Arabic which is understood throughout the Arab world has remained largely unchanged since the seventh century AD. It is the language of the Qur'ān and of literacy and is therefore associated with so-called 'high' domains such as religion and education. It exists in a diglossic situation with local varieties of Arabic (*cf* Ferguson 1959; Fasold 1984) which are reserved for 'low' domains such as everyday conversation with family and friends. Spoken Arabic varies within any Arab state according to social and geograpical factors. More important, however, is the linguistic variation between different parts of the

Arab world. For instance, Moroccan Arabic and Syrian Arabic are best considered autonomous language varieties and are by no means mutually intelligible.

The question of diglossia in Arabic is extremely complex. It is possible to argue, for instance, that a description in terms of 'low' and 'high' varieties is overly simplistic and cannot account for educated spoken Arabic and other intermediate varieties. We also need to take into account the development of modern standard Arabic (see, for instance, Kaye 1970; McLoughlin 1972), largely as a response to the mass media and the need for Pan-Arab spoken communication. None the less, the 'high–low' dichotomy has a psychological reality for many Arab speakers who point, for instance, to the practical applications of this model in the area of language and education.

Arabic has a large and prestigious literature which goes back to the pre-Islamic era. It is written from right to left with an alphabet of twenty-eight letters which are basically consonants. Vowels are indicated in the Qur'ān and elementary school-books by marks above or below the letters, but are often omitted elsewhere. This script is, of course, used in languages other than Arabic such as Urdu, Pashto, Sindhi and Farsi.

The extent of linguistic diversity varies from state to state. In Saudi Arabia, for instance, varieties of Arabic are spoken by the entire population. Libya and Egypt are also overwhelmingly Arabic speaking. However, varying degrees of bilingualism exist in many other Arab states. Languages such as Shluh, Tamazight and Riffian which belong to the Berber subgroup of the Afro-Asiatic family, are spoken, for instance, in parts of North Africa, particularly in Algeria and Morocco; French is spoken extensively among educated Tunisians, Algerians and Moroccans as a result of former colonial links with France; and Spanish is widely spoken in the former Spanish zone of Morocco (Katzner 1986).

Moroccans in Britain

The Arabic speech community in Britain will clearly reflect the heterogeneous nature of the Arab states. At one end of the scale, there are the long-established Yemeni Arabic-speaking communities of Birmingham and Newcastle; at the other end are the Saudi Arabian annual 'migrants' who live in some of the affluent areas of London. For present purposes, however, we will limit the discussion to the Moroccan Arabic community which has centred on the North Kensington and Ladbroke Grove areas of London since 1970.

Moroccan Arabs come mainly from small coastal towns in west Morocco on the Atlantic coast, especially Larache. Although France has tended to be the most popular destination for Moroccan Arabs, like most North Africans, many Moroccans were recruited individually during the 1960s to come and work in catering by agencies owned by Spanish partners based in London. They in turn, were instrumental in obtaining work permits for relatives. In most cases, men arrived first and found jobs in the hotel and catering industries. They were followed by their wives, who often worked as cleaners and chambermaids, and then their children. Both men and women tend to be involved in a great deal of shift work and long and antisocial hours are the rule.

There are no accurate statistics on the size of the Moroccan Arab community in London though ILEA *Language Census* data give some indication both of overall numbers and rate of growth (Table 16.1). There has been a steady increase in the numbers of Arabic-speaking children in London schools in the 1980s, and they now constitute the eighth-largest linguistic minority group. These figures, include, however, children from other Arabic-speaking communities, though the majority are likely to be Moroccan Arabs.

Changing patterns of language use

The Moroccan Arabic community is a relatively new arrival on the British scene and therefore still includes a high proportion of individuals for whom Arabic is the dominant language. Their situation is thus closer, for instance, to that of Turkish speakers who have arrived in the same period from mainland Turkey than ex-colonial migrant workers, such as Indians and Pàkistanis, or European immigrants, such as the Poles and Ukrainians, who arrived in the early post-war period.

The majority of first-generation Moroccans have a very limited knowledge of English. Very often they work in a situation where most of the work-force are not native speakers of English; com-

TABLE 16.1 Data on Arabic-speaking children from ILEA *Language Census* (1981–87)

Year	Number	%PHLOE*
1981	1,969	4.4
1983	2,345	4.7
1985	2,706	4.8
1987	3,067	4.7

* PHLOE = Pupils with a home language other than or in addition to English.

munication therefore tends to take the form of a simplified 'survival' English (*cf* Ch. 14).

Evidence of language shift in the second generation is, however, apparent. Moroccan children, like children from other language minority communities, are exposed to a predominantly English-speaking environment in the form of school, television and the larger community. This situation is exacerbated still further by the long working hours of many of the parents. The most obvious symptom of language shift is the conversational pattern which has become the norm for most families: parents speak to their children in Moroccan Arabic, but the children are likely to reply in English.

The degree of commitment to Arabic varies from family to family and individual to individual. None the less, there is no shortage of young British Moroccans who strongly support the maintenance of Arabic for literary and religious uses and are actively transmitting Moroccan Arabic as the language of primary socialization to their children.

Language, culture and community

Various events bring together the community and provide opportunities for the use of the mother tongue. These include religious festivals like 'Id al – Fitr; life-cycle celebrations, like weddings and engagement parties; and national feasts, including Monarchy Day, hosted by the Embassy. Social events equally focus on music and there is growing support for various London-based groups. Life thus revolves around the family and the long and antisocial working day which is the norm in the community makes it very difficult to establish more formal organizations or networks. Some developments in this direction, however, are under way. On the recreational level, for instance, the use of video cassettes in the community is thriving following the setting up of a video club. And on the level of community organization, the Moroccan Co-ordinating Committee (MCC) was set up in 1986 as a subcommittee of Nottinghill Social Council. It aims to develop into an independent organization by the end of 1990 and has as its main function the improvement of access to services for Moroccans within the Royal borough of Kensington and Chelsea. To this end, an information and advice centre was established in late 1987, providing an information service and personal advice service, including interpreting. Other services available at the centre are in the areas of employment, training and education. There are also projects for women, young people and the elderly.

Interpreting services are provided by the borough's interpreter, based at Westway Information and Aid Centre. There is, however, a serious concern about the lack of professional interpreters and, even with the use of volunteers as a stop-gap measure, it is not possible to meet the demand of the community. The MCC intends working very closely with the Paddington Migrants Unit which has been endeavouring to lobby MPs for extra funding.

Because Morocco is relatively accessible by air, most families manage to visit their countries once a year. Such opportunities enable children particularly to experience their language and culture at first hand. Visits by relatives from Morocco are also quite frequent.

Local public libraries have been able to stock a reasonable range of books in Arabic. There is no Moroccan newspaper but there are many London-based Arabic publications, notably *El Arab*, which often report on community affairs.

Education and language reproduction

Given the diglossic nature of Arabic and the fact that the spoken variety has rarely been taught formally in the Arab world, except as a survival kit for foreign visitors, the overriding pedagogical problem in the British context of a settled Moroccan community is how to promote both varieties. The teaching of Classical Arabic for religious purposes has traditionally been accepted as an educational priority. Outside of Morocco, however, to what extent is it reasonable to expect that the spoken variety will *ipso facto* be maintained in the community? This is emerging as a pressing issue for those who recognize the importance of both Moroccan and Classical Arabic as integral elements of their identity. The majority of community classes, in fact, focus on both Classical and Moroccan Arabic, as well as on cultural and religious questions.

The organization of Arabic classes started in a very uncertain and *ad hoc* way as the community wrestled with problems such as fund-raising and the shortage of appropriately trained and qualified teachers and adequate premises. Some progress, has, however, been made. The ILEA policy to grant-aid community language teaching has relieved a great deal of the financial burden, and the shortage of teachers has been resolved to some extent with the arrival of four teachers sponsored by the Moroccan Ministry of Education to work in the supplementary system. After-school Arabic classes are currently supported by the MCC.

Within mainstream education, Arabic is taught in a small number of inner London primary and secondary schools. At the time of writing, Classical Arabic is offered by the London and East Anglian Group as a GCSE subject and by the University of London Examinations Board as an 'A' level subject, with 130 and 29 entries respectively in the summer of 1988. Most of these examination candidates, however, will have prepared for their examinations outside mainstream state schools, where the extent of provision is very limited. Sometimes Arabic is part of the curriculum. Most often, however, it is an after-school or dinner-time activity. An interesting development is the setting up of family workshops where both parents and children take part in storytelling, reading and Moroccan cookery. A small number of bilingual texts are now available in Arabic and usefully promote the idea of bilingualism as a normal phenomenon and a skill which deserves recognition in the eyes of monolingual and bilingual pupils alike.

References

FERGUSON, C. A. (1959) 'Diglossia', *Word* 15: 325–4014

FASOLD, R. (1984) *The Sociolinguistics of Society*. Oxford: Basil Blackwell.

Inner London Education Authority (ILEA) (1981, 1983, 1985, 1987) *Language Census*. London: ILEA Research and Statistics.

KATZNER, K. (1986) *Languages of the World*. London: Routledge & Kegan Paul.

KAYE, A. S. (1970) 'Modern standard Arabic and the colloquials', *Lingue* 24:

MCLOUGHLIN, L. J. (1972) 'Towards a definition of modern standard Arabic', *Archivum Linguisticum*

Notes on the Contributors

AYDIN MEHMET ALI was born in Nicosia, Cyprus, in 1947. She has a degree in psychology from University College, Cardiff, but was also educated in Cyprus and the USA and has travelled extensively in Europe, the USA, India and Australia. In addition to her work as Head of Consultation and Information for the Education Department in Southwark, London, she is a translator, writer and community activist. She is a member of the Turkish Education Group and FATAL (For the Advancement of Turkish Arts and Literature) and has also helped to set up numerous projects for women, young people and children. She has written, lectured and participated in international conferences on anti-racism, bilingualism, community involvement and accountability, Turkish women and the Turkish community in London. She is currently translating the work of Turkish Cypriot women poets into English, conducting research into Turkish Cypriot women and war and preparing her first collection of short stories.

SAFDER ALLADINA was born in Tanzania. His paternal grandparents went from Gujarat to what was then the German colony of Tanzania at the turn of the last century. His maternal grandparents were Kachchi speakers whose family was settled in Zanzibar from the early part of the last century. He has fifteen years of teaching experience in a variety of primary, secondary and adult institutions and worked as Director of the Berkshire Support Service for Intercultural Education before moving to his present post as Principal Lecturer at the Polytechnic of North London. There he has been responsible for developing the PGCE in Multilingual Primary Education, unique to teacher education institutions in Britain, which prepares teachers for multilingual inner city primary schools. In 1983 he won the ILEA Teacher Fellowship to the Centre for Multicultural Education at the University of London Institute of Education. His publications are in the area of South Asian languages and multicultural education. His research interests include patterns of language maintenance and shift among children of South Asian origin in Britain.

JOSEPHINE A. BOYD (née Galackas – a corruption of the original Lithuanian surname, Galeckas), whose grandparents came to Scotland in 1900, has previously published articles on the survival of Lithuanian as a minority language. Born in Glasgow in 1936 and educated at the University of Glasgow, she graduated with an MA in English Literature and Language and Phonetics. Her linguistic skills extend beyond Lithuanian to include, among others, French and German. She currently teaches English to secondary school children in Scotland.

BRUNO CERVI was born in Italy in 1944. After 15 years' involvement with education in Italy he was assigned, in 1979, to the Education Department of the Italian Consulate General in London. He has been involved, both as teacher and coordinator, with the teaching of Italian language and culture to children of Italian immigrants. He completed an M.A. course in Applied Linguistics at Birkbeck College, University of London, with particular interest in bilingual development, multicultural education and need analysis of children of Italian origin. He took part in the E.C. Pilot Project: Community Languages in the Secondary Curriculum (1984–87) as coordinator of the team of *inseriti* teachers (Consulate sponsored teachers of Italian as a community language, operating in mainstream schools).

VIV EDWARDS was born in the Rhondda, South Wales. Experience of bilingualism within the family and the wider community acted as a catalyst for her interest in language as a whole and she went on to do first a BA and later a Ph.D in Linguistics at the University of Reading. She is currently lecturer in Applied Linguistics at Birkbeck College, University of London. Her research interests are in oral culture and language in education and publications include *The West Indian Language Issue in British Schools* (Routledge & Kegan Paul, 1979), *Language in Multicultural Classrooms* (Batsford, 1983), *Language in a Black Community* (Multilingual Matters, 1986) and *At Home in School: Parent Participation in Primary Education* (with Angela Redfern, Routledge, 1988). She is a parent governor in a primary school where the children speak some 22 different languages between them.

SALYADOR ESTEBANEZ was born in Pamplona, Spain, in 1954. He was educated in Spain and has an MA in Educational Studies. Between 1979 and 1984, he was the Headteacher of the Spanish Bilingual School in London which was created to provide the best possible solution to the educational needs of the Spanish community in London. There he felt the need to develop his knowledge of linguistics, with special reference to bilingualism, in order to formulate and implement the most appropriate educational policies. He completed an MA in Second Language Learning and Teaching at Birkbeck College in 1984 and is now working on his Ph.D. thesis. He is also involved in designing and teaching courses in English and Spanish in Spain and England respectively and is the Spanish language representative on the subject committee of the International Baccalaureate Organization (University of Bath).

IAN HANCOCK of British and Hungarian Gypsy descent, is Professor of English and Linguistics at the University of Texas at Austin. He has authored over 80 works on Romani life and language including *The Pariah Syndrome: An Account of Gypsy Slavery and Persecution* (Waroma Publishers, Ann Arbor, Michigan, 1987). He has spoken and written widely on the Romani Holocaust both in America and in Europe. He is American NGO and UNICEF representative to the United Nations for the World Romani Union, and has been active in the Romani civil rights movement since the mid-1960s. In 1979 he was awarded a citation of merit by Yeshiva University for his work for his ethnic community, and in 1981 was invited to serve on the Haifa-based Advisory Board of Jewish Affairs. Between 1985 and 1987 he served as Special Advisor to the U.S. Holocaust Memorial Council. He is a Board Member of the Austin Chapter of the National Conference of Christians and Jews for the Remembrance of the Holocaust through the Performing Arts and a founding member of the Centre for Cultural Studies Inc. He is currently working on the development of a Model Curriculum for Genocide and the Holocaust for the Central Texas school system.

TINA HICKEY was born in Arklow, in the Republic of Ireland. She studied psychology at University College, Dublin and completed her MA there. She was employed as a researcher by Institiúid Teangeolaíochta Éireann (ITÉ), where she was involved in the development of a criterion-referenced test of Irish ability among eight-year-old children, and its application to a national sample. She was awarded a fellowship from ITÉ for postgraduate study at the University of Reading, England, completing her Ph.D. in 1987 on the acquisition of Irish as first language, and its implications for theories of first language acquisition. At present she is working at ITÉ on the publication of the results of this study, drawing out their implications for cross-linguistic research.

ALI HAOUAS was born in Tunisia. He worked as a teacher of French and German in secondary schools before moving more recently into teacher training in community languages and English. At present he is involved in the piloting of a diploma in the teaching of community languages across the primary curriculum. He is also currently chairperson of the National Council for Mother Tongue Teaching.

MARTA JENKALA was born in London of Ukrainian parents. She holds a BA in French and Linguistics from University College, London and an MA in second language learning and teaching from Birkbeck College. She is currently teaching French at secondary level. She has, from an early age, been involved in the life of the Ukrainian community in Britain, working in Ukrainian scout, student and educational organizations, as teacher at the Ukrainian Saturday school in London and as editor of several publications. She has taught Ukrainian at the Polish University in Exile and continues to do so at the London College of the Ukrainian Catholic University. She also has an interest in Ukrainian folk art and has broadcast on the subject on radio and television.

JUDY KEINER was born in 1944, the daughter of Polish Jews who escaped to Britain from Berlin in the nick of time. She grew up in the Jewish East End of London, in a home where Yiddish was an everyday language and Hebrew was the language of blessings and ceremonies. She is Senior Lecturer in Education at the University of Reading Department of Educational Studies and Management. Her commitment to Yiddish and Ashkenazi Hebrew has been strengthened by the desire to teach both to her daughter, who was born in 1986.

PADDY LADD was born deaf. He went to mainstream schools and joined the BSL deaf community after education, something which he describes as 'a gradual process of coming home'. Since then he has worked in all sections of the deaf world, from social work to linguistics, from the British Deaf Association to broadcasting for the deaf with the BBC. A co-founder of the National Union of the Deaf, he is politically active, especially in the field of deaf children's education. At present he is consultant to the London Deaf Video Project and involved in the revival of BSL culture. He, with other deaf people, hopes to see other linguistic minority groups accepting BSL in the next decade as part of the wider struggle for a 'rainbow coalition'.

KENNETH MACKINNON was born in 1933 in the docklands area of London's East End of mixed Isle of Arran and Ulster descent. Following the blitz, he was a war evacuee in West Cornwall, where he first encountered a Celtic language. Later as a teenager, he developed an abiding interest in the Gaelic language of his family origins. Most of his working life has been in teaching: in secondary schools and technical colleges in Essex and East London, and more recently in teaching and research as Reader in the Sociology of Language at Hatfield Polytechnic. Since 1972 he has undertaken numerous research projects for the Economic and Social Research Council and other organizations into the sociology of Gaelic language and Gaelic-speaking communities. He has spent much of that time in various Gaelic communities both in Scotland and in Canada. His publications include: *The Lions Tongue* (1974), *Language, Education and Social Processes in a Gaelic Community* (1977), and *The Present Position of Gaelic in Scottish Primary Education* (1987).

MARILYN MARTIN-JONES has been teaching Linguistics at Lancaster University since 1983. From 1979 to 1983, she was a member of the Linguistic Minorities Project (LMP) research team based at the University of London, Institute of Education. She speaks Portuguese, and, in 1981, she was the member of the LMP team who coordinated the survey of Portuguese speakers in London. Her main area of research interest is bilingualism and language education. She is joint author of *The Other Languages of England* RKP (1985) and she is currently working on a book on bilingualism and linguistic minorities.

ELIZABETH MUIR was born in Poznan, Poland. She was awarded an M.Phil degree in psychology from A. Mickiewicz

University of Poznan in 1973. Her interest in psycholinguistics led her to the Department of Philology at the University of Poznan where she became involved in the study of bilingualism. In 1975 she came to Britain and pursued her interest in bilingualism, doing research on Polish/English children. She was awarded a Ph.D. from the University of Reading. She is actively involved in the Polish community in the UK, and especially with Polish Saturday schools.

EVIENIA PAPADAKI-D'ONOFRIO was born in Canaea on the Greek island of Crete. She was educated at primary and secondary levels in Greece but came to the UK for her higher education and was awarded a BA in Modern Languages from the Polytechnic of Central London in 1980. The birth of her daughter in 1982, and the decision to bring her up in a trilingual environment (English, Greek and Italian), encouraged her to follow the MA in Second Language Learning and Teaching from Birkbeck College, University of London which she completed in 1988. She currently works as a language support teacher at a community school in Hounslow and also teaches Greek as a mother tongue at a community school in South London. She has also worked as a freelance translator and acted as examiner for the RSA course in Modern Greek.

MARIA ROUSSOU was born in Nicosia in Cyprus. She did a Ph.D on the sociology of education at the University of London Institute of Education before going on to work for 4 years as the co-ordinator of the EEC funded Schools Council Mother Tongue Project. Her publications include *Working with Many Languages: a Handbook for Community Language Teachers* (co-authored with Paula Tansley and Hasina Nowaz, School Curriculum Development Council, 1985). She is senior lecturer in antiracist and antisexist education at the University of the Aegean. Her research interests include multilingualism, bilingualism, and the implications of European unity for education. She is currently investigating language maintenance among Greek Cypriots in London, based at Birkbeck College University of London.

PAULA SANTARITA has been involved in community work with Portuguese migrants in the London area since the early 1980s. From 1980–1984, she was employed as a development worker and social policy advisor by the Greater London Council and then by the London Strategic Policy Unit. She has also represented the interests of the Portuguese community at Kensington and Chelsea Community Relations Council. One of her main concerns has been with the health problems faced by migrant workers. She has recently published an article on 'Migrants and health' in *Radical Medicine*. Besides her involvement in community work, Paula Santarita has also acted as a Portuguese-English interpreter and translator on many occasions. She has also taught Portuguese to adults. She is presently working in Mozambique.

MARIKA SHERWOOD was born a Hungarian Jew in Budapest. In 1948, with the remnants of her family, she emigrated to Sydney, Australia where she eventually married – and divorced – an Australian. After a mainly part-time education at the University of Sydney, she re-emigrated to London with her son in search of a more European and less sexist lifestyle and to refresh her Hungarian roots. Since leaving Australia, she has earned her living in various sectors of the education system in London and New York. Presently she is teaching for Birkbeck College's Extramural Studies Centre and doing research for her third book which will be on Black organizations in Britain, 1938–1948. Her previous books are *Many Struggles – West Indian Workers and Service Personnel in Britain 1939–1945* (Karia Press, 1985) and *Genocide USA?* (Karia Press, 1989) which looks at the situation of Afro-Americans since the Civil Rights era.

Community Addresses

BSL

British Deaf Association, 38 Victoria Place, Carlisle, Cumbria CA1 1HU.

National Union of the Deaf, 120 New Road, Bedfont, Middlesex TW14 8QT.

LASER, 8 Church Lane, Kimpton, Hitchin, Herts SG4 8RP

London Deaf Video Project, Room 303, South Bank House, Black Prince Road, London SE1.

Gaelic

Acair Earranta (Anchor Ltd. – Gaelic educational publishing house), 7 James Street, Stornoway, Isle of Lewis, Western Isles PA 87 2QA

BBC Gaelic Department/BBC Radio Nan Gàidheal, Broadcasting House, Queen Margaret Drive, Glasgow G12 8DG

Comunn Na Gàidhlig (CNAG – The Gaelic Association); Comunn Luchd-Ionnsachaidh (The Learners' Association); Comhairle

Comhairle Nan Sgoiltean Àraich (Gaelic Playgroups Council). All at: 109 Church Street, Inverness IV1 1EY

Gaelic Books Council, Department of Celtic, University of Glasgow, University Gardens, Glasgow G12 8QQ

Guth Nam Parant (The Parents' Voice – parents for Gaelic education) c/o Mrs. Margaret Ishbel Macleod, 10 Airidhantuim, Shader, Barvas, Isle of Lewis, Western Isles PA 86

Greek

Embassy of Greece, 1a Holland Park, London W11 3TP

The Greek Embassy Bilingual School, Pierpoint Road, Acton, London W3
The Greek Institute, 34 Bush Hill Road, London N21 2DS
The Hellenic Cultural Centre, 12–14 Cottesmore Gardens, London W8 5PR
Cyprus High Commission, 93 Park Street, London W1

Hungarian

Embassy of the Hungarian People's Republic, 35 Eaton Place, London SW1
British-Hungarian Fellowship, 3 Hillside, 7 Burston Road, Putney, London SW15 6AR

Italian

Inspettorato Scolastico, The Italian Embassy, 14 Three Kings Yard, London W1
F.A.S.F.A. (Federation of Parents' Associations), 4 Southern Street, London N1 9AY
Uffici Scolastici Londra, 4 Upper Tachbrook Street, London SW1Y 1SH

Irish

Institiúid Teangeolaíochta Éireann, 31 Plás Mhic Liam, Baile Átha Cliath 2, Éire. (The Linguistics Institute of Ireland, 31 Fitzwilliam Place, Dublin 2, Ireland)
Bord na Gaeilege, 7 Cearnóg Muirfean, Baile Átha Cliath 2, Éire. Bord na Gaeilege, 7 Merrion Square, Dublin 2, Ireland.
Conradh na Gaeilge, 6 Sráid Fhearchair, Baile Átha Cliath 2, Éire (Irish Language Movement: Information on local branches and language classes in Britain and Ireland from this address)
Comdháil Náisiúnta na Gaeilge, 86 Sráid Gardner Locht, Baile Átha Cliath 1, Éire (Congress for Voluntary Irish language organizations)
Comhaltas Ceoltóiri Éireann, 32 Cearnóg Belfrave, Baile na Manach, Baile Átha Cliath, Éire (Irish music and culture. Information on British and Irish branches supplied)
British Association of Irish Studies, c/o Humanities Department, North Staffordshire Polytechnic, Beaconside, Stafford ST 18 OAD.

Institute of Irish Studies, University of Liverpool, PO Box 147, Liverpool L69 3BX

Lithuanian

Lithuanian Association in Great Britain, Lithuanian House, 2 Ladbroke Gardens, London W11 2PT
Supreme Committee for the Liberation of Lithuania, 1611 Connecticut Ave NW, Washington DC 20009, USA.

Moroccan Arabic

Moroccan Information and Advice Centre, 61 Golborne Road, London W10 5NR
Moroccan Arabic Interpreter, Westway Information and Aid Centre, 140 Ladbroke Grove, London W10 *or* Nottinghill Social Council, 7 Thorpe Close, London W10.

Polish

Biblioteka Polska, (The Polish Library), POSK, 238–246 King Street, London W6 OR
Polska Macierz Szkolna Za Granica (The Polish Educational Society Abroad), 238–246 King Street, London W6 ORF
Polski Osrodek Spoleczno-Kulturalny (POSK) (The Polish Social and Cultural Centre), 238–246 King Street, London W6 ORF
Polska YMCA (The Polish YMCA), 46/47 Kensington Gardens Square, London W2 4BA.
Stowarzyszenie Polskich Kombatantow (The Polish Ex-Combatants' Association), 238–246 King Street, London W6 OR

Portuguese

The Federation of Portuguese Associations in the UK, c/o the Portuguese Chaplaincy, 165 Arlington Road, Camden, London N1.
The Education Officer, Portuguese Consulate, 62 Brompton Road, London SW3.

Romani

Association of Gypsy Organisations/Romani Institute, 61 Blenheim Crescent, London W11 2EG
International Romani Union, US Office, PO Box 856, Buda,

Texas 78610–0865, USA.
National Gypsy Council. Life President: H. Smith, Greenmills,
Greengate Street, Oldham, Lancs.
National Gypsy Education Council, 32 Marshall Close, Feering,
Colchester, Essex CO5 9LQ
Romanestan Publications, 22 Northend Way, Warley, Brent-
wood, Essex CM14 5LA
Romany Guild, 62 Temple Mills Lane, London E15.
Romany Rights Association, Roman Bank, Walpole Saint An-
drew, Cambridge.
Write Here (Drop-in Literacy Centre), 697 Atcliffe Road, Shef-
field S9 3RE

Spanish

Spanish Embassy, 24 Belgrave Square, London SW1X 80A
Spanish Institute, 102 Eaton Square, London SW1
Spanish Education Office, 102 Earl's Court Road, London W8
Spanish School Vicente Cañada Blanch, 317 Portobello Road,
London W10

Ukrainian

Ukrainian Catholic Church, Duke Street, London W1Y 1YN
Ukrainian Autocephalous Orthodox Cathedral, 1a Newton Ave-
nue, London W3 8AJ
Association of Ukrainians in Great Britain, 49 Linden Gardens,
London W2 4HG
Federation of Ukrainians in Great Britain, 78 Kensington Park
Road, London W11 2PL
St. Clement Ukrainian Catholic University London College, 79
Holland Park, London W11 3SH
Ukrainian Publishers and Printers, 200 Liverpool Road, London
N1 1LF

Welsh

Cyd-Bwllgor Addysg Cymru/Welsh Joint Education Committee,
245 Western Avenue, Cardiff CF5 2YX
Cymdeithas Yr Iaith Cymraeg (Welsh Language Movement), Pen
Roc, Rhodfa'r Môr, Aberystwyth SY23 2AZ
Mudiad Ysgolion Meithrin (Welsh Playgroup Movement), 10
Park Grove, Cardiff CF1 3BN Y Swddfa Gymreig/Welsh Of-
fice, Crown Building, Cathays Park, Cardiff CF1 3NQ

Urdd Gobaith Cymru (Welsh League of Youth), Conway Road, Cardiff

Yiddish

Board of Deputies of British Jews, Woburn House, Upper Woburn Place, London WC1H OEP (The representative body of mainstream – but not fundamentalist – Jewish religious and cultural organizations. Operates a general information service on all aspects of Jewish communal life and culture in Britain)

Spiro Institute for the Study of Jewish History and Culture, Westfield College, Kidderpore Avenue, London NW3
(Organizes a wide range of adult education courses, including Modern Hebrew; also conducts research and organizes cultural events and school level courses)

YIVO Institute for Jewish Research, 1048 Fifth Avenue, New York, NY 1002, USA

Index